Entrepreneurship Development

Issues and Perspectives

Entrepreneurship Development

Issues and Perspectives

Edited by

Jaynal Ud-din Ahmed

Professor, Department of Management,
North-Eastern Hill University, Tura Campus, Meghalaya

and

Khundrakpam Devananda Singh

Assistant Professor, Department of Management,
North- Eastern Hill University, Tura Campus, Meghalaya

New Century Publications
New Delhi, India

NEW CENTURY PUBLICATIONS
4800/24, Bharat Ram Road,
Ansari Road, Daryaganj,
New Delhi - 110 002 (India)

Tel.: 011-2324 7798, 4358 7398, 6539 6605
Fax: 011-4101 7798
E-mail: indiatax@vsnl.com • info@newcenturypublications.com
www.newcenturypublications.com

Editorial office:
LG–7, Aakarshan Bhawan,
4754-57/23, Ansari Road, Daryaganj,
New Delhi – 110 002

Tel.: 011-4356 0919

First Published: **July 2015**

ISBN: **978-81-7708-414-6**

Published by New Century Publications and printed at Salasar Imaging Systems, New Delhi.

Designs: Patch Creative Unit, New Delhi.

PRINTED IN INDIA

About the Book

Entrepreneurship has been considered the backbone of economic development. It has been well-established that the level of economic growth of a region, to a large extent, depends on the level of entrepreneurial activities in that region. The myth that entrepreneurs are born, no more holds good. Rather, it is well-recognised now that the entrepreneurs can be created and nurtured through appropriate interventions in the form of entrepreneurship development programmes.

In the present era of liberalisation, privatisation and globalization along with ongoing IT revolution, capable entrepreneurs are making use of the opportunities emerging from the evolving scenario. However, a large segment of the population, particularly in the industrially backward regions/rural areas generally lags behind in taking advantage of these opportunities. Therefore, there is a need to provide skill development and entrepreneurship development training to such people in order to bring them to mainstream of economic growth.

Entrepreneurship is the quality of being an entrepreneur, i.e. one who *undertakes an enterprise*. The term puts emphasis on the risk and effort taken by individuals who both own and manage a business, and on the innovations resulting from their pursuit of economic success.

This volume contains 18 papers, authored by experts in the field of entrepreneurship and related areas, which provide theoretical and empirical insights into various aspects of entrepreneurship development.

About the Editors

Dr. Jaynal Ud-din Ahmed is presently Professor, Department of Management at North-Eastern Hill University, Tura Campus, Tura, Meghalaya. After completing his Post-graduation in Accounting and Finance, he obtained Ph.D. degree in Business Administration from Assam (Central) University, Silchar. He also holds Bachelor of Law (LL.B.) and Master of Law (LL.M.) degrees. He has successfully completed three research projects—one sponsored by the University Grants Commission (UGC), New Delhi and two other by Indian Council of Social Science Research (ICSSR), New Delhi.

Dr. Ahmed has published research papers in national and international journals, besides authoring five books and editing six books. He has attended and presented research papers at various international, national and regional seminars and conferences. He is the recipient of Best Thesis Award (2004) and Best Young Faculty Award (2005) in recognition of his teaching and research work.

Dr. Khundrakpam Devananda Singh is currently Assistant Professor in the Department of Management, North- Eastern Hill University, Tura Campus, Tura, Meghalaya. He did his M.Com. and MBA from Indira Gandhi National Open University (IGNOU), New Delhi and Ph.D. from Manipur University, Imphal.

Dr. Singh has published 2 books and 15 research papers. He has participated and presented papers at various national and international conferences/seminars. He is also engaged in two major research projects funded by ICSSR, New Delhi and NABARD, Mumbai.

Contents

Contributors

S.S. Khanka	National Institute of Financial Management (NIFM), Faridabad, Haryana.
Mohammad Saleh Jahur	Professor and Chairman, Department of Finance and Banking, University of Chittagong, Chittagong, Bangladesh.
Md. Abu Taher	Senior Fulbright Fellow Professor, Faculty of Business Administration, University of Chittagong, Chittagong, Bangladesh.
R.K.P.G. Singha	Head, Department of Commerce, Pachhunga University College, Aizawl, Mizoram.
Doneti Sivaji	Assistant Professor, Department of History and Archaeology, North-Eastern Hill University, Tura Campus, Tura, Meghalaya.
Sandeep Kumar Singh	Research Scholar, Department of Business Administration, Tezpur University, Napaam, Assam.
Lalhmingliana Renthlei	Research Scholar, Department of Management, Mizoram University, Aizawl, Mizoram.
Lalropuii	Assistant Professor, Department of Management, Mizoram University, Aizawl, Mizoram.
Angom Jeevan Singh	Assistant Librarian, North-Eastern Hill University, Tura Campus, Tura, Meghalaya.
Purnima Takhellambam	Department of Management, North-Eastern Hill University, Tura Campus, Tura, Meghalaya.
Rupam Roy	Head, Department of Management, Regional College of Higher Education, Dispur, Assam.

Hassan Mahmoud Hasan	Head of Internet Department, Department of ICT, Syrian Ministry of Foreign Affairs and Expatriates, Damascus, Syria.
Moirangthem Biren Singh	Research Scholar (SRF), Department of Commerce, Manipur University, Imphal, Manipur.
N. Tejmani Singh	Associate Professor, Department of Commerce, Manipur University, Imphal, Manipur.
Bidhu Kanti Das	Assistant Professor, Department of Management, Mizoram University, Aizawl, Mizoram.
SultanaB.A. Mazumder	Assistant Professor, Department of Management, North-Eastern Hill University, Tura Campus, Tura, Meghalaya.
Hedayatullah Choudhury	Assistant Professor, Department of Commerce, Nabinchandra College, Karimganj, Assam.
R.R. Blesson Hrangao	Research Scholar, Department of Commerce, Manipur University, Imphal, Manipur.
Robita Sorokhaibam	Associate Professor, Department of Commerce, Manipur University, Imphal, Manipur.
A. Ibemcha Chanu	Assistant Professor, Department of Commerce, Assam University, Diphu Campus, Assam.
Hunasing Engti	Research Scholar, Department of Commerce, Assam University, Diphu Campus, Assam.
Thrinadha Rao B.	Assistant Professor, Department of Management, North-Eastern Hill University, Tura Campus, Tura, Meghalaya.
Venkata Rao Y.	Associate Professor, Department of Tourism Studies, Pondicherry University, Puducherry.

Amir Jafar Assistant Professor, Department of Business Administration, University of Burdwan, West Bengal.

Partha Sarar Assistant Professor and Teacher-in-Charge, Department of Business Administration, University of Burdwan, West Bengal.

Anjan Kumar Ghosh Project Fellow, Department of Business Administration, University of Burdwan, West Bengal.

Trailokya Deka Research Scholar, Department of Economics, North-Eastern Hill University, Shillong, Meghalaya.

Preface

In economics, entrepreneurship is the quality of being an entrepreneur, i.e. one who *undertakes an enterprise*. The term puts emphasis on the risk and effort taken by individuals who both own and manage a business, and on the innovations resulting from their pursuit of economic success.

Entrepreneurship in this sense may result in new organizations or may be part of revitalizing mature organizations in response to a perceived opportunity. The most obvious form of entrepreneurship is that of starting new businesses. In recent years, the term has been extended to include social and political forms of entrepreneurial activities. When entrepreneurship is describing activities within a firm or large organization, it is referred to as intra-preneurship and may include corporate venturing, when large entities spin-off organizations.

The ability of entrepreneurs to innovate is thought to relate to innate traits such as extroversion and a proclivity for risk-taking. The capabilities of innovating, introducing new technologies, increasing efficiency and productivity, or generating new products or services, are characteristic qualities of entrepreneurs. Entrepreneurs are catalysts for economic change, and researchers argue that entrepreneurs are highly creative individuals with a tendency to imagine new solutions by finding opportunities for profit or reward. It is widely maintained that entrepreneurs are unusual individuals. In line with this view, there is an emerging research tradition investigating the genetic factors that are perceived to make entrepreneurs so distinctive.

This volume contains 18 papers authored by experts in the field of entrepreneurship and related areas.

The paper titled, *Changing Facets of Entrepreneurship Development*, by S.S. Khanka traces entrepreneurship in historical perspective and examines its changing facets in the modern world. Some of the successful entrepreneurs in India are also listed in this paper.

The paper, *Entrepreneurial Success in Small and Medium*

Enterprises (SMEs), authored by Mohammad Saleh Jahur and Md. Abu Taher, has identified the factors contributing to the entrepreneurial success in SMEs of Bangladesh by employing Varimax Rotated Factor Analytical Technique. The study has considered ten numbers of variables contributing to the success of entrepreneurs. It has identified relationship and organizational factors in order of magnitude for entrepreneurial success in Bangladesh.

In the paper, *Entrepreneurship in Informal Cross-border Trade,* R.K.P.G. Singha observes that the cross-border trade has a special significance since Mizoram is in the immediate vicinity of Myanmar and Bangladesh with as much as 72 percent its periphery forming international border with these countries. Owing to topography, poor infrastructural facilities, absence of mineral wealth coupled with other problems, the state has not been able to attract industries, virtually making it dependent upon the neighbouring states and countries. The paper has examined the socio-economic origins of the entrepreneurs involved in such trade, analyzed the problems faced by the traders and has finally offered some suggestions for the overall development of border trade.

Realising the tremendous potential of health care, Doneti Sivaji in a study, *Post-liberalisation Entrepreneurship in Pharmaceutical Business,* observes that healthcare is highly demanded to achieve a larger stock of 'health capital' which transforms service-oriented hospitals into business-oriented healthcare hubs. Hyderabad became a promising sector for new entrepreneurs who created trends in bulk pharma and retail pharma.

Sandeep Kumar Singh in his paper, *Problems and Prospects of Entrepreneurship,* has identified ten parameters which influence the growth of entrepreneurship and found that factors like red tape, high taxes, lack of capital and inadequate infrastructure act as deterrents. In view of the low-level growth of entrepreneurship in Assam, the paper has suggested that there is a need for change of perception for entrepreneurship growth.

The paper, *New Land Use Policy (NLUP) Beneficiaries in Petty Trade,* authored by Lalhmingliana Renthlei and Lalropuii has examined the beneficiaries of NLUP around Aizawl city in general and the beneficiaries in petty trade in particular. The paper observes that the petty trade plays a major role in the economy of Aizawl city. The paper recommends that understanding the problems and prospects of NLUP beneficiaries in petty trade around Aizawl city is the need of the day.

The paper, *Entrepreneurship Skills among the Information Professionals of College Libraries,* authored by Angom Jeevan Singh and Purnima Takhellambam, has explored the role played by information professionals in marketing the information products in college libraries of Garo Hills of Meghalaya. The paper throws light on the need to achieve the organisational and professional goals for the benefit of the users of information products in the region.

Rupam Roy in a case study, *Entrepreneurship Education of Cluster Industry,* has identified determinants of bell metal industry. The industry is presently facing acute problems in the procurement of raw materials, financial assistance from government and other sources, lack of training facilities, transportation and marketing difficulties. The artisans have been suffering from basic facilities like drinking water and sanitation. The paper has suggested adequate assistance and proper care to be given for its survival and growth.

Recognizing the potential of applying ICT to improve socio-economic development, Hassan Mahmoud Hasan in his paper, *Entrepreneurship and ICT in Developing Countries,* has provided a comprehensive view on the prospects of ICT including e-commerce in developing countries as an entrepreneurial tool for socio-economic development. The paper has also measured the national ICT readiness in Syria. It has diagnosed the relevant hindrances and recommended the practical solutions to make use of ICT in entrepreneurship development.

Moirangthem Biren Singh and N. Tejmani Singh in their paper, *Working Capital and Liquidity Management in Micro,*

Small and Medium Enterprises (MSMEs), point out that the efforts and success of an enterprise depends largely on its ability to manage working capital, which helps to maintain the balance between liquidity and profitability. The paper analyzes the working capital trends and liquidity management in MSMEs with special reference to selected plastic industries in Manipur.

The paper titled, *Role of Corporate Houses in Developing Entrepreneurship,* by Bidhu Kanti Das, has highlighted some of the initiatives taken by corporate houses in North-East India for the development of entrepreneurial activity. The paper also emphasizes the empowerment of the poor through entrepreneurial training.

The paper, *Remittances and Micro Enterprises,* by Sultana B.A. Mazumder, finds that remittances play a significant role in the economies of many countries and constitute the second largest financial inflow in many developing countries. The paper tries to link remittances with micro enterprise development in the Indian context.

The paper, *Tourism Industry and Entrepreneurship Development,* contributed by Hedayatullah Choudhury, emphasizes that tourism has the greatest potential for generating income and employment opportunities in North-East Indian states since the region is characterized by the blending of flora and fauna and is exceptionally rich in bio-diversity.

R.R. Blesson Hrangao and Robita Sorokhaibam in a specific study, *Tourism Entrepreneurship,* underline the role and responsibilities of tourism entrepreneurs in the state of Manipur with special reference to Senapati district and to bring up a concrete solution in developing Senapati district as one of the best tourist destinations in the country.

A. Ibemcha Chanu and Hunasing Engti in their paper, *Ecopreneurship Development through Ecotourism*, argue that since tourism sector is the fast growing service sector which provides huge employment opportunities— the promotion of this sector is an urgent call for the development of backward but beautiful places like Karbi Anglong district of Assam. However, in order to protect the beauty of the district in the process of commercialisation, the paper suggests to develop ecotourism as a part of ecopreneurship development.

Thrinadha Rao B. and Venkata Rao Y., in their paper, *Entrepreneurship, Employment Generation and Tourism,* state that the development of tourism upgrades the livelihood status and eradicates poverty. Interestingly, the tourism development programmes and projects are mostly concentrated in metropolitan cities, urban areas and highly developed destinations. The contribution of rural population towards the investment in tourism sector is very less—almost negligible. The involvement and contribution of the local people in tourism promotion will bring the real economic growth in the region.

Amir Jafar, Partha Sarar and Anjan Kumar Ghosh in an empirical study titled, *Entrepreneurship Development in the Indian Rice Mill Sector,* point out that entrepreneurship is the most critical factor contributing towards an economy's growth and development. The paper highlights the deterring factors for entrepreneurship development in India.

Trailokya Deka in his paper, *Entrepreneurship: Global Opportunities and Challenges,* has examined the global issues of entrepreneurship and observed that in the era of globalization and rapidly changing economic world, entrepreneurship has to be more dynamic. The globalized world markets and economies have encouraged entrepreneurial organizations of all sizes and national origins to foster entrepreneurship throughout their operations. However, due to all relevant economic, political and cultural factors, the conduit of business opportunities in entrepreneurial process is not smooth and even. Therefore, the paper concludes that the entrepreneurs need to be more dynamic to find the global as well as regional ways of profit derivation and optimization.

We place on record our deep appreciation for all the contributors to this volume. Their scholarly papers would surely add to the existing body of literature on the subject and ignite debate on its various dimensions.

We also place on record our gratitude to the following scholars for their help and guidance at different stages of the completion of this work: Professor Furqan Qamar, Secretary General, Association of Indian Universities (AIU), New Delhi; Professor Eugene D. Thomas, Pro-Vice-Chancellor, North-Eastern Hill University, Tura Campus, Tura, Meghalaya; Professor M.S. Jahur, University of Chittagong, Bangladesh; Professor S. Sikidar, Gauhati University, Guwahati; Dr. Kamal Uddin Ahmed, Retired Principal, Karimganj College, Karimganj, Assam; Professor G.P. Prasain, Manipur University, Imphal, Manipur; Professor S.S. Khanka, National Institute of Financial Management (NIFM), Faridabad, Haryana and Professor G. Singaiah, Department of Management, North-Eastern Hill University.

Finally, we are obliged to Mr. Sandeep Sury, chief executive, New Century Publications, New Delhi for accepting the manuscript and bringing out this book in the present form in a short time.

NEHU,
Tura Campus

Jaynal Ud-din Ahmed
Khundrakpam Devananda Singh

1

Changing Facets of Entrepreneurship Development

S.S. Khanka

Historical Perspective of Entrepreneurship Development

Entrepreneurship development is a relatively new term that emerged in economic literature, particularly during the 18th century. Its meaning has cradled and changed over time from risk-taking during 18th century, to coordination during the 19th century, to innovation during the 20th century and to wealth creation during the 21st century. The National Knowledge Commission (NKC) of India has defined entrepreneurship as, "the professional application of knowledge, skills and competencies and/or of monetizing a new idea, by an individual or a set of people by launching an enterprise *de novo* or diversifying from an existing one (distinct from seeking self-employment as in a profession or trade), thus, to pursue growth while generating wealth, employment and social good". Call it by any name, entrepreneurship is an activity of converting an idea into products and services to create jobs and wealth for the benefit of self and the society.

Entrepreneurship development essentially implies development of small-scale enterprises which are considered as seed-bed for industrial development of an economy. This, therefore, implies that entrepreneurship development precedes enterprise development. More often than not, both entrepreneurship development and small enterprise development are used interchangeably. The need for and significance of developing entrepreneurship and, in turn, small enterprises in the country can be imbued with multiplicity of justifications and not limited to the following only:

1. They generate immediate and large-scale employment opportunities with relatively low investment.
2. They eradicate unemployment problem from the country.
3. They encourage dispersal of industries to all over country covering small towns, villages and economically lagging regions.
4. They bring backward areas too in the mainstream of national development.
5. They promote balanced regional development in the whole country and thus achieve the adumbrated goal of inclusive growth.
6. They ensure more equitable distribution of national income.
7. They encourage effective mobilization of country's untapped resources.
8. They serve as seed-bed or nursery for development of medium and large-scale enterprises.

One way, perhaps the most plausible way of viewing at the role of small enterprises in economic development of an economy is to see its relative position in terms of country's total production, employment and exports in relative terms.

In India, small-scale enterprises and/or entrepreneurship development accounts for 35 percent of the gross value of the output in the manufacturing sector, about 80 percent of the total industrial employment and about 40 percent of the total exports of the country.

Given such significant role of entrepreneurship and small enterprise development in an economy, Ernst Friedrich Schumacher coined the phrase *"small is beautiful"*.

There are yet others who extol the significance of small enterprises, such as, *"an economy is the effect for which entrepreneurship is the cause"*.

Having appreciated the need for entrepreneurship development, let us briefly delineate the historical perspective of entrepreneurship development in India.

Entrepreneurship development in India started with the establishment of Small Industry Extension and Training Institute (SIET) in 1962 in Hyderabad. Thereafter, the major subsequent developments in the field of entrepreneurship development were Professor David C. McClelland's 3 months' training and research programmes in Rajamundi, Kakinada and Vellur towns of Andhra Pradesh and Tamil Nadu through which McClelland proved that, through proper education and training, the vital quality of an entrepreneur, i.e. 'need for achievement' (n'ach) can be developed. The fact remains that McClelland's successful experiment proved to be a seed for entrepreneurship development in India which have become popular today as EDPs (entrepreneurship development programmes) and have emerged as a national movement. Subsequently, the Gujarat Industrial Investment Corporation (GIIC) for the first time started a three month training programme on entrepreneurship development in 1970.

By the latter half of 1970s, the news of GIIC's EDP success spread to the other parts of the country. As a result, SIET and Small Industry Development Organisation (SIDO) through Small Industry Services Institute (SISI) and Industrial Development Bank of India (IDBI) through Technical Consultancy Organisations (TCOs) started organising EDPs. The encouraging results of these efforts culminated to the establishment of Centre for Entrepreneurship Development (CED), Ahmedabad in 1979. Inspired and influenced by the success of CED, Ahmedabad, the national level financial institutions such as IDBI, IFCI, ICICI and SBI with active support from the Gujarat Government, sponsored a 'National Resource Organisation', called Entrepreneurship Development Institute of India (EDI), Ahmedabad, in 1983.

This institute was entrusted with the responsibility of extension and institutionalization of entrepreneurship development activities in the country which the institute has since been discharging successfully. Almost at the same time, the Government of India also established National Institute for

Entrepreneurship and Small Business Development (NIESBUD) to coordinate entrepreneurship development activities in the country. In the course of time, some State Governments with the support from national level financial institutions established state-level Centre for Entrepreneurship Development (CED) or Institute of Entrepreneurship Development (IED). By now, CED or IED have been established in most of the states in the country. Today, India operates the oldest and largest entrepreneurship development programmes in any developing country and EDP has emerged as a nation-wide revolution in the country.

It is cliché to mention that in spite of the EDPs emerging as a national movement, there has not been any perceptible improvement in the entrepreneurial activities in the country. Unfortunately that is the case. The fact remains that in the garb of quantitative success, there is a qualitative failure in EDPs in India.

According to a nationwide study carried out by the Entrepreneurship Development Institute of India, Ahmedabad, the success rate of EDPs in India is just 25 percent i.e. one out of every four trainees actually started his/her enterprise after undergoing entrepreneurial training. It could have been considered satisfactory had it been otherwise, i.e. 3 out of every 4 trainees would have established enterprises. However, this underlines the need for looking back into our adumbrated efforts to develop entrepreneurship in the country.

Changing Facets of Entrepreneurship Development

Historically, there are two possible theories of entrepreneurship development doing the round. *One,* entrepreneurs are born. *Two,* entrepreneurs are made. These are also known respectively as the 'entrepreneur-based model' and 'the environment-based model' of entrepreneurship. The former model is based on the belief that the success or failure in business venture even in unfavourable business environment depends primarily on entrepreneur by making appropriate strategic decisions, rather than on the favourableness of the environment. The later model believes that entrepreneurship, or say, enterprise operates within an environment and, hence, gets affected by the environment. As such, entrepreneurship is an outcome of a given environment. Without contesting the two theories, the fact remains that entrepreneurs emerge from both origins and, as such, there is no typical entrepreneur.

If we go through the business history of India, we come across the names of some persons who have emerged as successful entrepreneurs like (Late) Dhiru Bhai Ambani of Reliance Industries Ltd., Azim Premji of Wipro, Narayan Murthy of Infosys Technologies Ltd., Kiran Mazumdar-Shaw of The Biocon India Group, Verghese Kurien of Gujarat Cooperative Milk Marketing Federation popularly known for utterly buttery delicious "*Amul*', Deepak S. Parekh of HDFC and many more. The entrepreneurial profiles of these business/industry men are found quite fascinating. They are a study in sharp contrasts. How? Some are highly educated; others are high school/college dropouts. Some are inheritors, others are self-made. Some topped their chosen field in their thirties; others did not approach the starting line until their fifties. Thus, there is no typical entrepreneur as such.

There has been over the period, a dynamic change in entrepreneurial perspective all over the world including India. The major paradigm changes in the entrepreneurial perspective in India have been highlighted in Table 1.1.

By now, entrepreneurship has been emerging in both business and non-business background and also in almost all spheres of human activity. So to say, the facet of entrepreneurship has been changing over time and clime. Rural entrepreneurship, tourism entrepreneurship, agri-preneurship, social entrepreneurship, etc. have been the prominent changing facets of entrepreneurship development in recent times.

No doubt, over the past half-century, there has been prodigious volume of research resulting in various models and/or theories of entrepreneurship development. Yet, entrepreneurship as a relatively young field is still rife with controversy and multiple paradigms. Nonetheless, the significance of practical experience gained in a particular paradigm (or say, context) to the existing knowledge and new learning can be, by no account, contested on mainly two counts. *One,* proceeding from the general to the particular is, more often than not, perilous because authenticating the particular from the general that too based on secondary sources may not fit in a particular context. *Two,* secondary sources often offer contestable interpretations and alternative views. This is because the problems and prospects of development in any respect are, to a great extent, context specific.

Table 1.1: Major Paradigm Changes in the Entrepreneurial Perspective in India

Earlier	Presently
Business background	Non-business background, also known as '*first generation entrepreneurs*'
Merchant	Manufacturing
Industry	Service
Caste-based, i.e. *Marwaris and Gujaratis*	Caste-less, i.e. broad-based
Gender-based, i.e. *male dominated*	Gender encompassing i.e. *women entrepreneurs*
General education	Professional and technical education
Local/regional/national	Global
Commercial, i.e. *profit motive*	Social, i.e. *social impact motive*

Therefore, the context-specific actual experiences in relation to theory assume relevance and significance in search of new learning and understanding of the phenomenon of entrepreneurship.

2

Entrepreneurial Success in Small and Medium Enterprises (SMEs)

Mohammad Saleh Jahur and Md. Abu Taher

Statement of the Problem

Entrepreneurs are directly involved into activities contributing to the development of the economy of any country. Entrepreneurship and economic development are highly correlated (Khan, 2000). Entrepreneurs are creating values for socio-economic development through employment generation, meeting demand of customers, contribution to national exchequer and foreign exchange reserves, poverty reduction etc. Hence, entrepreneurs play a vital role in bringing technological change, innovation and growth of output in general, and rapid employment generation in particular, which finally results in changing standard of living of the common masses (Park and Taher, 2010, p.17).

The success and failure in doing business has profound impact on the economic development of a country. Therefore, government and other development agencies are involved in generating a congenial business environment for entrepreneurs in a country. Entrepreneurial environment plays an important role in the development of industrial entrepreneurship (Tandon, 1975). A Study (Rahman, 1970) has mentioned that growth of industrial entrepreneurship is possible in an environment which regards the world as orderly, determinable and capable of being managed and manipulated. In fact, enabling business environment such as adequate supply of utility and infrastructural services, influence the entrepreneurs to come out with innovative business ideas and their success in doing business and contributing to the socio-economic development of the country (Ahmed, 1994).

Bangladesh is characterized by different business ventures—small, medium, and large. Small businesses are numerous in Bangladesh and form a large majority in the domestic markets. According the estimate of BSCIC, there are about 52,3000 small enterprises including cottage industries in the country employing about 2.3 million people, which is around 82 percent of the total industrial labour force [Khan, 1999]. Quoting informal Planning Commission estimates, the SMDF puts the number of medium enterprises to be around 20,000. Its development is largely dependent on the contribution of small and medium enterprises, and the role being played by the entrepreneurs of SMEs. The growing economic significance of SMEs as a source of development of entrepreneurship—traditional and technology social venture, and employment generation in the developed, OECD countries especially since 1970s—is now widely recognized in an increasingly growing volume of literature (OECD, 1997).

The world economy has been experiencing a paradigm structural shift from mass production to a more flexible production in order to cope up with the change and avail of opportunities in the market. This has led the SMEs to a notable resurgence in developing countries like Bangladesh. These sectors are expected to offer ample opportunities to a cross-section of people of the society to get involved into income generating activities—traditional, technological, vocational and other activities—and thereby strengthening the efforts towards achieving high and sustainable economic growth which are important prerequisites for triggering an exit from the vicious circle of poverty. This can be accomplished by establishing labour intensive SMEs in rural areas of the country where cheap labour can be a key competitive advantage.

SMEs of Bangladesh have been vulnerable to frequent policy changes of Government from time to time. Besides, they are facing severe competition in and outside of the country. As a result, the profitability of SMEs has got squeezed and many of them have got financially distressed. Besides, entrepreneurs of SMEs are experiencing both success and failure in different sectors for internal factors as well. Country's half of the ready-made garments units have fallen sick due to global crisis, slump in the business as well as other industrial constraints at home. The sick industries in various sectors include textile, leather, medicine, loom, food, chemical and rubber. At least 2,00,000 employees were employed in those industries, and now at least 50,000 of them are unemployed, leading an inhuman life in the absence of any alternative income source. Country's civil society that includes noted economists, entrepreneurs and chamber leaders called for revival of such sick industries in order to protect jobs and boost economy. In view of this, the present study has been undertaken aimed at identifying factors contributing to the success and responsible for the failure of entrepreneurs of SMEs in Bangladesh.

Objectives of the Study

The principal objective of the study is to identify the factors influencing the success of entrepreneurs of SMEs in Bangladesh. To accomplish this objective, following specific objectives have been covered:

1 To identify factors influencing the success of entrepreneurship;
2 To identify the factors contributing to the success of entrepreneurs of SMEs; and
3 To suggest some strategic policy measures for entrepreneurial success.

The following hypothesis have been developed and tested against the objectives set forth above:

Ha: Following Factors are hypothesized to contribute to the success of entrepreneurs of SMEs in Bangladesh:

X_1: Willingness to succeed.

X_2: Self-confidence.
X_3: Understands the competition.
X_4: Uses a targeted marketing strategy.
X_5: Clear idea about their next start up.
X_6: Wealthy managerial support.
X_7: Firms well with others.
X_8: Well structured in life and business.
X_9: Keeps close tabs on finances.
X_{10}: The business plan.

Methodology of the Study

Study Design: The main purpose of this study is to address the factors influencing the entrepreneurial success of SMEs in Bangladesh. A survey method is used to collect primary data for the study. Two phases of a pilot test was conducted with five individuals for the first phase and two individuals for the second who were experienced in SME business in order to determine the clarity of the survey questions.

Generally, the data was collected via two rounds of email invitation to the selected respondents. After the data collection, reliability estimates were done to determine the internal consistency of the sample data using Cronbach alpha technique. An EFA with principal component analysis (varimax rotation) were conducted to explain total variance and also to determine the inter-relationship among the factors. Finally, the ranking of each core factor was made on the basis of factor scores derived.

Sampling Procedure and Sample Size: The sample of SME entrepreneurs was drawn from the Directory of Chittagong Chamber of Commerce and Industry, Bangladesh. This directory provides full contact details of all entrepreneurs of SMEs.

Based on stratified and random sampling, 40 SME entrepreneurs were selected as a sample for this study. Researchers were able to take interview of 23 selected samples despite vigorous efforts (Table 2.1).

Table 2.1: List of Sample Entrepreneurs of SMEs

Industry Sub-Sector	Number of Samples	Percentage
Light Engineering Works	4	17.40
Printing and Publishing	5	21.75
Readymade Garments	8	34.75
Plastic Products	3	13.05
Automatic Servicing and Repairing	3	13.05
Total Number of Sample	**23**	**100**

Note: Data has been compiled by the researcher.

Survey Instrument: As no standard scales related to the influencing factors of entrepreneurial success exist, the researchers underwent a comprehensive literature review to identify the key factors to prepare the survey instrument. Based on the existing literature survey, discussions with some experts in relevant field and pilot testing, 10 factors were identified as a focal guide for this study. The instrument was developed keeping two criteria in mind: (a) that the instrument meets reasonable validity and reliability standards, and (b) that the instrument is short and practical to administer in terms of the amount of time required to complete. The survey instrument comprised of 10 factors plus demographic information. All the factors except demographic information were measured using a five-point Likert-type scale, ranging from "1" (least important) to "5" (most important) to rate their levels of importance with the statements.

Data Collection Procedure: Researchers prepared a questionnaire for collecting primary data on the basis of literature survey and opinions of experts/professionals. For that, the researchers selected 40 entrepreneurs of SMEs for the purpose of collecting data conveniently. They attempted to conduct interview of 40 entrepreneurs of SMEs. Finally, they were able to conduct interviews of 23 entrepreneurs of SMEs. In this case, the opinions of sample respondents were captured on a five point Likert-scale (5: most important, 4: important, 3: indifferent, 2: less important, and 1: least important). The study consulted existing literature, journals, magazines, websites, and annual reports of the sample SMEs for designing the questionnaire and rationalizing the present study.

Analysis of Data: The data thus collected was tabulated first. Thereafter, the data was analyzed by employing sophisticated multivariate techniques—Varimax Rotated Factor Analysis or Principal Component Method.

Factor Analysis: Factor analysis is a method of reducing a large number of variables (tests, scales, items, persons and so on) to a smaller number of presumed underlying hypothetical entities called factor (Fruchter, 1967). It tries to simplify a diverse relationship that exists among a set of observed variables by uncovering common dimensions or factors that link together the seemingly unrelated variables and consequently provides insight into the underlying structures of the data (Dillion and Goldstein, 1984). The purpose of factor analysis is mainly two-fold: data reduction and substantive interpretation. In the present study, 'Principal Components Varimax Rotated Method' of factor analysis was used in order to identify the factors influencing the success and failure of entrepreneurs of SMEs in Bangladesh.

Principal component factor explains more variance that the loadings obtained from any method of factoring. In order to define the group membership, an algorithm may be used to uncover a structure purely on the basis of the correlation structure of the input variables. The number of principal components to be retained in the study was decided on the basis of Kaiser's criterion (1958) of Eigen value ≥ 1. Principal components having higher reliability coefficients were more reliable in the sense that the corresponding factors would be replicable in other similar kind of studies. Consequently, communality, symbolized by h^2—was worked out which showed how much of each variable is accounted for by the underlying factors taken together. Subsequently, factor scores were generated on the basis of weighted average of 'Principal Factor' loadings and average of respective variables was included into the concerned group. Ranking of each factor was made on the basis of the scores derived.

Findings and Analysis

Entrepreneur and entrepreneurship are interwoven. Entrepreneurship is considered as an act of assuming the risk and the tasks of an entrepreneur (Khan, 2000, p. 4). The success and failure of entrepreneurs depends largely on the entrepreneurial capacity. Entrepreneur believes that success is possible because of: (i) the uniqueness of the idea; (ii) the strength of the product; and (iii) self-perception of quickness, and hard work, or some other fact known mainly to the entrepreneur which will guarantee success (Khan, 2000, p. 2). This is why the present study has attempted to identify the key factors for successful entrepreneurship in order to facilitate the study over the factors influencing the success and failure of entrepreneurs of SMEs.

The findings of the study have been discussed below.

Sample Profile: The sample for this study consisted of SME entrepreneurs located in Chittagong, Bangladesh. The 40 questionnaires were distributed, of which 23 SME entrepreneurs responded. The response rate was 58 percent. This response rate was similar to those obtained by others who have surveyed on SMEs (Makbul, 2011; Man, Lau and Snape, 2008; Park and Taher, 2010; Sen and Haq, 2010). The age of the respondents ranged from 22 to 63 years. A significant portion of respondents (35.48 percent) were in the 26 to 35 years age group. 17.74 percent of the respondents were single and 82.26 percent were married. In terms of education, 64.51 percent had completed high school, 24.19 percent had a college degree and only 11.30 percent had a university degree. The majority of the respondents (75.81 percent) had less than

10 years of working experience. Tenure in the SMEs ranged from 6 months to 18 years, with a mean 4.7 years (standard deviation 2.2 years).

Reliability and Validity: Before applying statistical tools, reliability testing of the scale is important. This was done by determining the association between scores obtained from different administrations of the scale. If the association is high, the scale yields consistent result, thus is reliable. Cronbach alpha is the most widely used method and its value varies from 0 to 1 but satisfactory value is required to be more than 0.6 for the scale to be reliable (Malhotra, 2002; Cronbach, 1951). The Cronbach alpha value for the instrument used in this study was estimated to be 0.793.

If we compare our reliability value with the standard value alpha of 0.6 advocated by Cronbach (1951), a more accurate recommendation of Nunnally and Bernstein (1994) or with the standard value of 0.6 as recommended by Bagozzi and Yis (1988) or with the standard value of 0.7 as recommended by Kline (2005), we find that the scales used are highly reliable for factor analysis.

Validation procedures involved initial consultation with expert researchers about the survey instrument. The expert's opinion was also incorporated. The experts judged the face and content validity of the survey instrument as adequate. The construct validity via Principle Component Analysis (PCA) with Varimax Rotation Method was also estimated.

Key Factors for Successful Entrepreneurship of SMEs: Successful entrepreneurship is not an unmixed pleasure and blessing. The success of business depends not only on internal and external conditions; but also on the capability and quality of entrepreneurship. The study consulted different literatures (Khan, 2000; Hold, 2002; Khanka, 2001 and Ahmed, 1994) for identifying the key factors for successful entrepreneurship. It collected opinion of 23 entrepreneurs of SMEs on these factors on a five point Likert-scale. The study expressed the collected opinions of the sample entrepreneurs in terms of percentage weight (Table 2.2).

Table 2.2: Key Factors for Successful Entrepreneurship

(percentage)

Factors	MI	I	In	LI	LeI
1. Prior Work Experience	58	30	-	12	-
2. Lessons Learnt from Failure	48	20	11	05	16
3. Own Luck	41	30	3	18	08
4. Professional Networks	36	41	12	6	5
5. Availability of Financing	36	30	14	12	08
6. Lack of Willingness or Ability to Take Risks	48	30	12	6	4
7. Ease of Management	54	18	10	8	10
8. Difficulty in Raising Capital	56	16	8	8	12
9. Business Management Skills	36	40	6	12	8
10. Knowledge to Start a Business	56	26	4	4	10
11. Industry and Market Knowledge	30	56	-	14	-
12. Pressure to Keep a Traditional Steady Job	32	30	20	18	-

MI = Most Important; I = Important; In = Indifferent; LI = Less Important; LeI = Least Important.

Note: Data has been compiled by the researcher.

It is evident from the analysis of the above table that most of the sample entrepreneurs had given highest importance to factors like prior work experience, difficulty in raising capital, ease of management, lessons learnt from failure and ability to take risk, in order of magnitude. Aggregately on important side, most of the sample entrepreneurs were of the opinion that prior work experience, industry and market knowledge, knowledge to start a business, ability to take risk, professional network, and business management skills were key successful factors for entrepreneurship.

This implies that these entrepreneurial factors were most important for entrepreneurship. The entrepreneurs had to concentrate more on to these entrepreneurial factors in order to have a profitable niche in the competitive business environment.

Identification of Factors Contributing to the Success of Entrepreneurs of SMEs: Apart from entrepreneurial factors as have been mentioned previously, the success of an entrepreneur depends on both internal and external factors. A Study (Ahmed 1981) had segmented the various factors for the success into four categories. These are: (a) psychological factors, (b) socio-cultural factors, (c) personal factors, and (d) opportunity factors. A summary of the success factors of entrepreneurs based on available literature is shown in Table 2.3.

Identification of Factors Influencing the Success of Entrepreneurs of SMEs

Entrepreneurs are subject to both systematic and unsystematic risks. They are to deal with the different issues like moral hazard, adverse selection, agent cost and conflicts thereof. Entrepreneurs can succeed in the business taking all the risks arising out of these issues and conditions with reasonable care. The present study has consulted available literature, and considered the opinions of experts while determining the factors contributing to the success of entrepreneurs of SMEs. The study collected opinions of 23 entrepreneurs of SMEs and analyzed them by employing 'Varimax Rotated Factor Analysis'.

Analysis of Correlation Matrix: The study has estimated zero-order correlation of all 10 variables that contributed to the success of entrepreneurs of SMEs, considered for the study. The correlation matrix has shown that variables under study had formed several groups on the basis of relationship lying between different variables. Variables within the group were found to have significant relationship at different levels of significance ranging from 1 percent to 10 percent.

Table 2.3: Success Factors of Entrepreneurs

Factors	Canti-Llon, R. 1975	McClen lland, D. 1961	Rahman, A, 1979	Ahmed, S.U. 1981	Hornaday, J.A. 1982	Kao, J.J. 1989
Risk Taking	√	√	√	√	√	√
Innovativeness	√		√	√	√	
Well-Coordination				√	√	√
Self-Awareness		√		√	√	√
Self - Confidence	√	√			√	
Personal Initiative	√		√	√	√	
Knowledge Information					√	
Dynamism		√			√	
Long-term Involvement				√		
Perseverance and Determination					√	
Opportunity Seeking						√

It is observed that variables X_2 was found significantly correlated with variables X_3 and X_5 at 1 percent level; variable X_4 was found correlated with variable X_8 at 1 percent level of significance; and variable X_{10} was found significantly correlated with variables X_5 and X_6 at 1 percent level of significance. These relationships between variables finally led to the formation of different orthogonal factors.

Principal Component Analysis: The correlation matrix of all 10 variables was further subjected to principal component analysis. The Eigen values, the percentage of total variance, and rotated sum of squared loadings and the factor matrix as obtained by the principal component analysis was further subjected to Varimax Rotation. An examination of Eigen values led to the retention of four factors. These factors accounted for 24.45 percent, 23.05 percent, 19.90 percent, and 13.32 percent of variation respectively. This implies that the total variance accounted for by all eight factors was 80.71 percent and the remaining variance was explained by other factors.

Factor Analysis: The rotated factor matrix shows that variables under study constituted four groups/factors. It can be mentioned that the variable with factor loading of 0.50 and above was considered for inclusion into the factors. These have been discussed in the following paragraphs.

Factor-I: Organizational Factor: Factor-I explains 24.45 percent of the total variation existing in the variable set. This included variables such as X_5, X_6 and X_{10}. This factor had significant factor loadings on these variables which have formed this major cluster. This factor incorporated idea generation and managerial support for implementation through effective business plan for SMEs. Hence, this factor provides a basis for conceptualization of a dimension, which may be identified as 'organizational factor'.

Factor-II: Strategic Management Factor: Factor-II explains 23.05 percent of the total variation existing in the variable set. This included variables such as X_4, X_8 and X_9. This factor also had significant factor loading on these variables which formed the second important cluster with respect to the variations. This factor was concerned with strategic relationship and fund factors of entrepreneurs of SMEs. Therefore, it provided a dimension of conceptualizing these strategic variables, which may be identified as 'strategic management factors'.

Factor-III: Personal Factor: Factor-III explains 19.90 percent of the total variations existing in the variable set. This includes variables X_1, X_2 and X_3. This factor has high to higher factor loadings on these variables which have formed a third important cluster. This factor is related to basic entrepreneurial capacity of entrepreneurs of SMEs. Hence, it has provided a dimension of conceptualizing capacity related variables as a 'Personal Factor'.

Factor-IV: Relationship Factor: Factor-IV explains

13.32 percent of the total variations existing in the variable set. This includes only one variable, namely X_7. This factor also had higher factor loadings on the variable which formed a fourth important cluster. This factor also provided a basis for conceptualization of dimension which may be called 'Relationship Factor'.

Finally, the rankings obtained on the basis of factor-wise average scores are shown in Table 2.4.

Table 2.4: Rankings of the Factors Influencing Failure of Entrepreneurs of SMEs

	Factor	Average Score	Rank
I	Organizational Factor	3.30	2
II	Strategic Management Factor	3.28	3
III	Personal Factor	1.10	4
IV	Relationship Factor	3.7	1

Note: Data has been compiled by the researcher.

The factor ranking shows that Factor-IV, viz. the 'relationship factor' is the most important factor that leads the entrepreneurs of SMEs towards the success of business. This factor includes only one variable, namely X_7. This implies that an entrepreneur with competitive advantage and core competence can be a market leader and can maintain a very good relationship even with the competitors among others. This has really reflected the true picture of an entrepreneur's success in managing SMEs. The second most important factor is the 'organization factor'. This factor includes variables such as generation of innovative ideas, good business plan and healthy management support. These variables have been found contributing in the success of entrepreneurs in managing SMEs. The third important factor is the 'strategic management factor' which includes variables like well-structured in life and business, tabbing funds and strategic marketing of products. These three variables can be considered to be significant factors in an entrepreneur's success.

The study has adopted one alternative hypothesis for testing against the objective. The methodology, the researcher has employed, does not allow taking all variables as significant for policy and decision-making. The study has identified first two ranking factors, influencing the success of entrepreneur in managing SME. The study has found a few numbers of variables under study, being significantly correlated. This led the researcher to conclude that all variables under study, are not contributing significantly to the entrepreneurial success of SMEs in Bangladesh.

Summary, Policy Implications and Conclusion

The inference of the study is confined to the economies of SMEs in Bangladesh. The present study has been an explorative one. It has tried to explore the variables contributing to the success of entrepreneurs of SMEs by employing sophisticated multivariate technique, viz. Varimax Rotated Factor Analysis. In this case, the study has used SPSS. The study has found following factors as significant for entrepreneurial policies and strategies:

1. Relationship factor.
2. Organization factor.

The study has suggested present and future entrepreneurs to take above factors into consideration while making policies and strategies for SMEs. This is expected to give entrepreneurs a competitive and sustainable advantage of understanding and doing business in a global environment.

References

Ahmed, M. (1994), 'Economic and Cultural Environments for Industrial Entrepreneurship Development in Bangladesh: An Explorative Study', Dhaka, Bangladesh.

Ahmed, S.U. (1981), 'Entrepreneurship and Management Practices among Immigrants from Bangladesh in the UK', *unpublished doctoral thesis*, Brunel University.

Bagozzi, R. and Yi, Y. (1988), 'On the Evaluation of Structural

Equation Model', *Journal of the Academy of Marketing Science,* 16(1), 74-95.

Cog, C. and Jennings, R. (1995), 'The Foundation of Success: The Development and Characteristics of British Entrepreneurs and Intrapreneurs', *Leadership and Organizational Development Journal,* 16(7), 4-9.

Cronbach, L.J. (1951), 'Coefficient Alpha and the Internal Structure of Tests', *Psychometrika,* 16(3), 297-334.

Hornaday, J.A. (1982), 'Research about Living Entrepreneurs', Encyclopaedia of Entrepreneur, (ed.) Kent et al., Eagle Cliffs, New Jersey: Prentice Hall, 20-24.

Khan, A.K. (2000), 'Entrepreneurship, Small Business and Lives of Successful Entrepreneurs', Dhaka: Rubi Publications, Bangladesh.

Kao, J.J. (1989), 'Entrepreneurship, Creative and Organization: Text Cases and Readings', New Jersey: Prentice Hall.

Khanka, S.S. (2001), 'Entrepreneurial Development', New Delhi: S. Chand & Company Ltd.

McClelland, D.C. (1961), 'The Achieving Society', New York: The Free Press, 210-215.

Markman, G. and Baron, R. (2003), 'Person-Entrepreneurship Fit: Why Some People are More Successful as Entrepreneurs than Others', *Human Resource Management Review*, 13(2), 281-301.

Man, T.W, Lau, T. and Snape (2008), 'Entrepreneurial Competencies and the Performance of SMEs: An Investigation through a Framework of Competitiveness', *Journal of Small Business and Entrepreneurship,* 21(3), 257-276.

Makhbul, Z.M. (2011), 'Entrepreneurial Success: An Exploratory Study among Entrepreneurs', *International Journal of Business and Management,* 6(1), 116-125.

OECD (1997), 'Globalization and SMEs', Volume 1, Synthesis Report, Paris.

Palmer, K.N. (1994), 'Financial Information used by Small Retailer', *The CPA Journal*, Volume 64, No. 4, 70-72.

Park, K. and Taher, A. (2010), 'Encouraging Entrepreneurship Development and Its Impact on HRD in Emerging Economies', *Korean Journal of Business Ethics,* The Korean Academy of Business Ethics, Volume 12, No. 1, June.

Rahman, A. (1970), 'Private Sector of East Pakistan: An Analysis of Lagged Development', Research Monograph, No. 3, Karachi:

UBL, March 4.

Rahman, A.H. (1979), 'Entrepreneurship and Small Enterprise Development in Bangladesh', Bureau of Business Research, Dhaka.

Tandon, B.C. (1975), 'Environment and Entrepreneurs', Allahabad: Chugh Publications, p. 1.

3

Entrepreneurship in Informal Cross-border Trade

R.K.P.G. Singha

Introduction

Informal cross-border trade takes place mainly outside the legal framework. It is a fact that formal border trade is considered expensive because of the high level of taxation, which reduces potential profits. At the same time, there are many state services which try to extort bribes from the traders. This type of situation pushes the cross-border traders into illegality, as they try to stay away from such cumbersome formalities. Cross-border entrepreneurship activity plays an important role in community economic development programmes. The emergence of business groups and trade activities will generate employment, create wealth, contribute to tax revenue and stimulate the construction of infrastructure such as transportation. Indirectly, this will improve the standard of living in the border communities (Abd Hair Awang et al., 2013). Coming to Mizoram, cross-border trade has a special significance as it is in the immediate vicinity of Myanmar and Bangladesh and is far from the mainland. Mizoram's 72 percent of the boundary (1,006 km.) shares international border with these two countries.

Owing to topography, poor infrastructural facilities, absence of mineral wealth, coupled with other problems, the State has not been able to attract industries, virtually making it dependent upon the neighbouring states and countries. Further, the physical distance, the prevailing road conditions, and poor communication facilities acts as barriers in quick supply of goods and services from the neighbouring states, resulting in higher costs. Besides, the practice of charging higher profit margin by traders makes these goods and services too expensive (Felfamkima, V.L., 2009).

On the contrary, the trade centres of neighbouring countries being nearer, offer ease to traders in transportation and cost less. The affinity of the people with these countries owing to their similarity in ethnicity, lifestyle, habits, culture and religion, has also facilitated trade and commerce with these neighbouring countries (Kabra and Singha, 2006). Due to the prevailing situation, informal trade is flourishing in various markets of Mizoram and is flooded with foreign goods, specially coming through Champai and Tlabung, bordering with Myanmar and Bangladesh respectively (Singha and Kabra, 2007).

Objectives of the Study

The main objectives of the present study are:

1. To discuss the importance of informal cross-border trade in the context of Champhai and Tlabung in particular and Mizoram in general.
2. To study the socio-economic origins of the selected entrepreneurs.
3. To analyze the factors that have motivated and facilitated the entrepreneurship in informal cross-border trade.
4. To offer suggestions for improving the cross-border trade in Mizoram.

Methodology

The research work is based on the data collected from both primary as well as secondary sources. The primary data was collected from personal interviews with traders, researchers and other stakeholders and from market surveys of Champhai and Tlabung of Lunglei district of Mizoram. Samples of 60 traders were selected and who are involved in border trade particularly from Champhai and Tlabung market from Lunglei district. The data was also collected through structured questionnaire for this study. The information thus collected was tabulated and analyzed using various statistical tools and techniques, especially SPSS software for arriving at a meaningful conclusion and suggestions which may foster the overall economic development of the state of Mizoram.

About Champhai and Tlabung

Champhai is one of the 8 districts of Mizoram state in India. The district is bound on the north by Churachandpur district of Manipur state, on the west by Aizawl and Serchhip districts, and on the south and east by Myanmar. The district occupies an area of 3185.83 km^2. Champhai town is the administrative headquarters of the district. The district comprises 4 rural development blocks, namely, Champhai, Khawbung, Khawzawl and Ngopa. The district has 5 legislative assembly constituencies. These are Champhai, Khawbung, Khawhai, Khawzawl and Ngopa. There are 88 inhabited villages in the district.

According to the 2011 Census, Champhai district has a population of 1,25,370, roughly equal to the nation of Grenada. The population of Champhai town is 32,630 consisting of 16,205 males and 16,425 females (Census, 2011). The district has a population density of 39 inhabitants per square kilometre. Its population growth rate over the decade 2001-2011 was 16.01 percent. Champhai has a sex ratio of 984 females for every 1,000 males, and a literacy rate of 95.91 percent. The major religious groups in the districts are: the Christians (1,05,061), the Hindus (2,248) and the Muslims (432). In 1991, Champai district became home to Murlen National Park, which has an area of 200 km^2 (77.2 sq. miles). It is also home to the Lengteng Wildlife Sanctuary, which was established in 1999 and has an area of 120 km^2.

On the other hand, Tlabung is a census town in Lunglei district in the Indian state of Mizoram. Tlabung was also known as Demagiri. The area was unsettled but was considered to be the hunting ground of a Lusei Chief Rothangpuia and his subjects and was understood to be under his rule and jurisdiction. The township was first established and settled in November 1871 when the Superintendent of the Chittagong Hill Tracts, Lt. Col. T.H. Lewin ordered his Assistant Mr. Crouch and 150 soldiers from the Frontier Battalion to build a fort at Tlabung which is to serve the Battalion headquarters of the Southern Column of the Lushai Expedition to rescue a young girl named Mary Winchester from the Lushai Chief Bengkhuaia. It was made a part of the South Lushai Hills on April 1, 1898, while it was part of the Chittagong Hill Tracts earlier. It became a flourishing trade centre during 1860-70 when Mizo in north and south had less knowledge of commerce. It was used as the main river port to import goods from what is now Bangladesh through Chittagong city. It had an old fort constructed during British time at the advice of Lt. Col. T.H. Lewin.

As per Census 2011, Tlabung town has a population of 4,414. Males constitute 2,216 of the total population and females 2,198. Tlabung is 97 kilometres from Lunglei, the district headquarters and 332 kilometres from Aizawl, the state capital. The Khawthlangtuipui River flows through Tlabung and it is navigable up to Rangamati, Bangladesh but due to construction of Kaptai Dam, access to Port of Chittagong is not possible by boat. A border trade facilitation centre in Tlabung is in operation which helps with trade between Chittagong, Bangladesh and Tlabung, Mizoram. There are future plans to open the route from Tlabung to Chittagong port. It has been estimated that Mizoram can export raw and semi-raw materials like bamboo while it can import iron, steel and crockery and is accessible by road.

Socio-economic Origins of the Entrepreneurs

It is very crucial to understand that the entrepreneurship activity is dependent upon complex and varying combinations of the socio-economic, psychological and other factors like, age, educational level, occupation, religion, earning at the time of entry into the trade etc. The post economic liberalization has witnessed tremendous change in socio-economic as well as in business and trade environment in India as well in North Eastern Region also (Prasain and Singh, 2007). Therefore, an analysis of factors which promoted the entrepreneurs in informal cross-border trade under the study may provide a clue to the influences to which these particularly local entrepreneurs reacted to. The socio-economic origins of the entrepreneurs in informal cross-border trade are discussed in the following paragraphs.

Age of Traders: Table 3.1 shows district-wise classification of the age of the traders involved in cross-border trade. The table reveals that 46.7 percent of traders of Champhai fall in the age group of 35-45 years which is the highest, followed by 23.3 percent and 16.7 percent in the age group of 30-35 and below 30 years respectively. 50 years and above accounted for only 3.3 percent which is the least under the study. Tlabung has the maximum number of traders in 50 and above age group with 33.3 percent, followed by 35-45 age groups accounting for 30 percent and 23.3 percent in age group of 45-50 years. The least is 15.0 percent in the age group of below 30 years. The analysis shows that entrepreneurs in Champhai are younger than Tlabung of Lunglei district. Another reason is that Tlabung bazaar is older than Champhai.

Gender of Trader: Table 3.2 shows the gender-wise classification of traders in two districts of Mizoram. We can observe from the Table that Tlabung has an equal proportion of male and female traders out of the sample collected. However, in Champhai, 53.3 percent of the traders are females and 46.7 percent are males. At the same time, the combined percentage of women traders of both the districts is 51.67 percent. From the study, it is found that female participation in informal cross-border trade is quite significant.

Level of Education: In Champhai, 53.3 percent of the

traders have a bachelor's degree followed by 33.3 percent with HSSLC and 6.7 percent with primary level qualification.

Table 3.1: Age of the Trader: District-wise Classification

District of the Trader			Age of the Trader					Total
			Below 30	30-35	35-45	45-50	50 and above	
	Champhai	Count	5	7	14	3	1	30
		percent within the district of the trader	16.7	23.3	46.7	10.0	3.3	100
	Tlabung	Count	4	0	9	7	10	30
		percent within the district of the trader	13.3	.0	30.0	23.3	33.3	100
Total		Count	9	7	23	10	11	60
		percent within the district of the trader	15.0	11.6	38.3	16.6	18.3	100

Source: Field Survey.

Table 3.2: Gender of Traders: District-wise Classification

District of the Trader			Gender		Total
			Male	Female	
	Champhai	Count	15	15	30
		percent within the district of the trader	50.0	50.0	100.0
	Tlabung	Count	14	16	30
		percent within the district of the trader	46.7	53.3	100.0
Total		Count	29	31	60
		percent within the district of the trader	48.33	51.67	100.0

Source: Field Survey.

However, in Tlabung, 40.0 percent traders had primary

level of education followed by 36.7 percent with HSLC and 23.3 percent with HSSLC. Interestingly, no one has got a bachelor's or a master's degree qualification in Tlabung. It is crucial to mention here that Tlabung is the least developed town in terms of educational facilities bordering Bangladesh.

Religion: It was revealed that majority of traders in the two districts are Christians. In Champhai, all traders i.e. 100 percent are Christians by religion. Whereas, Tlabung has 30 percent Hindu traders, the remaining 70 percent traders are Christians. Interestingly in Tlablung, quite a good number of non-Mizos reside.

Generation in Trade: 85 percent of the entrepreneurs were first generation entrepreneurs, followed by 13.3 percent as second generation and only 1.7 percent as third generation entrepreneurs in both the districts. In Champhai, 83.3 percent of the traders belonged to first generation followed by 10.0 percent and 6.7 percent to second and third generations. Again, in Tlabung, 80.0 percent were first generation traders followed by 20.0 percent as second generation traders. There were no third generation traders found in Tlabung. The study shows that business and trade is still at in infancy as entrepreneurs mostly belong to the first generation only.

Motivating Factors: In Champhai, majority of the traders, i.e. 53.3 percent, were motivated as they wanted to make money out of the trade. The next factor was to fulfil their ambitions with a percentage share of 20 percent followed by 10 percent traders who decided to continue their family business. Again in Tlabung, 60.0 percent of them started the business to make money, followed by 30.0 percent to continue the family business and 10.0 percent to secure self-employment.

Reasons for Choosing the Trade: In Champhai, 56.7 percent of the traders started their business because it was easy to do such type of trade. Again 20.0 percent of the traders claimed that it is due to the related past profession or occupation and 10.0 percent of them opted for the trade because it was easy to start as there was not much competition in this line of business. Similarly, in Tlabung, 70.0 percent of the traders selected the trade because it was easy to start this type of business followed by 20.0 percent who started due to a higher margin of profit and 6.7 percent started because of previous employment in the same line.

Compelling Reasons for Starting the Trade: In Champhai, 53.3 percent claimed that they opted for the trade because of unemployment followed by 30 percent traders stating that they wanted to make use of their technical and professional skills, and 10.0 percent of them became traders to make use of idle funds lying with them. On the other hand, in Tlabung, majority of the traders i.e. 70.0 percent, opted for the trade due to the unemployment followed by 16.7 percent who wanted to make use of their idle funds and 6.7 percent who wanted to utilize their technical and professional skills.

Country of Origin of the Products: In Champhai, 36.7 percent of the traders claimed that their products were from China, 26.7 percent from Myanmar followed by 23.3 percent who sourced from Thailand. On the other hand, in Tlabung, 40 percent of the products were sourced from Myanmar followed by 30 percent of the products from China and 26.7 percent of the products from Bangladesh.

Major Products in the Trade: In Champhai district, it is evident that a majority of the traders dealt in miscellaneous consumer goods accounting for 36.7 percent which was followed the category of textiles, readymade garments, blankets etc. and food products and beverages respectively. Meanwhile, in Tlabung, majority of the traders dealt in textiles, readymade garments, blankets etc. accounting for 36.7 percent followed by food products and beverages with a 30 percent share and cosmetics and toiletries with a 16.7 percent share.

Conclusion

The emergence of entrepreneurs—men or women—in a society depends to a large extent on the social, economic, religious, cultural, psychological and environmental factors prevailing in the society. Entrepreneurs with their inherent intelligence, drive and hard work can make the best use of the opportunities that are made available through the above factors. In the context of Mizoram, local trader participation in trading activities is quite visible when we studied the market place (Singha, 2012). The recent phenomenon is that more and more local entrepreneurs are joining in informal cross-border trade in the state. It can be observed from the above discussion that cross-border trade stabilizes the market price of the goods supplied with the additional demand from the recipient country and provide job opportunities to the local people.

Trade and business is growing day by day and successful entrepreneurs have proved that they are no less when compared to entrepreneurs in other parts of the country in terms of efficiency, hard work and intelligence. In this study, it is very interesting to note that almost 50 percent of the traders in the districts are women, which is very significant from the socio-economic development as well as from the women empowerment point of view (Singha, 2014).

With growing awareness about business and trade and due to growth of education level and professional qualifications, industrialisation, urbanisation and democratic values, the traditional bond of our society has undergone a change and entrepreneurs have shifted their entrepreneurial activities to non-traditional trades like informal cross-border trade to benefit from the economic liberalization.

References

Abd, Hair Awang, Junaenah Sulehan, Noor Rahamah Abu Bakar, Mohd. Yusof Abdullah and Ong Puay Liu (2013), 'Informal Cross-Border Trade: A Catalyst for Border Community's Development', *Asian Social Science,* Volume 9, No. 4, Canadian Centre of Science and Education.

Kabra, K.C. and Singha, R.K.P.G. (2006), 'Border Trade in Mizoram: Emerging Trends and Future Prospects', in David, R. and Syemlieh et al. (ed.), 'Challenges of Development in North-

East India', Regency Publications, New Delhi.

Felfamkima, V.L. (2009), 'Border Trade in Mizoram: Emerging Trend and Future Prospects', M. Phil dissertation (Submitted to Madurai Kamraj University, Tamil Nadu).

Singha, R.K.P.G. and Kabra, K.C. (2007), 'Prospects of Indo-Bangla Border Trade: A Case Study of Mizoram', in Prasain, G.P. (ed.), Global Convergence on Commerce of Commerce Education.

Singha, R.K.P.G. (2014), 'Women Entrepreneurship in Informal Cross-Border Trade: A Mizoram Perspective', Paper presented at the National Seminar on ''Millennium Development Goals and North-East India' organized by Department of Political Science, Government J. Buana College, Lunglei, Mizoram on May 1, 2014.

4

Post-liberalisation Entrepreneurship in Pharmaceutical Business

Doneti Sivaji

Introduction

The roots of entrepreneurship of the pharma sector can be traced back from the establishment of (IDPL) Indian Drugs and Pharmaceuticals Ltd. It was established in 1960 in Hyderabad along with some other centres for achieving India's march towards self-sufficiency and self-reliance in the field of drugs and pharmaceuticals. The branch in Hyderabad focused primarily on R&D activities. IDPL has played a pioneering infrastructural role in the growth of the Indian drug industry.

The company contributed significantly towards this objective in the area of such essential and life saving drugs as narrow spectrum antibiotics, tetracyclines, anti-fungal, sulphonamides, vitamins, analgesics, anti hypertensive, diuretics, hypnotics, anti malarial and fluoroquinolones.

The Hyderabad branch had three patents on drugs related to diarrhoea, arthritis, depression and muscle relaxants. Nevertheless, IDPL gave a tremendous boost to indigenous efforts in the private sector of the pharmaceutical industry. Since the synthetic drug plant of IDPL was located in Hyderabad, the city has developed as the main bulk drug manufacturing centre in the country.

Objectives of the Study

- To study the fast growth of entrepreneurship in pharma industry with reference to the city of Hyderabad.
- To analyze the trends and factors in promoting

entrepreneurship in pharma industry in view of the post-liberalization policies in Hyderabad.

- To know, how the city of Hyderabad became the testing ground for the new entrants.

The method followed is of qualitative analysis by collecting information and opinions, taken from entrepreneurs and also their private and published papers and also referred business magazines and biographies along with internet sources.

Bulk Pharma

The entrepreneurs of many of the private sector bulk drug manufacturing firms had at one time worked with IDPL's production or R&D departments. These include Dr. K. Anji Reddy, the founder of the highly successful Dr. Reddy's Laboratories. [1] After the introduction of the new economic policy and with the onset of liberalization in 1991, the IDPL went into severe losses as it continued to sell its generic drugs at very Low prices. This was opposed by the MNCs and private sector firms who sold the drugs at higher prices. The new climate for enterprise emerged in the wake of liberalization and it was evident that huge opportunities existed in India. It was natural and these conditions for new enterprises created the most successful entrepreneurs. Dr. Anji Reddy's of Reddy's Laboratories, a health care and pharmaceutical company at Hyderabad was predominant among them. [2] Dr. K. Anji Reddy [3] who is the founder chairman of Dr. Reddy's Laboratory, created a worldwide wave in the pharma business. He served in the state owned Indian Drugs and Pharmaceuticals Ltd., from 1969 to 1975, was founder managing director of Uniloids Ltd. from 1976 to 1980 and Standard Organics Ltd. from 1980 to 1984, before founding Dr. Reddy's in 1984.

Dr. Reddy opened the new vistas in the pharma business by starting a research foundation in Hyderabad with the team of brilliant scientists from various disciplines of life sciences in 1993. The research program at this foundation was focused on diabetes and cancer. They accomplished admirable success in their chosen fields. Several other companies also started drug discovery research and made significant investments in the field in Hyderabad. The opportunities from new biology revolutionized the management of human healthcare, offering much greater potential to create wealth.

Around 600 pharma units, including a dozen big ones like Dr. Reddy's Labs which has won international recognition, mushroomed in Hyderabad and some of them in Telangana also, catering to the demand for bulk drugs and making them cost effective. The cost effectiveness of Indian manufacturers and the availability of skilled labour are among the major advantages that had put Hyderabad on the world map of pharma research and production, opines Dr. Anji Reddy. [4]

Under Dr. Anji Reddy's leadership, Dr. Reddy's Laboratories has become a pioneer and a trendsetter in the Indian pharmaceutical industry. It has turned the Indian bulk drug industry from import-dependent in the mid-1980s to self-reliant in the mid-1990s and finally into an export-oriented industry as of today. Dr. Reddy's was the first company to begin drug discovery research in India in 1993 and has led the industry in turning from 'copycats' into innovators. Dr. Reddy's was listed on the New York Stock Exchange in April 2001—the first non-Japanese Asian pharmaceutical company to be listed on the NYSE. The present turnover of the company is in excess of US$ 1 billion. Perhaps, Dr. Reddy was strongly influenced by Jawaharlal Nehru, who set the foundation of modern India and had the vision and courage to steer the nation on the path of democracy and scientific progress. He himself told that he was energized and inspired by Nehru's call to advance the frontiers of science and technology to build a strong and self-reliant nation. [5]

G.V. Prasad is another important entrepreneur in Hyderabad pharma industry. He spent his initial years in managing various construction projects in Karnataka. His first exposure to the world of pharmaceuticals was in 1985 with Benzex Labs, a pharmaceutical enterprise that he co-founded. Benzex was later acquired by Dr. Reddy's and Prasad returned to the construction business, only to come back to pharma in 1990—this time as the CEO and MD of Cheminor Drugs Ltd. Prasad infused professionalism, good governance and transparency to transform Cheminor into a world class active pharmaceutical ingredient and generics manufacturer. In 2001, Cheminor Drugs merged with Dr. Reddy's Laboratories and Prasad took over as the vice-chairman and CEO of the merged entity. As CEO, Prasad strategized the metamorphosis of the mid-sized pharmaceutical company into a globally respected pharma major. He nurtured new lines of business, built a high-talent organization, expanded the global footprint and crafted best-in-class practices in corporate governance.

Prasad is widely credited as the architect of Dr. Reddy's successful global generics strategy. He envisioned newer business platforms like the custom pharmaceutical business and speciality pharmaceuticals. He has been a strong advocate of his company's vision to be "a discovery-led global pharmaceutical company" and is currently focused on building the innovation side of the business. Prasad has made dramatic and emphatic moves to expand his organization's size and scale of operations through sustained global alliances and well-calculated mergers and acquisitions.

Prasad has over the years, built a diverse, talented and experienced senior management team in India, Europe and the US. A strong believer in his people, he has encouraged dynamic HR practices in the organization. Today, Dr. Reddy's is widely acknowledged as one of the best companies to work for in India across various 'best employer' surveys. Even as he builds business, Prasad strongly champions sustainable development at Dr. Reddy's and supports new technologies and investments in transforming Dr. Reddy's into an environmentally conscious and socially responsible organization. [6]

Companies such as Matrix Laboratories, Hetero Drugs Ltd., Divis Labs, Aurobindo Pharma Ltd. and Vimta Labs being housed in the city also come under the bulk drug business. A large number of entrepreneurial start-ups have emerged very strong and have started churning out new drug discoveries for the world. A few Hyderabad companies have also become leaders in the global generics markets. Predominantly, Hyderabad has emerged as a major centre for pharmaceuticals business with multinational standards in both bulk drug and retail business.

Vimta Labs Ltd. was established in 1984 by Dr. S.P. Vasireddi. Vimta Labs is a leading provider of multi-disciplinary contract research and testing services in India. With its international quality systems, world class infrastructure and expert human resources, today Vimta is the preferred choice for many market leaders across the globe. Vimta has an envious track record of providing its services to several prestigious clients across the world, including six 'Fortune 500' companies, and three of world's 'Top Ten' generic drug development companies. [7]

Aurobindo Pharma was born out of a vision. Founded in 1986 by Mr. P.V. Ramaprasad Reddy, Mr. K. Nityananda Reddy and a small, highly committed group of professionals, the company became a public venture in 1992. It commenced operations in 1988-89 with a single unit manufacturing of semi-synthetic penicillin at Pondicherry. Aurobindo Pharma went public in 1995 by listing its shares in various stock exchanges across the country. The company is a market leader in semi-synthetic penicillin drugs. It has a presence in key therapeutic segments like SSPs, cephalosporins, antivirals, CNS, cardio-vascular, gastroenterology, etc. Over the years, Aurobindo Pharma has evolved into a knowledge-driven company. It is R&D focused, has a multi-product portfolio with multi-country manufacturing facilities, and is becoming a marketing conglomerate across the world. Aurobindo Pharma has created a name for itself in the manufacture of bulk drugs—its area of core competence.

After ensuring a firm foundation of cost effective production capabilities and a clutch of loyal customers, the company has entered the high margin specialty generic formulations segment, with a global marketing network. The formulation business is systematically organized with a divisional structure, and has a focused team for each key international market. Aurobindo believes in gaining volume and market share in every business/segment it enters. Aurobindo has invested significant resources in building a mega infrastructure for APIs and formulations to emerge as a vertically integrated pharmaceutical company. Aurobindo's five units for APIs and four units for formulations are designed for the regulated markets. [8]

Retail Pharma

The retail business is a new trend and took shape in the pharma business along with the development of the bulk drug pharma entrepreneurship during the liberalization period. The companies like Apollo, Goodlife, Medplus etc. have made hay in the retail market.

The reason for this new trend of retail business is that many patients, suffering with different health problems, pulled over to the retail shops as they were habituated to buy medicines over the counter at the medical stores even without consulting doctor. People were scared at the very thought of taking appointments one day or two days (weeks in some cases) in advance, and then wait in the long queues. They either postponed their visits to the doctors or became dependent on the medical stores for quick fixes. Recognizing this problem, some pharmacy chains started evolving plans to offer the services at the locations convenient to the people to turn up. There are many entrepreneurs who have come forward to start their ventures and to open pharma stores in Hyderabad.

The key role has been played by the Apollo Hospitals by establishing its pharmacy chain in the city. Apollo Hospitals have aggressive plans for expansion of its pharmacy business, which is a high-return growth sector, commanding high valuations of the retail business. Apollo Health and Lifestyle, Apollo Pharmacies and Apollo Health Street have done financially well.

Ms. Shivani Kanneganti, chief operating officer of Goodlife, promoted by Global Hospitals chain runs five regular pharmacies in the twin cities, providing health check-ups, diagnostic services, dental care and medical counselling, besides selling pharma and wellness products. '*We offer the patients the first line of defence. They can see a physician without an appointment. They will be referred to a specialist only if it is warranted'.* [9] Goodlife is in advanced stage of talks with the retail major Future Group. '*We are planning to locate these convenience clinics at the malls or in the high streets*', Ms. Shivani said. With Global Hospitals planning to enter all major cities, Goodlife sees a strong backing as it goes to those cities. The company is proposing to set up 30 such clinics in the next 12 months. Another city-based pharmacy chain, MedPlus has already rolled out similar clinics. [10]

It, however, is not an easy task, Dr. Surendra Mantena, CEO, of MedPlus Path Labs, felt. '*We agree that in the current scenario, people have a tendency to seek out a specialist rather than a generalist as they have a wrong perception that a specialist is better than a generalist for treating any ailment',* he said. *'We believe that our conveniently located MedPlus Clinics can change this mentality, but it will take time and education',* he pointed out. MedPlus, which operates 15 such integrated clinics is expecting to open at least 50 such clinics by March 2009. [11]

Conclusion

Hyderabad turned out to be a fruitful destiny and became a promising sector for new entrepreneurs. It created trends in bulk pharma and retail pharma. Dr. Reddy's Laboratories opened new vistas in creating a profitable business in bulk pharma; many MNC companies also focused on Hyderabad to test their fate in the pbusiness.

The policies pursued by the local government(s) in Andhra Pradesh, particularly by Naidu and subsequently by Reddy, provided the support one can quote in setting up of exclusive zones for pharma industries around Hyderabad. This could be one reason and some of the initial successes made by the first generation entrepreneurs in the pharma field in Hyderabad gave the courage and push to other investors to plunge in the industry. Dr. Reddy paved the way for new entrepreneurs to come in the pharma sector. The other factors could include availability of well educated employable workforce.

More so, Hyderabad has also offered a platform for many intelligent young minds who took up these courses when they could not get admission to the first tier medical education. Another factor could be the need of quality basic medicines at a much cheaper cost and naturally to produce such basic medicines at nearby location to save transportation costs. Pharma industries in Hyderabad could enter into agreements with overseas leading pharma companies for supply of basic formulations and basic medicines. The well developed countries chose to sub-contract manufacture and supply such medicines/formulations for less costly locations. Hyderabad happened to be one among them.

Endnotes

1. Rao, R.S., Rao, V. Hanumanta and Gopal, N. Venu. (ed.), 'Fifty Years of Andhra Pradesh 1956-2006', Centre for Documentation Research and Communication (CDRC), Hyderabad, 2007, pp. 324-325.
2. Tripati, Dwijendra and Jumani, Jyothi, 'The Concise History of Indian Business', Oxford University Press, New Delhi, 2007, pp. 224-225.
3. A Bachelor's of Science in Pharmaceuticals and Fine Chemicals from Bombay University and a Ph.D. in Chemical Engineering from the National Chemical Laboratory, Pune.
4. 'Fifty years of Andhra Pradesh', *op. cit.*, p. 265.
5. Speech delivered by Dr. Reddy at international symposium on

"Innovating Drugs: Emerging Perspectives", 2004, at Hotel Viceroys, Hyderabad.

6. Visited: Wikipedia free encyclopaedia.
7. April 2004, Reachout Hyderabad.com, News Bureau.
8. http://www.aurobindo.com/companyhistory.htm.
9. The Hindu Business Line: July 8, 2008.
10. Ibid.
11. Ibid.

5

Problems and Prospects of Entrepreneurship

Sandeep Kumar Singh

Introduction

Entrepreneurship is derived from the French word 'entreprende' meaning to 'undertake'. It is the process of identifying and exploiting business opportunities by organizing the human and non-human resources, while taking both the risks and rewards associated with the venture. It is concerned with the establishment of new organizations, also known as start-ups, in response to a perceived business opportunity. According to GEDI, "Entrepreneurship is a dynamic interaction of entrepreneurial attitudes, entrepreneurial activity and entrepreneurial aspiration that vary across stages of economic development". In recent years, various new forms of entrepreneurship have emerged, dealing with specific issues, such as women entrepreneurship, rural entrepreneurship, green entrepreneurship, social entrepreneurship and intrapreneurship. However, our study deals only with the problems and prospects associated with entrepreneurship, in general.

Entrepreneurship is regarded as an engine of growth. It creates social value, economic value, promotes innovation and leads to job creation, all of which eventually helps in improving the economy of the state. But very often, it has been seen that we have ignored the importance of entrepreneurship. This is evident from the fact that very few start-ups have come up in the state and a majority of them have failed to sustain their growth, eventually shutting down their operations. One must remember that goodwill from the government is not enough to re-create what other prosperous states have done. We need to create a friendly climate for our entrepreneurs by providing them with financial assistance and technical support so that their ventures do not fail prematurely.

The common notion held is that anyone who starts a new venture is an entrepreneur. One should keep in mind that although the creation of business is certainly an important dimension of entrepreneurship, it is not the complete picture. There is a thin line of difference between self-employment and entrepreneurship. A person who starts a new venture with the sole objective of earning livelihood for himself cannot be classified as an entrepreneur. An entrepreneur is more than that. He is an innovator, organiser, risk-taker and a change agent for the society. He is not here for short-term gains, but in pursuit of sustained growth. He believes in creating opportunities for others and brings in an overall change in the society. In this process, he contributes to personal, economic as well as human development.

A few years ago anyone could become an entrepreneur. Entrepreneurship required three elements—a unique idea, basic infrastructure and a funding source which would help translate one's idea into action. However, things are not that easy now. There are a lot of licenses, clearances and certificates that must be obtained before one can start his own venture and it consumes a lot of time, money and energy to get it all done with. Also because of liberalisation and globalisation, there has been a huge inflow of funds and firms from other parts of the world and competition has increased to an altogether different level. The essence of innovation of entrepreneurship comes from economic hardship: the actual desire to improve oneself. And it is this basic feature that is very rarely found. As a society, we have a more casual and laidback approach towards life. The entrepreneurial scene in Assam will improve only if we stop trying to shift the entire blame on the State and start viewing entrepreneurship as an alternate career choice.

Objectives of the Study

- To examine the role of government in promoting entrepreneurship in Assam.
- To list the problems faced by budding entrepreneurs in starting a new venture.
- To establish standard criteria for measuring the ease of doing business in Assam.
- To come up with remedial measures that will help foster entrepreneurship and contribute to the state's growth story.

Literature Review

An exhaustive review of the available literature lays the foundation for our study on entrepreneurship in Assam. The quantity of research that has been carried out in this area is very high as it is regarded as a burning issue. The key references have been listed below in a chronological order.

Chakraborty, Dipanjan (2014): The study analyses the impact of socio-economic background on growth of rural entrepreneurship. The findings revealed that factors like age, gender, education, annual income of rural entrepreneurs etc., had a direct impact on the growth of rural entrepreneurship. It advocated the need for concerted efforts by the government and rural masses to promote entrepreneurship.

GEDI (2014): This study was conducted to help understand where entrepreneurs are operating, where they are not operating, and why. This information can then be used to reduce the cultural, economic and institutional barriers that stand in their way. It would also help expose areas where policy improvements would improve the entrepreneurship ecosystem the most.

Goswami and Devi (2014): The article traces the development of women entrepreneurs in Assam and the various problems that they have to face in order to start a new venture. The number of women entrepreneurs in Assam is greater than the national average but still a lot can be done to augment entrepreneurial growth through awareness and assistance.

Lalhunthara and Kumar (2012): This study was designed to examine if there is any correlation between the socio-economic background of people and their entrepreneurial ambition. The findings revealed that factors like educational level, economic standing and social forces indeed have a bearing on entrepreneurship.

Zoltan J. and Laszlo Szerb (2010): While small businesses and entrepreneurship are not the same, the two concepts are frequently used interchangeably. In fact, job creation cannot be expected to flow from the creation of numerous tiny businesses; they are instead the result of a small number of high-growth entrepreneurial ventures. According to them, a small business is basically a quantitative activity whereas entrepreneurship is a qualitative phenomenon.

Srivastava (2008): This study analyses the development of small-scale industrial sector in the rural areas of Assam. The findings reveal that the concentration of SSI activities is higher in rural areas than in urban areas. Also it was found that, manufacturing sector is more dominant in such areas.

Walter Kuemmerle (2002): According to Walter, the path of an entrepreneur isn't for everyone and you will be much more likely to succeed in your venture if you have the answer for five small questions. Are you comfortable stretching the rules? Are you prepared to make powerful enemies? Do you have the patience to start small? Are you willing to shift strategies quickly? and Are you a closer?

Mali (1998): The findings of the study revealed that small, medium and micro enterprises based in Assam would have to face increasing competition as globalisation facilitated the entry of new firms. They have to specifically upgrade their capabilities and improve themselves in the fields of marketing, product research, infrastructure development and technological well-being.

Thus, from the above literature review, it can be inferred that entrepreneurship should not be confused with small businesses. In context of Assam, entrepreneurship is yet to gain acceptance as an alternate career choice. Earlier research work has focussed on specific research areas like green entrepreneurship, social entrepreneurship, women entrepreneurship and rural entrepreneurship. There are a number of problems that potential entrepreneurs will have to face and it is only through the support of all stakeholders that these problems can be countered in a timely manner.

Justification of the Study

There hasn't been a lot of research work focusing on the role of the state in promoting entrepreneurship and the real problems faced by prospective entrepreneurs in setting up a new business venture in the state. A number of questions still remain answered. Why are most people reluctant to take up the entrepreneurial role? Is it only because the state has failed miserably in its actions and its policies have had a very minimal impact? Or are there other difficulties that have been faced by prospective entrepreneurs in setting up their business. This study aims to unravel the real issues that are responsible for the negligible number of start-ups in the state and their failures.

Again, there is a wide research gap between the existing literature and the desired quality of research which reinforces the need for more quantitative and qualitative research in the field of green marketing. Moreover, the state is now aware of the fact that promoting entrepreneurship will help the state in more ways than one. It helps in creating economic value and generates employment opportunities for the state. As such, a proper evaluation of the state's role is need of the hour. Proper feedback from the entrepreneurs' side will help us understand where it all went wrong. The desire to solve unsolved problems and reducing information asymmetry on government schemes is the biggest motivation for conducting research in this area.

Limitations of the Study

- There is a wide research gap between the existing

literature and desired quantity. The researcher does not have enough research material to bank upon.

- Another big obstacle was the refusal of some persons to disclose information when asked whether they had to pay kickbacks in order to obtain licenses and clearances.
- Another common error that was noticed in the data collection process was that though people were really angry at the minimal support extended by the state, they did not give extremely poor ratings.

Research Methodology

The research is exploratory and empirical in nature. The study has been carried out keeping in mind various demographic characteristics such as age, gender, marital status, educational level, income level etc. of the respondents. An exhaustive review of the existing literature lays the foundation for the study. For the purpose of study, non-probability approach is adopted and a sample is selected from the population using the convenient sampling method so as to ensure that there is adequate representation from all genders, age groups, income levels and educational backgrounds.

For the purpose of the study, a sample of 120 budding entrepreneurs was selected from Barpeta, Baksa and Bongaigaon districts. The sample was selected through convenient sampling method as most of the entrepreneurs were hesitant to talk about certain issues such as payment of bribes in state departments so as to speed up the process of obtaining clearances etc. Data was gathered first hand with the help of a questionnaire, consisting of questions which were in the form of statements. The entrepreneurs had to provide ratings for ten different parameters that were identified as determinants of regional entrepreneurship. The parameters were:

- Entrepreneurship education.
- Management training.
- Financial support.
- Technical support.

- Tax incentives.
- Physical infrastructure.
- Licensing.
- Statutory laws.
- Regional issues like terrorism.
- Family support.

The questionnaires were self-administered and handed out to the respondents individually, through household drop-off, just like personal surveys. After a brief time period during which the respondents were expected to fill up the questionnaires, the questionnaires were collected back from them. The responses were totalled and analysed to arrive at the conclusion. The study was conducted during the period April to May 2014.

Data Analysis

The data obtained from the respondents was then tabulated, digitised and analysed using a combination of research tools and techniques such as scaling techniques (Five Point Likert scale), descriptive statistics (mean and standard deviation), tables and pie-charts in order to achieve a better understanding of the research area. In the beginning, we observe the demographic profile of respondents keeping in mind parameters like age, gender, marital status, educational qualifications, income levels, location etc (Table 5.1).

From Table 5.1, it can be inferred that:

- Among the respondents, males clearly outnumber females, the ratio falling at 54:46.
- Amongst the respondents, graduates emerge as the biggest category as they constitute about 45 percent of the sample.
- Majority of the respondents (33.3 percent) earn between ₹ 10, 000 to ₹ 20,000 per month. About 29.17 percent of the respondents fall in the income bracket of ₹ 20,000 to ₹ 40,000.
- At the time of the survey, 62.5 percent of the respondents were single and the remaining 37.5 percent were married.
- Amongst the respondents, 45.84 percent were living in

villages, 33.33 percent lived in towns and about 20.83 percent lived in city. The idea was to make the sample as geographically widespread as possible, so as to ensure diversity and obtain a broader perspective.

Table 5.1: Demographic Profile of Respondents

Characteristics		Number	Percentage
Gender	Male	65	54.16
	Female	55	45.84
Age	21-25 years	25	20.83
	25-29 years	45	37.50
	30-35 years	30	25.00
	Above 35	20	16.67
Education	Higher Secondary	15	12.50
	Graduate	45	37.50
	Post-graduate	40	33.33
	Professionals	20	16.67
Family Income	No Income	30	25.00
	₹ 5,000-₹ 9,999	15	12.50
	₹ 10,000-₹ 19,999	40	33.33
	₹ 20,000-₹ 39,999	35	29.17
Marital Status	Married	45	37.50
	Unmarried	75	62.50
Residence	Village	55	45.84
	Town	40	33.33
	City	25	20.83

Ease of Doing Business

In order to determine the ease of doing business in Assam, ten specific parameters were created and responses were obtained from the respondents on them, on a five point Likert scale ranging from excellent-good-average-fair-poor. The respondents were asked to provide honest ratings according to their experiences. The responses thus obtained were then converted into percentages and charted for better understanding as shown in Table 5.2.

Table 5.2: Parameters to Determine Ease of Doing Business

Responses Obtained on:	E	G	A	F	P
Quality of Entrepreneurship Education	10	20	30	25	15
Quality of Management Training	15	30	10	30	15
Financial Support	20	30	10	18	22
Tax Incentives	10	23	18	29	20
Technical Support	10	15	20	35	20
Physical Infrastructure	15	24	30	21	10
Licensing	10	22	28	15	25
Statutory Laws	15	18	20	27	20
Regional Problems like Terrorism	05	10	18	12	55
Family Support	20	35	15	10	10

E = Excellent; G = Good; A = Average; F = Fair; P = Poor

From the data obtained, the following inferences can be made:

- The biggest problem plaguing entrepreneurship in Assam is that of terrorism. Assam is a victim of terrorism. Every now and then, we keep hearing about kidnappings of businessmen for ransom, killings of innocent people just because they speak a different language. It is known to one and all that terrorism creates uncertainty and delays investments in any part of the world. People refrain from investing their money out of fear and insecurity.
- The physical infrastructure of the state is pretty average. Most of the roads and bridges are in a deplorable condition. Rail connectivity still does not exist in some parts of the state. It becomes very difficult to transport finished goods and raw materials to and from the market. Using waterways for transportation of cargo is still not a common practice as some of the rivers are not navigable and the inter-linking of rivers is still underway.
- Other major problems include lack of awareness about the financial schemes floated by the state at the local level,

delay in obtaining licenses and clearances and the state of entrepreneurial education in Assam. These processes must be streamlined and made more user-friendly.

Challenges to Entrepreneurship

Major findings of the study reveal that there are a lot of hurdles, namely red tapism, high taxes, and lack of capital. There is not as much support for business start ups as compared to other states. In fact, it should be noted that Assam ranks much behind in the 'Ease of Doing Business Index'. The various problems plaguing entrepreneurship with specific reference to Assam are listed as under.

Lack of Credit Facilities: Potential entrepreneurs find it really difficult to acquire funds for their businesses. Though there are a number of institutions offering assistance, they usually charge high interest rates and set heavy collateral conditions, deterring the aspiring entrepreneurs.

Corrupt System: Widespread corruption in the state departments is another source of trouble. The procurement of licenses, permits and clearances is very difficult without paying bribes and kickbacks. Either pay or there will be delays in getting the necessary permits.

Inconsistent Government Policies: Government inconsistency is really a challenge an entrepreneur has to face if he is planning to start a new venture. Political instability has a huge bearing on businesses. All entrepreneurs can do is to influence government's policy with respect to enacting favourable business law, provided he has the political clout for it.

Heavy Taxation: Another sensitive challenge that is encountered by majority of entrepreneurs here is the high rates of taxation. Although entrepreneurs in a country have a responsibility for funding the government by paying taxes on time, the rates at which taxes have to be paid, is too high, especially for the outsiders.

Inadequate Infrastructure: The infrastructure in Assam and other neighbouring states is pathetic, to say the least. With the existing infrastructure deteriorating and in some places non-existent, the cost of doing business has tremendously gone up because of higher transportation cost. Also, the erratic supply of electricity is a big problem.

Failure to Adapt to Change: A majority of entrepreneurs lack relevant and adequate information about the business they engage in and the environment they operate in. As such they end up taking wrong decisions based on incomplete information. Moreover, they lack sufficient problem-solving skills and in the end, find it hard to survive the competition.

Low Standard of Education: It is known to one and all that education plays a crucial role in entrepreneurship. The world today is a global village and since an intending entrepreneur must be conversant with the events and happenings around him, education becomes a critical factor in preparing the entrepreneur with the qualities required of him.

Lack of Awareness: Very few budding entrepreneurs know about the institutional and financial support that is available to them under various schemes and from different sources. The number of venture capital firms is also very few and it is equally difficult to approach them or arrange a meeting with them for funds.

FDI Restrictions: Restrictions on FDI act as a barrier to entrepreneurship too as it slows down flow of funds from outside the state. Outsiders start viewing it as an unsafe investment zone and refrain from investing in the region, which would have indirectly led to creation of more employment opportunities.

Based on Necessity: The purpose with which you start a business tells a lot about how far the business will go. In Assam, most people start a business only because they want to make fast money or that is the only thing left for them to do. The key ingredient is missing in most of them, that of passion.

Female Entrepreneurs: Women are often underestimated and overlooked despite having the talent and skills required to start a new venture. The main reason behind this is the cultural barriers such as male/female role definitions that label women as inferior to men. As such, it gets very difficult for them to acquire funds and manage resources.

Poor Planning: There is one thing that binds all successful entrepreneurs together. They are good planners. Unfortunately, it is seen that most of the entrepreneurs do not plan their actions well in advance. Even if they do, they are myopic in their views, leaving out possibilities of contingencies in the near future.

Troubled Exit: Starting a company in Assam is a one way journey with no exits. Indian laws do not let go so easily. Non-closure will lock your Director's ID number blocking all chances of starting up again. On the other hand, early closure saves you from repeated tax demands and need for filing returns each year. It keeps books clear for engagement in another venture and to raise funds. It helps in amicable parting of co-founders and investors.

Ignoring NRIs: Assam's tendency to shun its diaspora must rank as among the most disastrous decisions by a state in modern times—disastrous in the sense that a successful group of people are willing to give time, money, energy, and good will to their state of origin and are being pushed away. Fortunately, this situation has been changing in the last 4 to 5 years.

Market Issues: Individual ideas and people are integral to the success of entrepreneurship, but there are three main problems with Assam's entrepreneurial scene that its government could work on—Absence of a big and homogeneous market; relative shortage of capital for start-ups and growing firms; and lack of entrepreneurs who combine technological expertise, business acumen and risk-taking ability.

Casual Attitude: Most of the people in Assam have a very casual and laidback approach towards life. They are highly averse towards risk and as such do not view entrepreneurship as an alternate career choice because it does not guarantee any stable source of income. They would ignore even lucrative business opportunities, if there are risks associated with it. Most of the people want to take up a job in the government sector as it provides job security.

Entrepreneurship Education: There are only a few entrepreneurship institutes operating in the region, offering limited courses. Even in schools and colleges, the entrepreneurial courses that are being taught are very basic in nature and do not hold much practical value. The number of workshops being organised by the entrepreneurship institutes is also very less in number.

Solutions to Counter Entrepreneurial Problems

The study revealed a number of problem areas relating to entrepreneurship with specific reference to Assam. Based on the responses obtained and a detailed analysis, the following remedial solutions are offered to counter these problems.

1. The state must ensure that financial assistance is made available to promising entrepreneurs who have a viable economic idea to start with. Exorbitant rates of interest rates or higher collateral should not be charged as it discourages entrepreneurs to go ahead.
2. The state must make sure that, the funds once approved, gets transferred immediately to the entrepreneur's account. Many a times, it is seen that the funds get delayed and does not reach the entrepreneur, when he requires it the most. Direct transfer of funds helps in this regard.
3. The procedure to apply for licenses, permits and various clearance certificates must be simplified and if possible, made online. Any instances of wrong doing such as canvassing or demanding bribes to obtain the required documentation must be reported and punished. This will set a precedent for others and similar incidents would not occur again.
4. We need to invest heavily in entrepreneurship education. There should be more entrepreneurship-based seminars

and workshops at the school and college level to create interest in the minds of the younger generation. We need to reinvent entrepreneurship education and bring in structural changes through educational reforms. Students must be taught about the benefits of entrepreneurship from a very early age.

5. The government must pass new measures to help credit flow into the real economy, remove administrative charges and boost the competitiveness of firms operating here by investing in research and development. We cannot be reliant on world technology always. We must make efforts to develop indigenous technology.
6. Alleviating financing constraints for would-be entrepreneurs should also be an important goal for policymakers. Assam has always had a shortage of venture capital funds. Therefore, it has a low entrepreneurship rate. The state can get away with this weakness by creating a good investor climate. That will be an important stepping stone to further development.
7. It can be stated unequivocally that terrorism creates uncertainty and delays investments in any part of the world and this problem still persists in most parts of our state and the neighbouring states too. We need to act tough and resolve our conflicts with these militant groups so as to create a sound business environment.
8. We need to encourage individuals to start more high-growth firms and technology based firms and to introduce products that are new to more people. More entrepreneurs will lead to more economic value and job creation, eventually contributing to the economic growth of the state.
9. We must recognise the role of co-operatives, new partnerships and emerging collaborative spaces for social innovation. Only then can we transform the face of the state.
10. The spatial determinants of local entrepreneurship in

Assam for both manufacturing and services sector has two elements: local education level and physical infrastructure quality. We must make a balanced investment towards both to facilitate the entry of new firms.

11. Investors here are distracted by a myriad of other opportunities that earn a high return. There are a lot of competing investment opportunities, such as public equity markets, currencies or dead assets like land and gold. We must encourage investors to channelize their investments towards more productive sources which will help turnaround the economy of the state.
12. Like previous research, this paper also links strict labour regulations in India to slower economic growth and development. This pattern is especially apparent for the organized manufacturing sector where these laws are most binding. We need to make the laws more business friendly. Very often, it is seen that projects are put on hold even when they are in minimal conflict with environment protection laws.
13. The state must focus on improving the image of entrepreneurs and improve the incentive structure to reward productive rather than unproductive activities.
14. We must challenge the existing social and cultural norms that make it less conducive for women to become entrepreneurs. The Internet provides new ways of networking which can eliminate temporal and geographic as well as gendered social constraints, which limits women's access to information and resources. In order to promote women entrepreneurship, we must first invest in women education.
15. We need to encourage rural entrepreneurship by extending financial support to farmers, artisans and craftsmen who work at the rural level. They need to be made aware of the various incentives, concessions and subsidies that are being offered by the government for them. Very often, they are not even aware of these incentives that are

available to them and cannot avail them.

16. We need to reverse the brain drain that resulted in the outflow of skilled students from Assam to other states or countries. According to a study published by the Harvard Law School, 50 percent of NRI returnees are coming back to India for entrepreneurship and business start-up reasons. We need more such people. The state government must introduce financial incentives like tax holidays and provide them with the adequate infrastructure required to start their own venture.
17. We need to improve our physical infrastructure. The roads and bridges are in a deplorable condition. Some parts of the state are still not connected by railways. There are many big rivers in the state but most of them are not navigable. Direct flights to many international destinations are not available to us. All of these factors have a huge bearing on the transportation time and cost.

Conclusion

Assam has never been known as an *entrepreneurial* hub. It is high time we change this perception. This change will come about not through government initiatives alone, but personal resolutions too. The government's primary role will be to provide financial assistance, build physical infrastructure, impart entrepreneurship education and create an investor-friendly environment. At an individual level, the people here need to be more enterprising, ambitious, passionate and risk-taking. They need to scan the environment on a regular basis so as to identify business opportunities and exploit them before anyone else does, so as to experience the first mover advantage.

Of late, the signals have been good. There has been a sharp increase in the number of women entrepreneurs and rural entrepreneurs in the state. In fact, it is surprising that majority of the new ventures that have come up, are in the rural areas. Now for the first time ever, the Indian government has instituted a new ministry of entrepreneurship to promote entrepreneurial culture. Things are looking up. We are moving towards a better future.

References

Barua, A. Nissar and Mali, Archana (2011), 'Entrepreneurship and Its Role in the Growth of Micro and Small Enterprises: A Case Study of Assam', *Small Enterprise Development, Management and Extension Journal*, Volume 38, No. 2, pp. 69-83.

Chakraborty, Dipanjan (2014), 'Socio-economic Determinants of Growth of Rural Entrepreneurship in Sonitpur District of Assam: An Empirical Study', *Journal of Behavioural Economics, Finance, Entrepreneurship, Accounting and Transport*, Volume 2, No. 2, pp. 26-34.

Desai, Vasant (2010), 'Entrepreneurship and Small Business Management, Himalaya Publishing House, New Delhi.

Devi, Anjali and Goswami, Gayatri (2014), 'Women Entrepreneurship Development in Assam with Special Reference to Kamrup District', *The Clarion*, Volume 3, No. 1, pp. 149-156.

Khanka, S.S., (2009), 'Entrepreneurship in India: Perspectives and Practice', Akansha Publishing House, New Delhi.

Namboodiri, K.V.N. and Singh, B.M. (2006), 'Unleashing Rural Entrepreneurship', ICFAI University Press, Hyderabad.

Szerb, L. (2009), 'The Global Entrepreneurship Index (GEINDEX)', *Foundations and Trends in Entrepreneurship,* Volume 5(5), pp. 341-435.

Websites:
www.forbes.com
www.inc.com

6

New Land Use Policy (NLUP) Beneficiaries in Petty Trade

Lalhmingliana Renthlei and Lalropuii

Introduction

Mizoram is a land of rich flora and fauna and the rolling hills and mountains form majestic landscape that is breath taking, but human civilization has taken its toll drastically over the years and due to the form of cultivation called Jhum cultivation, the vegetation is cleared bare from the land and burnt year after year for many decades for cultivation of vegetables and this form of cultivation has caused the land to lose its top soil fertility and beauty. This has caused massive deforestation all over the state and in fact contributes tremendously to one of the causes of global warming that has resulted in a rise in the temperature in Mizoram. It is because of this major problem that the government launched the New Land Use Policy (NLUP) to tackle the problems caused by Jhum cultivation by providing the people with other source of livelihood and providing them with better alternatives and new methods of cultivation without actually harming the vegetation through the latest and new technology in farming and other sources of livelihood to support their families.

NLUP was launched on January 14, 2011 with a budget of 2873.13 crore. NLUP is targeted to benefit 1,20,000 families over a period of five years. During the Independence day speech, the Chief Minister claimed that the target had been achieved in the first three years and 15,000 more beneficiaries were proposed to be covered in the financial year 2013-14. He also claimed that the project had made significant impact on the economy by providing alternative and sustainable livelihood opportunities to farmers by reducing their dependence on Jhum practice. The main objectives of the new policy include keeping 60 percent of Mizoram's total land area as rain forest, to lure away farmers from destructive Jhum practices and assist the workforce and to improve the incomes of both urban and rural poor through sustainable farming, non farming activities and micro enterprises including promotion and modernization of small-scale and cottage industries.

The population of Aizawl city has experienced a drastic increase over the past decades and the number of rural population moving from rural to urban areas is increasing day by day and therefore the roles played by the petty traders in the economy of Aizawl city is immensely significant (Mbisso, D. 2011). Petty trading can be referred to as an economic activity that involves selling (and buying) goods and services in small-scale, ranging from agricultural produce to imported consumer goods and due to this very simple but important reason, that among the beneficiaries of NLUP, the petty traders of the area have been selected for an in-depth study on the problems and prospects of these traders in Aizawl city.

Petty trade has been further divided into petty trade I (grocery), petty trade II (vegetable shops), petty trade III (tea stall) and petty trade IV (food stalls).

Literature Review

NLUP is a flagship program of the government that provides the people with sustainable source of income and livelihood through the Industries Department that promote and encourage people to become entrepreneurs which is an important step to improve the economy of the region. Since NLUP is a program that was initiated in its first phase in 2010 -2011 and the second phase in 2011-2012, hence there is very little literature on NLUP in published books. Various reports by the Government of Mizoram and news agencies are available and besides that, the NLUP implementing board issues a yearly concise summary about the programme.

NLUP is guided by the state government's focus to introduce a reform process in the economy so that: (i) overall poverty rate is reduced, (ii) community's financial inclusion is ensured, (iii) a land use policy based on statutory rights is introduced, and (iv) optimal use of scarce resources such as land and water is encouraged. The Report elaborates the importance of NLUP in sustaining the scarce resources and instead focus on other sources of living that will provide food for the people without actually having to destroy the natural vegetation through Jhum cultivation and ultimately reduce the poverty rate in the state.

In another article from a newsletter from Imphal, NLUP has been referred as a method of inculcating systematic method of cultivation and trade, based on local resources (Lanpao, H., 2014). The main objective of this noble project is major overhauling of the State economy through structural replacement of devastating shifting cultivation by introducing systematic method of occupation based on local resources and ingenuity of the local people (The Hindu, 2013). The core objectives of the NLUP is to wean away farmers from Jhum practices and assist them to be employed in economic ventures to create productive assets in each family and to keep 60 percent of Mizoram's total land area under rain forest and to improve the income of both rural and urban poor through sustainable farming, non-farming, micro enterprises and small and cottage industries.

NLUP is a programme that encourages the people to venture out and become entrepreneurs. As Jean Baptiste, opined, 'the entrepreneur is an agent who unites all means of production and who finds in the value of the products...the reestablishment of the entire capital he employs, and the value of the wages, the interest, and rent which he pays, as well as profits belonging to himself'. Capital is being provided to the people through NLUP to propel their petty trades and make a living for themselves without having to depend on Jhum cultivation in Mizoram (Mbisso, D. 2011). Petty trading is a prevailing socio-economic activity serving a multitude of the low income population in rapidly urbanising developing countries. Petty trading marketplaces thus, have an important role to play in urban development processes. And likewise, Aizawl city is a rapidly developing city and the roles played by the petty traders is absolutely important for the economy of the state which the government intends to fulfil by promotion of entrepreneurs through NLUP beneficiaries.

Petty traders/merchants represent perhaps the fastest growing segment of the labour market in Africa, attracting the unemployed, the displaced and the impoverished. Therefore, petty trading in Aizawl city also solves a tiny bit of the unemployment problems and provides a means for the people to earn a living in the city and therefore this study intends to analyse the performance of NLUP petty traders and their perspective towards the program in terms of its success or failure in the state.

Research Methodology

This study was carried out in the city of Aizawl and a set of questionnaires was distributed to pool beneficiaries of NLUP in petty trade and also information was collected based on interview of the respondents and secondary data collected mainly from published journals and various articles found in internet.

Petty trade is further divided into four categories:

1. Petty trade I (grocery shops).
2. Petty trade II (vegetable shops).
3. Petty trade III (tea stalls).
4. Petty trade IV (food stalls).

The method of sampling used for this study is random sampling method as samples were collected from a pool of samples randomly.

Nevertheless, this study has a few limitations as the time period for the study was very limited and covers only the region around the city and hence cannot be assumed relevant for the whole of Mizoram and of other trades in NLUP as only petty traders have been taken as samples for the study.

Results and Discussions

Most of the petty traders had lesser number of family members—48.90 percent of them had 3-5 members only and 40.40 percent had 6-8 members. When asked further as to why they had smaller families, they responded by saying that the level of income can only provide for a few people as it is not high enough to support a bigger family.

Most of the beneficiaries (48.90 percent) were forty years and above and therefore we found that these beneficiaries had a lot of experience in carrying on the trade.

48.90 percent of the beneficiaries relied on the business for their main source of income to feed the family and that they had no other source of income.

55.30 percent of the beneficiaries earned more than ₹ 6,000 in a month from their business to support their families.

A majority (61.70 percent) of the beneficiaries lived in rented houses and 38.30 percent lived in their own houses.

38.30 percent of the beneficiaries chose groceries, 12.80 percent chose tea stall, 10.60 percent chose food stall, 8.50 percent chose vegetable shops and 27.70 percent of the beneficiaries were into activities similar to food stalls in the form of house to house vendors or ice cream carts etc.

Majority of the beneficiaries chose these particular trades to upgrade their already existing businesses or trade and 31.90 chose to start new venture.

53.20 percent of the beneficiaries had the skills needed to run the trade/activity that contributed tremendously to the success of the trade/activity.

A majority (51.00 percent) of the beneficiaries responded by saying NLUP is beneficial to their trade, whereas 25.50 percent said its very beneficial to trade and 21.30 percent responded by saying that it is somewhat beneficial.

57.40 percent responded that NLUP is beneficial to their family and others responded by saying that it is indeed very beneficial to their family. It is important to note that under NLUP, there has been a massive improvement in the family's standard of living.

There often was a rumour that the government is not fair in the selection of NLUP beneficiaries and is showing partiality towards selection of beneficiaries.

53.20 percent responded by saying that the government is fair enough in selection of the beneficiaries, whereas 36.20 percent were neutral to this question and had no response which might depict that some of them felt that it was not always fair.

Data analysis also shows that 55.30 percent were again neutral and 14.90 percent of them agreed to the fact that some level of corruption does exist in the selection of NLUP beneficiaries and this may suggest that some level of partiality existed in selection of the beneficiaries by the government.

68 percent of the beneficiaries agreed to the fact that NLUP did uplift the livelihood of the beneficiaries and that it must be carried on in the future years.

NLUP has drastically improved the family's economic condition and 78.70 percent agreed that their economic condition has improved significantly and that it has improved their incomes. 55.30 percent of them responded that the family increased its income by 25-50 percent under NLUP whereas 27.70 percent opined that it increased their income by just 25 percent.

Finally when the beneficiaries were asked the final question, 74.50 percent responded that NLUP is an important tool for the development of Mizoram and that it must be continued in the future with better management. They responded that this flagship program of the government will uplift the state and develop it in a tremendous way.

Conclusion

The study found that from all the beneficiaries that responded to the questionnaires, most of them were highly benefited by the NLUP and the trade they chose and it increased their source of income and improved their standard of living. The study also shows that majority of the beneficiaries used NLUP funds for upgrading their existing trade/activity and that 31.90 percent of them used it to start a new venture of their own. Furthermore, we can analyze from the information collected that most of the beneficiaries were aged 40 and above and therefore had the skills to carry on the trade without difficulty which gradually contributed to their success.

Majority of the people were very neutral when asked about using fair means and corruption in selecting the beneficiaries by the government etc. This led us to the inference that some minimum level of partiality and corruption goes on and exists in selection of NLUP beneficiaries and must be tackled with caution in the future. Finally, when they were asked if NLUP was an important tool for the development of Mizoram, a majority (74.50 percent) of the beneficiaries agreed that it is indeed very important and significant for the development of the state and would help in raising the standard of living and ultimately fulfil the core objectives of NLUP which is to wean away farmers from Jhum practices and assist them to be employed in economic ventures to create productive assets for the family.

References

Little, Peter D. (1999), 'Selling to Eat: Petty Trade and Traders in Peri-Urban Areas Of Sub-Saharan Africa", University of Kentucky and Institute for Development Anthropology.

Mbisso, Daniel (2011), 'Petty Trading in Market Places: Space Generation, Use and Management', at Temeke Stereomarket Places, Dar-es Salaam, Tanzania.

NABARD Consultancy Services Ltd. (2013), 'Mid-term Assessment Report on NLUP of Government of Mizoram, 2012-2013'.

NLUP Implementing Board (2013), 'New Land Use Policy: A Concise Summary', Aizawl, Mizoram.
'Statistical Handbook of Mizoram, 2012', Government of Mizoram.

7

Entrepreneurship Skills among the Information Professionals of College Libraries

Angom Jeevan Singh and PurnimaTakhellambam

Introduction

Entrepreneurship is a dynamic process of vision, change and creation. It requires application of energy and passion towards the creation and implementation of new ideas and creative solutions. Entrepreneurship is an act and art of being an entrepreneur or one who undertakes innovations or introduces newer things using finance and business acumen, in an effort to transform innovations into economic goods. The most obvious form of entrepreneurship is that of starting new business or businesses. However, in recent years, the term has been extended to include social and political forms of entrepreneurial activity. Entrepreneurial activities are substantially different depending on the type of organization and creativity involved. In more recent times, the term entrepreneurship has been extended to include elements not related necessarily to business formation activity such as conceptualizations of entrepreneurship as a specific mindset resulting in entrepreneurial initiatives e.g. in the form of social entrepreneurship, political entrepreneurship, or knowledge entrepreneurship.

In recent years, the concept of applying marketing skills in the field of library profession has become very crucial for extending the right information products to the right user or customer. Further, the advent of information and communication technology (ICT) has posed a challenge to the uses of physical information resources in the libraries.

Everyone has easy access to any information product from the comfort of their own home as is the case in online business activities. ICT has forced libraries across the world to re-assess and reconfigure the ways in which they supply information to the users or end customers. Thus, for the survival of the libraries in the long-run in this fast changing environment, it is very crucial for the information professionals to develop entrepreneurship skills and put it to practical application in college libraries.

An information professional is a person who works in non-profit organisations like libraries and plays a vital role in selection, collection, organisation, promotion, preservation and dissemination of information products to the users or customers.

A business entrepreneur deals with different products or commodities whereas an information professional deals with information products. In both cases, it is a human activity that inculcates creative, innovative, productive and managerial skills with a vision to bring new changes in the society.

Brief Profile of Garo Hills, Meghalaya

Meghalaya became full-fledged state on January 21, 1972. It comprises of Khasi Hills, Jaintia Hills and Garo Hills. The Garo Hills cover an area of 300 sq. Miles, is lower in elevation and rises gently from the southern plain. The Garo Hills are a part of the Garo-Khasi range in Meghalya, India. They are mainly inhabited by tribal dwellers, the majority of whom are Garo People. The Garos call themselves *Achik-mande*. In the Garo language, *Achik* means hills and *Mande* means man. So, *Achik-mande* means the hill people. The Garo Hills district comprises of five districts. They are: (i) East Garo Hills, (ii) West Garo Hills, (iii) South Garo Hills, (iv) North Garo Hills, and (v) South-west Garo Hills. Tura is the largest town with a population of about 70,000 located at the foothills of Tura peak. Tura has an amazing landscape of hills against a backdrop of low-lying plains. The society is matrilineal like the Khasis and the Jaintias.

There are many schools, colleges, universities and other educational institutes in Garo Hills. Most of the colleges in Garo Hills Districts are affiliated to NEHU, which caters to the academic needs of the community. Libraries play a vital role in fulfilling the academic need of the region (Table 7.1).

Table 7.1: Colleges of Garo Hills Districts, Meghalaya

S. No.	Name of the College	Estd. Year	Collection		Users	Information Professionals
			Books	Journals		
1.	Tura Government College	1958	60,000	25	3,070	4 (DL-1, LA-3)
2.	Don Bosco College	1987	30,000	15	2,587	3 (PA-1, LA-2)
3.	Tura Law College	1975	1,256	6	258	2 LA
4.	Durama College	1993	3,600	3	512	1 LA
5.	College of Teacher Education	1993	8,000	4	56	2(PA-1, LA-1)
6.	Don Bosco College of Teacher Education	2004	3,000	3	123	2 LA
7.	Mendipathar College	1971	12,500	9	1,404	2 LA
8.	AchengRangmanpa College	1986	1,311	3	521	1 LA
9.	Trikrikilla College	1988	15,000	12	425	2 LA
10.	Kazi&Zaman College	1992	2,541	6	225	1 LA
11.	Capt. Williamson Memorial College	1994	1,250	5	325	2 LA
12.	Williamnagar College	2001	2,453	7	997	2 (DL-1, LA-1)
13.	Phukan Memorial College	2003	1,325	3	243	1 LA
14.	Ampati College	2007	2,541	4	325	1 LA
15.	Nongrum College	2008	1,451	2	235	1 LA
16.	Loyola College	2013	2,500	4	250	2 (PA-1, LA-1)

L = Librarian, DL = Deputy Librarian, PA= Professional Assistant, LA= Library Assistant)

Source: CDC, NEHU, www.nehu.ac.in, and data collected from different colleges, July, 2013.

These college libraries have a minimum of one to three information professionals working with the information products and resources. Unfortunately, most of them are not trained professionals in the field of information management. These information professionals should develop entrepreneurial skills for maximising the use of information resources in the colleges. Business entrepreneurship and library entrepreneurship are like the sides of a coin. Application of entrepreneurship skills in the profession can bring the much desired for the user community of the region.

Characteristics of Entrepreneurship Applicable to Library Entrepreneurship

Table 7.2 presents the important characteristics of entrepreneurship applicable to library entrepreneurship:

Table 7.2: Characteristics of Entrepreneurship Applicable to Library Entrepreneurship

Character-istics	Entrepreneurship	Library Entrepreneurship
Decision-making	Decision making activity is one of the fundamentals characteristic features of an entrepreneurship. It is a course of action which is consciously chosen from among a multiple of alternatives to achieve the desired result. Decision-making is crucial on the part of the entrepreneurs to establish and run the enterprise successfully.	Decision-making is also equally important in the field of library management. Information professionals working in college libraries should focus on achieving the goals of the library. Proper planning on location, budget, type of users or customers, information needs should be taken into consideration. This will decide the future and success of the library.
Accepting Challenges	Entrepreneurship means accepting challenges amidst risk and uncertainty. While accepting entrepreneurship as a career, an entrepreneur accepts the challenges of all odds and puts his efforts to convert the odds into viable business opportunities by pooling together the resources for building and running an enterprise.	Information professional should accept challenges as the user needs and environment changes. They should put maximum effort amidst odds like, budget cuts, increasing users demand, fast changing environment of digital information format and so on. They should be able to organise the available resources to be put to maximum utilisation.
Risk Taking	One of the important	Information professionals face

	characteristics of entrepreneurship is risk taking or risk bearing. This characteristics feature implies assuming the responsibility for loss that may occur due to unforeseen contingencies of the future. Entrepreneurs, by their deep insight and scientific approach, analyse the situation objectively and reduce the risk considerably on one hand and enhances the profit factor on the other.	risk due to loss and damage of reading material, equipments due to human activity and adverse environmental condition. They should accept and take risk for all these unpredicted happenings in the library. The sole responsibility lies with the information professionals so they can have a deep insight to reduce such risks and put resources to the maximum benefit of the users.
Building Organiza-tion	Entrepreneurship pre-supposes the initiative and skill on building an organization. It is by delegation of authorities and proper leadership that an organization can be built up.	Information professionals should possess adequate skills and leadership quality and should be willing to take initiative to build up the college library. In other words, they should be well trained or educated in the field of library and information science. This will enable them to build a healthy college library.
Skillful Manage-ment	Entrepreneurship involves skillful management. The basic managerial skill is the most important characteristic feature of an entrepreneurship. For effective management of an enterprise, the role of an entrepreneur to initiate and supervise design of organization-improvement projects in relation to upcoming opportunities is very much important.	Information professionals should be good managers. They should be able to plan, decide, organise, and control the resources as well as the staff. Only through skilful management, an organisation's goals can be achieved.
Innovation	Innovation is one of the most important characteristics of entrepreneurship. It involves doing things in a new and better way and involving decision- making under uncertainty.	Information professionals should be innovators. They constantly put their effort to initiate new techniques and systems according to the environment and user needs. They should be able to analyse the fast changing environment and should reorganise the resources according to the user demands.

Mobilization of Resources	Resource mobilization is also a fundamental characteristic feature of an entrepreneurship. They are found in scattered manner in the environment and required to be perceived, identified and mobilized by entrepreneurs to attain business goal. Thus, entrepreneurs make themselves distinct from the rest of population because of their innate capability to mobilize resources. This is because resources are needed to ensure success which has the highest priority in the minds of entrepreneurs.	Information professionals should be able to mobilise the information products and resources. They should be able to develop an identity for themselves in the existing environment through their service and new innovation in providing information to the users. Through this, users will be attracted towards the resources. Thus, the goal of the professionals can be achieved at the highest level.

Importance of Entrepreneurship Skills for Information Professional

To be a successful library entrepreneur, an information professional should develop entrepreneurship skills. These skills should be put into practical application in the library profession to bring the right information product to the right user and maximising the use of information resources.

Market Research and Survey: Market profiling is an important activity, which is done to obtain marketing information for that particular area or locality. It is necessary to identify the market scope to formulate appropriate policies. Information professionals should have a much better understanding of customer or user needs and should have a closer liaison with them to identify their requirements of information. Analysis of the customers or users' need should be conducted regularly to identify who the users or customers are, the products and services they want, their expectations and the benefit they are seeking for individual satisfaction.

Development of Products: Product development or planning is the marketing activity concerned with developing a product that satisfies customers or users. The products may include information from books, research reports and articles, thesis and dissertation, CDs, teaching and learning materials.

Information professionals should play a vital role in acquisition, organisation, preservation and dissemination of information products and plan to facilitate its full service to the target customers or users.

Pricing of Products: Pricing is another marketing activity that determines the price of the product on the basis of cost as well as market factors such as distribution channels, discount structure, competitors' prices, ability or willingness of customers to pay, and so on. Pricing of information services and products is one of the important aspects of marketing. It is a relatively new concept and is least applicable to marketing since library services are generally offered free of cost. But to add value to the resources and services, the college libraries may charge an annual membership fee, consultation charges etc. However, discussions and consultation with the college authorities is the only way to decide on pricing of their information products.

Promotion of Products: Promotion is an activity that covers all aids to sales. Promotion stimulates demand and increases sales. Usually promotion moves the product towards the customers. It involves mechanisms that inform the target groups about the resources available and services and products offered by the college libraries. Information professionals can use various methods for promoting information products and services such as publicity through brochures, pamphlets, journals, handbooks, annual reports and magazines, exhibitions at library week, workshops and seminars, orientation programs etc. College users can be divided into: under-graduate students, faculty members and non-teaching staff etc. Each individual has different needs. The services that the library offers must be made known to as many users as possible, so that they think of the library when they need information for any individual satisfaction.

Distribution or Dissemination of Products and Services: Distribution is a marketing activity concerned with distributing the products from the manufacturer to the customer. In other words, it is making the product available to the customers or users. Distribution pertains to dissemination of information through various channels. An information professional can use such channels like, interpersonal delivery, group personal delivery, in-house dissemination, mass media, mail, telephone etc. to reach the right user of the information resource.

Evaluation of Products and Services: A marketing approach cannot be effective without evaluation. Therefore, an information professional should evaluate the effectiveness of the products and services in relation to organisations' objectives, internal strengths and weaknesses and customers' satisfaction and demand. Regular customers or users' surveys enable the information professionals to review how well each information product and service matches with customers' needs and expectations and plan the action required to correct any discrepancies.

Suggestions

Information professionals should adopt the following suggestions to achieve their professional goals.

1. Proactively seek partnerships with faculty, students and staff in their colleges.
2. Selection of information products according to the needs of the faculty and students.
3. Taking leadership role in developing collection in support of education mission.
4. Possessing good knowledge of the information products and services.
5. Possessing good communication and presentation skills.
6. Possessing the professional knowledge and skills for marketing information products and services.
7. Well-versed with technical knowledge such as internet use and other information sources and channels to help the users or customers.
8. Perception of users' need and ability to obtain feedback from users or customers.

Conclusion

Entrepreneurship skills are very crucial at this juncture for the information professionals working in the college libraries of the Garo Hills region. Information professionals must be more political, more socially engaged and active rather than staying neutral as a custodian of books and other information products. They should be able to reassess and reconfigure the ways in which they identity, collect, process and supply information to the customers. They should develop entrepreneurial skills to maximise the use of the college information resources. Apart from having knowledge of the in-house information products and resources, they should study the changing environment and should be able to direct the users to various information sources also to fulfil the customers or users' need. The key to library's success is in proper planning, implementation of services and resources, identifying user needs, promotion, marketing and constant evaluation for further improvement. Developing entrepreneurship skills among the information professionals working in the college libraries can bring many changes in the use of information resources and this will benefit the academic community of the Garo Hills region.

References

Eke, H.N., Igwesi, U. and Orji, D.I. (2011), 'Information Professionals as Agents for Promoting Entrepreneurship and Technology Education in Actualizing Vision 2020 for Nigeria', *Library Philosophy and Practice,* retrieved on March 5, 2014 from http://www.webpages.uidaho.edu/~mbolin/eke-igwesi-orji.htm.

Entrepreneur (2013), retrieved on May 4, 2013 from http://en.wikipedia.org/wiki/Entrepreneur.

Entrepreneurship (2013), retrieved on May 4, 2013 from http://en.wikipedia.org/wiki/Entrepreneurship.

Garo Hills (2014), retrieved on March 4, 2014 from http://en.wikipedia.org/wiki/Garo_Hills.

Hisrich, R.D. (2002), 'Entrepreneurship' 5th edition, New Delhi: Tata McGraw-Hill Publishing Company Limited.

Madhusudhan, M. (2008), 'Marketing of Library and Information

Services and Products in University Libraries: A Case Study of Goa University Library', *Library Philosophy and Practice,* 1(1), 1-6.

Mishra, R. (2011), 'Marketing of Library and Information Service: Trends and Issues in Digital Environment', *IASLIC Bulletin,* 56(2), 79-87.

Mohanty, S.K. (2013), 'Fundamentals of Entrepreneurship', New Delhi: PHI Learning Private Ltd.

Rani, S., and Kaur, A.P. (2005), 'Marketing of Information Products and Services: A Study of the Attitude of the Professional Staff working at Guru Nanak Dev University Library', *Journal of Library and Information Science,* 30(1&2), 101-113.

Smith, A.H. (2014), 'Library Entrepreneurship and Community Awareness', retrieved on March 5, 2014 from http://www.moyak.com/papers/library-entrepreneurship.html.

Spalding, H.H. and Wang, J. (2006), 'Marketing Academic Libraries in USA: Challenges and Opportunities', *Chinese Librarianship: An International Electronic Journal,* retrieved on March 4, 2014 from http://www.iclc.us/cl22SpaldingWang.htm.

8

Entrepreneurship Education of Cluster Industry

Rupam Roy

Introduction

A cluster is a geographic concentration of interconnected businesses, suppliers, and associated institutions in a particular field. Clusters are considered to increase the productivity with which industries can compete, nationally and globally. In urban study, the term agglomeration is used. The main principle is about collaborating while competing in a similar product and opportunities in particular area with the same flexible specialization. Clusters are considered to increase the productivity with which industry can compete, nationally and globally. A sectoral and geographical concentration of enterprises, in particular, small and medium enterprises (SMEs), face common opportunities and threats.

The term industry cluster, also known as a business cluster, competitive cluster, or Porterian cluster, was introduced and the term cluster was popularized by Michael Porter in the book, *The Competitive Advantage of Nations* (1990). The importance of economic geography, or more correctly geographical economics, was also brought to attention by Paul Krugman in the book *Geography and Trade* (1991). Cluster development has since become a focus for many governmental programmes. The underlying concept, which economists have referred to as agglomeration economies, dates back to 1890.

Cluster Approach in India

The brass and bronze metal utensils cluster of Mirzapur

city is one of the oldest clusters in the country. The cluster actors report that the cluster dates back 150-200 years or more involving almost four generations. We observed that the main reason for the development of brass industry is due to availability of raw material and traditional skills required. At present, there are more than 300 enterprises manufacturing brass utensils or similar work and most of the persons belong to 'Kasera' and 'Agrawal' caste. The total direct employment in the cluster is approximately 5,000 persons and indirect employment is close to 6,000 persons. Urban and rural industrialization is the most aspect in our country for development of small-scale industries.

The bell metal of Sarthabari (Assam) cluster is also one of the oldest clusters of the country. The main reason for the development of bell metal is due to the skill sets of the artisans who had been working for ages.

The Entrepreneur

The word entrepreneur is derived from the French word, *"Entreprendre"* which means to "undertake" i.e., the person who undertakes the risk of new enterprise. The word entrepreneur, therefore, first appeared in the French language in the beginning of the sixteenth century. The word was also applied to leaders of military expedition. But it was Richard Cantilon, an Irishman, living in France who first used the term entrepreneur to refer to economic activities. According to Cantilon, 'An entrepreneur is a person who buys factor services at certain prices with a view to selling its product at uncertain prices'. Thus, to Cantilon, an entrepreneur is a bearer of risk, which is non-insurable. A.H. Cole defined entrepreneurship as, 'the purposeful activity of an individual or group of associated individuals, undertaken to initiate, maintain, or earn profit by production and distribution of economic goods and services'.

McClelland, like other specialists, too identified the characteristics of entrepreneurship, i.e. first, doing thing in a new and better way and secondly, decision-making under uncertainty. He more explicitly emphasized achievement motivation as the most critical factor for the growth of entrepreneurship. According to Peter Druckur, 'entrepreneurship is neither a science nor an art. It is a practice. It has a knowledge base. Knowledge in entrepreneurship is a means to an end. Indeed, the ends that are by practice largely define what constitutes knowledge in practice. Entrepreneurship is not just about many. It is about imagination, flexibility, creativity, willingness to think conceptually, readiness to take risks, ability to mobilize agents of production and the capacity to see change as an opportunity. It is also about marrying passion and process with a good dose of perseverance'.

Entrepreneurship = Entrepreneur + Enterprise
(Process) (Person) (Object)

Entrepreneurship in India

The review of ancient literature has proved that ancient Indians took up a variety of commercial vocations akin to present day entrepreneurial activities. The first phase of entrepreneurship emerged when the Aryan conquerors settled down in this country by suppressing the non-Aryans. They appropriated the products of village communities to themselves leaving a little for the villagers or natives. Thus, the main conflict of ancient Indian society had begun. The Aryans were faced with the problem of innovating new crafts and occupation and also evolved some kind of division of labour for new handicrafts, breeding of cattle and cultivating land.

The ancient literature like 'Manusmriti' has provided a clear idea about entrepreneurial class of people during the ancient period (pre-Vedic). According to Manusmriti, "people belonging to Vaisya caste were regarded as entrepreneurs who specialized in maintaining livestock, giving charity, performing sacrifices, studying scriptures and undertaking business and banking". Hence, Vaisya was the specialized class of people carrying entrepreneurial activities in those days. They carried on trade in agriculture, industry and banking sectors.

Agriculture, crafts and handicrafts were the basic source of the occupation for the people in Gupta and post-Gupta period. The occupational development during this period comprised of ownership of land, pasture grounds, trees, forests, water reservoirs, mines, etc. There is clear evidence about the use of technical knowledge in water use namely, Persian water (Arahatta) in Northern India during the early medieval period.

In India, an emergence of manufacturing entrepreneurship is viewed by some social scientists as the consequence of the arrival of East India Company followed by colonial British rulers. It gave a new stimulus to businessman by injecting various changes in the economy and accelerating the export of raw material and import of finished goods.

In 1905, Indian leaders adopted the concept of 'Swadeshi' and boycott to counter the discriminatory policy of the British Government. The Swadeshi method was based on *Atma Sakti* (the principle of self-reliance), which mean manufacturing and using indigenous goods by the Indians.

Entrepreneurship Development in North-East

The concept of Entrepreneurship development in the North-Eastern region of India endued around or in about 1973. North-Eastern Council (NEC) seems to have played an important role in evolution of this movement over the years.

The region is industrially backward and has been declared as category 'A' (industrially backward region). Industrial backwardness of this region is reflected in the fact that the contribution of the manufacturing sector to the state domestic product of the region is much smaller than the contribution of this sector to the GDP of the country.

In the North-East, the Government of Assam is early 1970s carried out a small experiment on entrepreneurship development under the leadership of the Chief Minister of

Assam, Mr. Sharat Chandra Sinha. During the past few years, the Government and various institutions have been facilitating the development of entrepreneurship in the region by providing assistance in setting up of small and medium enterprises (SMEs) through financing, technical know-how, marketing training etc. North-East Council (NEC) set up in the year 1972 has carried out the important role of promoting entrepreneurship in the region. It has made a study on the entrepreneurial and managerial needs of the region through SIET Institute. Apart from NEC, now their also exist other institutions and organizations which work or function for the development of entrepreneurs, namely Industrial Development Bank of India (IDBI), Industrial Financial Corporation of India (IFCI) and Industrial Credit and Investment Corporation of India (ICICI).

Bell Metal Industry in Assam

At first, bell metal industry in Sarthebari was carried on under the patronization of rich traders called *mahajans*. These rich traders under whom the workers were doing the jobs were not given their fair share of remuneration. In the year 1933, a farsighted gentleman named Kohiram Das started a co-operative society among the brass and bell metal workers because the workers were deprived of the proper share and the benefits. The artisans were not given proper remuneration in proportion to their work. They were always deprived of proper wages. This co-operative was known as the Assam Co-operative Bell Metal Utensils Manufacturing Society Ltd. He was the first secretary in this establishment. The society was registered under the Co-operative Act, 1939. Mr. Kohiram Das died on July 27, 2012 at the age of 77 years. He had three sons and was the first artisan to receive an artisan pension by the Assam government.

During the research when I approached the workers, most of the workers expressed that they were not given proper remuneration in proportion to their work, even after the

Society was formed. However, Mr. Kohiram Das said that the society was providing other benefits like available raw materials, credit facility, distribution facility etc. However, there were many other important needs like training, standardization of the product, capacity building etc. Contrarily, there were many people who were satisfied with the income generated in association with the co-operatives.

There other group of *mahajans* is also vital for the procurement of raw materials from various suppliers. Both players, the co-operatives and the *mahajans* are equally important for the procurement of raw materials and it is difficult to find out how many employees are working in which group, as they fluctuate according to their needs and free will. Hence, it is important for the government to organize the sector and set rules as they have done for the tea industry. To improve the quality of standards, an approved institution should be set up by government. Just like the Swalkuchi Institute of Fashion Technology, an institute on similar lines for the bell metal industry should be set by the government of Assam.

The *mahajans* involved in this business, cannot have a direct control over the artisans like before since the formation of the co-operative society. The raw material brought by the co-operative society or other *mahajans* are given on credit to various artisans. According to their requirement, on an average, 30 grams extra is given in every 1 kg. of raw material. The artisans have the liberty to give back their finished products according to their time, and in return they are given wages according to the already set price for various shapes and sizes of the products in the market. Under this co-operative society, about 1,720 people are working daily and earning their livelihood.

According to the rules of the society, the payments to be made to the artisans is checked and calculated after every 6 months and a lump sum of the total earnings is given to the artisan for their daily needs and the rest remains with the co-operative. The artisans collect their raw material from the society to give different shapes and sizes to meet the needs of the society. The artisans are given remuneration according to the grades of the works, of their products. Their remuneration varies from ₹ 300 to ₹ 400 per kilogram. The average annual income of artisans ranges between ₹ 10,000 and ₹ 15,000 per month. Most of the artisans have been working since the age of 13 to 15 years.

The products made from bell metal are distributed among the 11 co-operative societies all over Assam, namely Guwahati Fancy Bazar, Ganeshguri Chariali, Dispur, Paltan Bazar, Jorhat, North Lakhimpur, Sarthebari New Market, Sibsagar, Tezpur, Golaghat and Pathshala. The products of bell metal are given to the retailers by the co-operative within their area of jurisdiction. At the same time, the retailers or individual customers can purchase the product directly from the co-operative society. The turnover of the Assam Co-operative Bell Metal Utensil Manufacturing Society was around ₹ 3.79 crore in fiscal year 2009-2010.

There is no control of price of the products and the retailers can sell the products according to the price fixed by them. The Assam Co-operative Bell Metal Utensils Manufacturing Society Ltd. can avail bank loans but they do not get any subsidies. Under the initiative of NEDFI, expert artisans of the industry are selected for training in different places of India, but training is not at all fruitful, because it does not suit the local requirements. The artisans are unable to meet the huge orders given by NEDFI and other institutions and also orders from states like Arunachal Pradesh because the products are made by hand. It is recommended that the government should set up training centres to uplift this dying tradition.

Objectives of the Study

- To find out the customer perception about the bell metal products.
- To find out the problems faced by the artisans and the Co-

operative.

- To study the prospect of bell metal industry in Sarthebari.

Database and Methodology

The bell metal industry in Sarthebari generally runs on a small-scale. There are about 280 units constituting the entire industry—most of them were active at the time of field survey. Most of the units are not registered with the Directorate of Industries nor with the Government of Assam. The information was collected through questionnaire and on the spot personal interview with artisans, government officials, and officials of Assam Co-operative Bell Metal Utensils Manufacturing Society. Field survey as well as empirical studies was used for collecting various types of data and information. The two sources of data collected were secondary and primary.

The secondary data was collected from the Directorate of Industries, Directorate of Assam Small-Scale Development Corporation, Assam Co-operative Bell Metal Utensils Manufacturing Society and District Industrial centre, Barpeta. Relevant books, journals, souvenirs, papers and various reports from different agencies, like Khadi and Village Industries Board and Assam Khadi and Village Industries Commission was also consulted.

The primary data was collected from direct field observation and survey of bell metal units. For this purpose, a questionnaire was prepared. The questionnaire included questions on socio-economic conditions, annual income, wages, recreation, raw material, tools, business capital, marketing system, production and process etc.

Sample Size was 300, namely.

- Artisans: 100.
- Customers: 100.
- Co-operative: 100.

Trends in Production

The trends in the production of bell metal from 1994-95 to

2011-2012 have been considered for analysis. From 1994-95 to 2011-2012, the industry has shown some progress in terms of value and variety of production. The relative progress of production trend can be gauged from Table 8.1.

Table 8.1: Production Trends of Bell-metal Utensils in Sarthebari under Co-operative Society (1994-95 to 2011-2012)

S. No.	Year	Finished Products (in kgs.)
1.	1994-1995	20,665,000
2.	1995-1996	22,186,000
3.	1996-1997	22,278,000
4.	1997-1998	24,314,000
5.	1998-1999	25,866,000
6.	1999-2000	22,580,000
7.	2000-2001	28,888,000
8.	2001-2002	35,018,000
9.	2002-2003	35,183,000
10.	2003-2004	35,237,000
11.	2004-2005	35,120,000
12.	2005-2006	33,154,000
13.	2006-2007	34,838,280
14.	2007-2008	24,807,580
15.	2008-2009	31,441,580
16.	2009-2010	32,005,590
17.	2010-2011	36,923,300
18.	2011-2012	41,638,820

Source: The Assam Co-operative Bell-Metal Utensils Manufacturing society Ltd, Sarthebari.

Table 8.1 indicates that during the period under study, the industry as a whole made a steady progress. The only exception took place in the year 1999-2000 where it showed a little decline of 22,580,000 kgs. as against 25,866,000 kgs. in the preceding year indicating a fall of 2,286,000 kgs. The production of bell metal in Sarthebari however, does not show any fall during the period 2001 to 2007, but shows a fall in 2008. The figure shows an increasing trend from 1994 to 2001, except in 1999 which was down to 22,580,000 showing a net fall of 2,286,000 kgs. From 2001 onwards, there was a rise from 28,888,000 to 35,018,000 kgs. From 2001 to 2005, the production depicts a stagnation. During the year 2005-2006, the production showed a decline of 35,120,000 kgs. to 33,154,000 kgs., which is insignificant. There was a gradual increase in production from the year 2009 to 2012.

Table 8.2 shows price of bell metal raw materials for different years.

Table 8.2: Price of Bell Metal Raw Materials for Different Years (per kg.)

S. No.	Year	Price (in `)
1.	2006	500
2.	2007	550
3.	2008	720
4.	2009	640
5.	2010	650
6.	2011	670
7.	2012	690
8.	2013	730

Different types of problems faced by the Association as well as the artisans are as under.

- Since there exist many financial institutions and the illiterate artisans cannot grab the opportunity, only few educated people take all the opportunity.
- The product is facing competition from those made by machineries and high equipments since their price is lesser as compared to the products made manually. This requires a steady implementation of technology in order to cope with the pricing of the product. Hence, the cost of finished products remains higher in comparison to the products

from Moradabad where machineries are used for processing.

- Training achieved by the artisans is not that much effective due to the constraint of time and other limitations.
- Since Sarthebari is well known in Assam as well as in India for its bell metal products, the distance from the heart of the Assam is about 92 km. which leads to higher transport cost and the resultant increase in selling price.
- Since there are already 11 units of bell metal of the Assam Co-operative Bell Metal Utensil Manufacturing Society Ltd. in different places of Assam, it is recommended that more such units of shop be opened in Assam as well as outside Assam for better exposure of the products.
- Also since the price of the raw materials is rising at a faster rate it would be prudent to revise the prices of the products at regular intervals to minimise loss in the market share.

Findings

1. The major problems faced by the industry are raw material, training, and funds from the state government. There is also no financial help from financial institutions like NEC, SBI, SIDBI etc. and no further steps have been taken by government to improve the situation.
2. The co-operatives supply products made of bell metal to eleven branches of co-operative and retailers. Mr. Nakul Talukdar, president of Assam Metal Guild Association opined that most of the middlemen decide to fix the price of bell metal product on their own and there is a lot of duplicate products that are now flourishing in the market. It is suggested that the government should route the supply of raw material through its own channels instead of the middlemen.
3. Most of the artisans have been working for more than ten years with the bell metal industry.

4. There are almost three to four members of the artisans' family engaged in bell metal industry.
5. The products like Bati and Taal are the highest manufacturing products in the bell metal industry.
6. Most of the artisans earn about ₹ 10,000 to ₹ 15,000 per month. The artisans face problems in manpower and timely payment of dues by the co-operatives. The artisans do not want their children to follow the same profession because it is very laborious and they think they are not being paid accordingly. They also think that by just passing H.S.L.C. or H.S., their children can earn as much or more.
7. Earnings of most of the artisans has slightly improved after joining the cooperative but it is not enough and they want artisan pension and life insurance from the government.
8. Most of the customers occasionally use the bell metal products in their day to day life.
9. The consumers find handling/cleaning as a major problem followed by price and weight.
10. Most of the consumers know the advantage of using bell metal products as most of them think that it improves digestion and kills germs.
11. Most consumers are not aware of the maintenance as most of them use detergents and traditional herbs.
12. The customers want change in the design, shape and size to suit modern lifestyle and small kitchens.

Recommendations

Raw material is a major concern for this sector since due to the lack of raw material, the price of the product is high and thus, ultimately the consumers find it hard to purchase the same. Thus, if an organization can be developed or a source of easy way of getting materials can be provided so that the product can be produced or manufactured in an less expensive way so as to compete in the market with those made by machines.

Although there does exist some financial institutions in Sarthabari or in and around it, yet the Association is not getting any help from it because the institutions are not willing to give loans to them easily and so they are dependent on the private co-operative societies which give them loans at a higher rate of interest.

There is still a need for technical up gradation. The entire process is done manually which is time consuming and involves a lot of hard labour. No doubt manual work is required but still some processes like melting etc. cannot be done at all.

Training which was provided to the artisans by various training institutions is not sufficient for them because of the very short duration of the courses. Hence, the training should be provided in an efficient way so that they can manufacture new type of innovative products.

Since the place is already famous for its products and traditional antique pieces and moreover it already has an outside market approach, the area can be a good spot for attracting the tourists. It can be developed also into an eco-tourism site where people can get the real taste of the place and at the same time they can also see the entire village unit engaged in the manufacturing of the product. Thus, it can provide an exposure to the people of this sector and at the same time create a platform of markets where tourists can, at the same time purchase the products in bulk.

Conclusion

It seems that the condition or the situation of the bell metal sector is not in a good state since there is lack of raw material which is very scarce and is being imported from outside the country. The present scenario manifests that the cost of the raw material is a major problem and it is also seen that a unit requires approximately 15 kg. to produce finished goods (300 units × 15 kg. = 4,500 kg.) but they are unable to produce the finished goods due to the scarcity of raw material. People use manual techniques to produce the finished goods, which takes a longer time to bring out the final product. This is primarily due to the lack of availability of new technology due to which goods cannot be produced in bulk.

It is evident from the above discussion that bell metal industries of Sarthebari block, Barpeta district have been suffering from various problems related to backward and forward linkages. It is no longer lucrative as a sequel and the educated youth of the region are not interested in carrying forward the legacy. In future, with its gloomy situation, it may be continued with the few handful people who have the traditional knowledge only. The artisans have been suffering from basic facilities like drinking water and sanitation also. As a result, health of the workers including their family members is not in a good condition, as they have been suffering from various ailments too.

References

Adhikari, A. and Laskar, B.I. (1999), 'A Study of Strategic Management of Mizoram State Transport', *Journal of the North East Council*, Volume 19, No. 4, October-December.

Agarwal, A.K. (1987), 'Economic Problems and Planning in North-East India', Sterling Publishers Pvt. Ltd., New Delhi.

Agarwal, A.K. (1988), 'North-Eastern Economy: Problems and Prospects', Mittal Publications, New Delhi.

Agarwal, A.K. (1999), 'Industry of Mizoram', in A. Banerjee and B. Kar (ed.), Economic Planning and Development of North-Eastern States, Kanishka Publishers, New Delhi.

Agarwal, A.K. and Prasad, R.N. (2003), 'Modernisation of the Mizo Society', Mittal Publications, New Delhi.

Agarwal, A.N. (1995), 'Indian Economy: Problems of Development and Planning', Wiley Eastern Ltd. Delhi.

Ahmad, Nisar (1987), 'Problems and Management of Small-scale and Cottage Industries', Deep and Deep Publications, New Delhi.

Ahmed, J.U. (2007), 'Industrialisation in North-Eastern Region', Mittal Publications New Delhi.

Ahmed, S.F. (1989), 'Problems and Prospects of Cottage Industry in

India', Anmol Publications, New Delhi.

Ali, M.Z. (2004), 'Absenteeism in Small-scale Industries', *Small Enterprise Development, Management and Extension (SEDME) Journal*, Volume 31, No.4, December.

Alvesson, M. and Ka¨rreman, D. (2001), 'Odd Couple: Making Sense of the Curious Concept of Knowledge Management', *Journal of Management Studies*, Volume 38, No. 7, pp. 995-1018.

Choudhury, P.C. (1959), 'The History and Civilization of the People of Assam: To the Twelfth Century A.D.', Department Of History and Ancient Studies, Government of Assam, Guwahati.

Deka, K.N. (1995), 'Aeekhan Sartthebari', Pratyush Printers, Baniyakuchi Bazaar, Sarthebari.

Deka, P.K. (1986), 'Contribution of Bell Metal Workers on Assamese Society', Souvenir, Golden Jubilee Celebration of the Assam Co-Operative Bell Metal Utensils Manufacturing Societies Ltd.

9

Entrepreneurship and ICT in Developing Countries

Hassan Mahmoud Hasan

Introduction

Technology is no longer a mere enabler, it is now central to the way we work, live and play. Actually, a new economy has evolved (PPI, 2000). Hence, the inability of a section of the world's population to benefit maximally from the popular opportunities that information and communication technologies (ICTs) and its vast youth population provide in promoting economic transformation and poverty is of great concern (Sesan, 2009). Recent studies and reports have rightly placed reducing emphasis on the need for developing countries to use ICTs for development, such as the United Nations Development Program's Human Development Report which stated that, "...information and communication technology (ICT) can also make an important development impact, because it can overcome barriers of social, economic and geographical isolation, increase access to information and education, and enable poor people to participate in more of the decisions that affect their lives" (Human Development Report, 2001).

In other words, ICTs have become useful in the delivery of social value (Sesan, 2009). On the other hand, in recent years, developing countries and their partners in the international development community have devoted considerable attention to the role that information and communication technologies (ICTs) might play in promoting economic growth, combating poverty, and strengthening their participation and competitiveness in the global economy. Spurred by the example of developing countries, such as India, that seem to be "riding the ICT wave" successfully, many developing countries are looking to emulate these successes and reap the benefits of ICT-led growth for their own economies (Info Dev, 2005). Many small and medium enterprises (SMEs) in developing countries have the possibilities to benefit enormously from mobile telephony, the Internet and other forms of information and communication technology (ICT) in their day-to-day business activities.

UNCTAD's Information Economy Report, 2010 shows how ICT used by micro enterprises and SMEs has improved not only the business performance but has helped improve livelihoods in some of the world's poorest regions and communities. Many entrepreneurs in developing countries now have a real possibility to benefit from ICT in their business activities. In many cases, this has resulted in gains in enhanced productivity in a number of areas. Mobile technology, for example, can be utilized by SMEs operating in the agricultural and fisheries sectors. It also has uses for labour and transport mobilization, for micro credit services and for mobile money. Kofi Annan, Secretary General of the United Nations stated in 2002 that "e-commerce is one of the most visible examples of the way in which information and communication technologies (ICTs) can contribute to economic growth. It helps countries improve trade efficiency and facilitates the integration of developing countries into the global economy. It allows businesses and entrepreneurs to become more competitive. And it provides jobs, thereby creating wealth" (Okoli and Mbarika, 2003, p. 44).

Recent Trends in ICT Developments

In fact, over 3.07 billion people were using internet by the end of December 2014, constituting about 42.4 of the world population. Mobile technology and services continue to be the key driver of the information society and the number of mobile broadband subscriptions is close to over 2 billion. Mobile-broadband networks are allowing more people to connect to high-speed networks and benefit from a growing number of applications and services. While both fixed- and mobile-broadband speeds continue to increase, the price of services is falling and ICTs are becoming more affordable: in the space of four years, fixed-broadband prices have dropped by an impressive 82 percent.

At the same time, ICT uptake remains limited in many developing countries, and particularly in the world's least connected countries (LCCs)—a group of 39 countries (home to 2.4 billion people) with particularly low levels of ICT development. In this group of countries, ICTs can become key enablers for achieving international and national development goals and have the greatest development impact—more policy attention needs to be directed towards them. On the other hand, young people all over the world are the most active users of ICTs. Today, 30 percent of the youth population are digital natives—the young people with solid ICT experience who are drivers of the information society. Within the next five years, the digital native population in the developing world is expected to double (ITU, 2013).

Overview of Electronic Commerce and its Recent Trends

"The truly revolutionary impact of the internet revolution is just beginning to be felt. But it is not "information that fuels this impact. It is not artificial intelligence. It is not the effect of computers and data processing on decision-making, policy making, or strategy. It is something practically no one foresaw or, indeed even talked about 10 or 15 years ago; e-commerce that is, the explosive emergence of the internet as a major, perhaps eventually the major, worldwide distribution channel for goods, services, and surprisingly, for managerial and professionals jobs. This is profoundly changing economics, markets and industry structure, products and services and their flow; consumer segmentation, consumer values and consumer behaviour; jobs and labour markets. But the impact may be even greater on societies and politics, and overall, on the way we see the world and ourselves in it" (Turban et al., 2004, p. 5).

Just like the way Industrial Revolution radically changed the nature of work, created enormous wealth, altered family structure, spawned new lifestyles and eventually affected even the primary form of government throughout the world, the e-commerce has brought about changes no less profound, especially for digital products (such as e-tickets, stock trades and mp3s) rather than molecular products, which mainly deal with the logistic costs of transporting physical products (Blackwell et al., 2009).

Internet based e-commerce began in the mid-1990s when companies like Federal Express, Cisco, Dell and GE started to focus on online sales, customer service and procurement. These companies recognized the advantages of the internet as an alternative to electronic data interchange systems (EDI). It allowed them to expand their electronic trading to smaller organizations, and transactions have now started to flow on the Internet (Conor et al., 2004).

By definition, e-commerce is the use of internet and web to transact business. More formally, the focus will be on digitally enabled commercial transactions between and among organizations and individuals (Laudon and Traver, 2005). But, a broader definition of e-commerce is found in Turban et al. (2002) and Adam et al. (1998), which encompasses a wide range of interactive business processes that occur before and after actual sales transactions. Having said that, electronic commerce is the electronic exchange (delivery or transactions of information, goods, services, and payments) over telecommunication networks, e-commerce activities include establishing and maintaining online relationships between an organization and its suppliers, dealers, customers, strategic partners , regulators and other agents related to (or in support of) traditional delivery channels (Warkentntin, 2001). In other words, e-commerce is anything that involves an online transaction. This can range from ordering online, through online delivery of paid content, to financial dealings such as movement of money between bank accounts (Hariharaputhiran, 2012).

In fact, e-commerce is commonly thought to include e-tailing, online banking and shopping—it involves transactions where buyers actually buy and shoppers actually shop. Others suggest that e-commerce is any transaction such as a support enquiry or an online catalogue search (Smith and Chaffey, 2002). In other words, e-commerce is often thought to refer simply to buying, selling and using the internet; people immediately think of consumer retail purchases from companies such as Amazon. However, e-commerce involves much more than electronically mediated financial transactions between organizations and customers. Many commentators now refer to e-commerce as both financial and informational electronically mediated transactions between an organization and any third party it deals with (Chaffey, 2002).

By this definition, non-financial transactions such as customer enquiries are also considered to be part of e-commerce (Marketing Online, 2006). In fact, electronic commerce or e-commerce encompasses all business conducted by means of computer networks. Advances in telecommunications and computer technologies in recent years have made computer networks an integral part of the economic infrastructure (Hariharaputhiran, 2012). From contemporary point of view, e-commerce can be defined as follows: "technology mediated exchanges between parties (individuals or organizations) as well as the electronically based intra-or inter-organizational activities that facilitate such exchanges" (Rayport and Jaworski, 2004, p. 4).

Actually, a new lexicon has developed for different e-commerce business models. Firstly, "bricks and mortar" companies are those that have a presence only in the physical world and are without a commercial internet presence (virtually every major company now has a website but a bricks and mortar company typically uses its site for passive promotional purposes rather than to engage in online commercial activity). Secondly, "bricks and clicks" companies are bricks and mortar companies that combine a physical offline presence with one online. Thirdly, "clicks-only companies" or "dot-coms" operate exclusively online. Amazon.com is one of the increasing numbers of formerly clicks-only firms that are now also operating traditional facilities or entering into alliances with partners that have traditional facilities. The company has alliances with Toys "R" Us, Wal-Mart and Walt Disney Stores among others (Evans and Berman, 2010).

It is important to acknowledge that the major types of e-commerce market categories are: B2C (business to consumer), B2B (business to business), C2C (consumers to consumers), P2P (peer to peer) and M-Commerce (mobile commerce). Amazon.com, esteel.com, eBay.com, Gnutella software and wireless mobile devices respectively are examples of the different major types of e-commerce. For the most part, the different types of e-commerce are distinguished by the nature of the market relationship—who is selling to whom. However, the exceptions are P2P and m-commerce, which are technology-based distinctions (Laudon and Traver, 2005).

Business-to-consumer companies (B2C) are involved with individual consumers in a retail or service setting (Rayport and Jaworski, 2004). Following WTO (1998), B2B e-commerce is defined as any transaction carried out between organizations in which at least one of the following activities—production, distribution, marketing, sale or delivery—takes place by electronic means. Compared to business-to-consumer (B2C), business-to-business (B2B) e-commerce is larger, growing faster and has less unequal geographical distribution globally. Indicators refer that increases in the freedom of the movements of goods, services, capital, technology and people coupled with rapid technological development resulted in an explosion of global B2B e-commerce (Kshetri and Dholakia, 2002).

Consumer-to-consumer companies (C2C) facilitate

transactions between individual consumers. eBay, an online auction site that serves the C2C market, generates revenue from transactional fees, ancillary services and advertising (Rayport and Jaworski, 2004). Peer-to-peer (P2P) e-commerce is the use of peer-to-peer technology, which enables internet users to share files and computer resources directly without having to go through a central web server in e-commerce. Napster.com, which was established to aid internet users in finding and sharing online music files known as MP3 files, is perhaps the most well known example of peer-to-peer e-commerce (Laudon and Traver, 2005).

Mobile e-commerce (also called mobile commerce or m-commerce) was defined as all activities related to a (potential) commercial transaction conducted through communication networks that interface with wireless (or mobile) devices. Current wireless devices include wireless or smart phones, laptop computers, vehicle-mounted technologies, personal message pager devices, and wireless-enabled handheld computers (so called pocket, palmtop and tablet computers). Mobile e-commerce can also be conducted using portable non-wireless mobile devices, such as personal digital assistants (PDAs) and laptop computers that can interface with other devices and networks through wired synchronization (Tarasewich et al., 2002). Diffusion researchers have found several characteristics of a new technology that influence its diffusion: relative advantage, compatibility, complexity, observability and trial ability (Rogers, 1983).

In most developing countries, mobile phones are easier to obtain than traditional fixed landline telephones. Therefore, the movement of the internet and internet applications into mobile phone systems will have a tremendous technological implication for these countries (Quibria et al., 2003). In addition, wireless (or mobile) telephony has emerged as a potential solution to the rural telephone deficit and as a possible "bridging" technology from unwired world to an Internet-accessible one (Goldstein and O'Connor, 2000).

Indicators demonstrate that, because mobile phone technology is an effective and relatively inexpensive path to telecommunications, countries with emerging economies can leapfrog industrlized countries in terms of usage (Strauss et al., 2006).

The data from IDC showed that PC sales worldwide have tumbled. Global sales of PCs fells 14 percent in the first three months of the year 2013, the biggest fall since research firm IDC started tracking the industry in 1994. IDC said 76.3 million units were shipped, a figure that underlines the appeal of tablets and smart phones as alternatives to PCs (BBC, 2013). Worldwide revenues from mobile payments are expected to increase significantly. Firms that track this space, including Juniper Research, Gartner and Yankee Group, have used different methodologies and forecast periods, but they concur that the segment is poised for a robust growth. For example, Juniper has expected that worldwide mobile payment volume to rise to US$ 670 billion by 2014 from US$ 240 billion in 2011. Looking more specifically at point-of-sale transactions made using mobile phones, Yankee Group has expected that worldwide volume would increase to US$ 40 billion by 2014 from US$ 27 million in 2010 (e-Marketer, 2011).

Telecom players, payment gateway companies and enterprises need to note the growth potential in mobile payments. While only 16 percent of smart phone and tablet users are currently using mobile payment services, 74 percent are aware of such services and an additional 39 percent indicated they would be interested or plan to use mobile payment apps. Indeed, mobile banking (m-banking) features are quite high among the more favoured mobile internet activities. The survey showed that 46 percent of the respondents have used their mobile device for banking transactions. Banks are also increasingly adding the mobile platform to their mix of distribution channels to meet the growing demand for mobility.

Not surprisingly, marketplace estimates put the number of m-banking users globally at 500 million in 2010 (Accenture, 2012). However, just having a cell phone does not eliminate the challenges of wireless e-marketing. E-marketers must still determine how to modify existing website content for the smaller screens on cell phones displays; how to resolve potentially cumbersome text entry using tiny keypads; how to develop new content that consumers will want; how to price services; and how to develop easy and secure payment methods. E-marketers also must understand that consumer behaviour with the mobile internet differs from consumer behaviour with stationary desktop computers or even laptop computers. Therefore, new content and new marketing strategies must be developed for wireless internet access (Strauss et al., 2006).

Furthermore, while the ubiquitous availability of mobile-telephone services is undeniable, with close to 100 percent of the population covered by a mobile signal, not everyone has a mobile phone. From a measurement point of view, the ongoing challenge thus remains to identify those who are still left without access to ICTs. By end-2014, there will be an estimated 3.07 billion people using the internet worldwide. In other words, there are still 4 billion people who are not yet online. Priority attention needs to be given to the unconnected, and action needs to be taken to improve to the accessibility and affordability of broadband internet services everywhere in order to usher in an inclusive information society.

Particularly, one promising application of the internet is in the area of e-commerce (OECD, 2004). Exactly as predicted by e-gurus 15 years ago, e-commerce is hotter than ever. Whether in mature markets, where consumer spending is shifting online, or in growth markets where rapid urbanization and increasing (mobile) internet penetration are unlocking new shopping habits, shoppers are 'e-commercing' it up (Trends Watching, 2012). 2012 was a great year for e-commerce, for both consumers and marketers alike. And from the looks of it,

2013 is shaping up to be even better (Simpson, 2012). Online purchase continues to rise, as global adoption and penetration levels of internet technology continuously increased (Rose et al., 2011).

Estimating B2B and B2C e-commerce transaction volumes to a reasonable level of accuracy has been a challenge. Based on data triangulation from several sources, it appears that global B2B e-commerce is more evenly distributed than global B2C e-commerce (Computer Economics, 2000; Nua Internet Surveys, 2000). Although North America dominates the global B2B e-commerce, the gap between North America and the rest of the world is much smaller for B2B e-commerce than for B2C e-commerce. Moreover, the inequality is narrowing rapidly. For instance, North's America share of the B2B market was 66 percent, twice the share of rest of the world in 1999 (BCG, 1999). This is estimated to shrink to 39 percent by 2004 (Lewis, 2000).

In fact, the share of the global B2B e-commerce which a country is likely to receive depends upon the following factors: country-level factors such as income and population size, the availability of credit, venture capital, and telecom and logistical infrastructure, tax, and other incentives, tariff/non-tariff barriers, government emphasis on the development of human capital, regulations to influence firms' investment in R&D, organizational level politics, language and the activities of international agencies (Kshetri and Dholakia, 2002). Global B2B transactions comprise 90 percent of all e-commerce.

According to research conducted by the US-based International Data Corporation (IDC), it is estimated that global B2B e-commerce, especially among wholesalers and distributors, amounted to US$ 12.4 trillion by the end of 2012. If the expansion in e-commerce continues at this rapid pace in developed markets as is expected, then B2B and B2C e-commerce transactions will account for about 5 percent of all inter-company transactions and retail sales by 2017 (WTO, 2013). On the other hand, global B2C e-commerce sales in

2012 grew 21.1 percent to top US$ 1 trillion for the first time. In 2013, sales will grow 18.3 percent to US$ 1.298 trillion worldwide, ten times less than B2B transactions, as Asia-Pacific surpasses North America to become the world's No. 1 market for B2C ecommerce sales (eMarketer, 2013).

According to a new report by the Interactive Media in Retail Group (IMRG), the United States remained the world's single biggest e-commerce market, followed by the United Kingdom and Japan. IMRG estimated that growth rates in those countries will be approximately 10-15 percent a year. But with China's e-commerce sales growing more than 130 percent in 2011, it is only a matter of time before the Asian giant becomes the single largest market in the world. IMRG, meanwhile, is forecasting that France, Italy, Spain, Russia, Turkey and Poland will be the fastest-growing markets in Europe. It also anticipated substantial growth in Latin America, led by Brazil and Mexico, and the Middle East, led by Israel and the UAE (iR, 2012). Interestingly, India's e-commerce market was worth about US$ 2.5 billion in 2009, it went up to US$ 6.3 billion in 2011 and to US$ 14 billion in 2012. About 75 percent of this is travel related (airline tickets, railway tickets, hotel bookings, online mobile recharge etc.).

Online retailing comprises about 12.5 percent (US$ 300 million as of 2009). India has close to 10 million online shoppers and is growing at an estimated 30 percent CAGR vis-à-vis a global growth rate of 8-10 percent. Electronics and apparel are the biggest categories in terms of sales. Although B2C e-commerce only accounts for only a small share of e-commerce as a whole, it continues to grow. B2C e-commerce is highest in Norway, Denmark, Sweden, the United Kingdom and the US and covers mainly computer-related products, clothing and digitized products. Despite the low value of its transactions, B2C e-commerce has received the most attention, partly because issues such as consumer trust and data protection have received considerable concern from policy makers (WTO, 2013).

However, e-commerce is the new wave of commerce and, depending on the industry; e-commerce represents either an opportunity for big profit or a death knell for the brick-and-mortar business. The landscape is changing, and businesses must adapt to survive (Simpson, 2013). Aad Weening, head of international marketing at Interactive Media in Retail Group (IMRG), acknowledged that mature markets in Europe and North America face challenges from faster-growing economies elsewhere in the world, but says the growth of internet usage and online shopping presents new opportunities in many countries. However, "the future of e-retail is global and with the inevitable slowing of growth in several major markets in the likes of North America and Europe, it is important for businesses to understand where the future opportunities will be", Weening stated. "Worldwide, we are increasingly seeing trust and confidence in purchasing online growing and government and private initiatives brought in to support the development of the global digital economy". He added, "online is now becoming an integral part of any country's economy and should be considered so" (iR, 2012).

In fact, rapid transmission of information is alerting the speed at which new trends develop and the direction in which they travel-especially since the virtual world allows consumers to participate in the creation and dissemination of new products (Solomon, 2007). Gil Levy, founder and managing partner, presented the latest trends in e-commerce including five common, yet rapidly evolving areas: social commerce, mobile commerce, enhanced media, personalization and segmentation (Birnbaum, 2013). Out of these trends for 2012, mobile and Facebook took the centre stage as online retailers focused on customers' digital experiences (Oracle White Paper, 2012). According to ITU estimates, there will be 6.8 billion mobile-cellular subscriptions by the end of 2013—almost as many as there are people on the planet (ITU, 2013).

The technological advances in mobile devices now enable customers to access information instantly, communicate with each other, receive up-to-the minute services, download relevant information, make online purchase and engage in a range of educational and entertainment services (Rose et al., 2011). Mobile devices are fast becoming the preferred method of accessing the web (Oracle White Paper, 2012). Further to that, the 2012 edition of measuring the Information Society prepared by the International Telecommunication Union (ITU) showed that, between 2010 and 2011, mobile-cellular subscriptions registered continuous double-digit growth in developing country markets. The number of mobile-cellular subscriptions increased by more than 600 million, almost all of them in the developing world, to a total of around 6 billion, or 86 per 100 inhabitants, globally (ITU, 2012a). On the other hand, Facebook took the top spot for emerging areas to invest in (Oracle White Paper, 2012).

Not surprisingly the CEO of Facebook, Mark Zuckerberg announced on September 14, 2012, a historic milestone of 1 billion Facebook users. Facebook had just officially registered one-seventh of earth's population (Vance, 2012). However, with regard to B2B e-commerce, the Forrester Research (2012) listed four B2B marketing trends and predictions for 2012. These include new tools that will empower B2B CMOs to have greater impact on revenue growth, marketers will quest after mobile due to smart phone and tablet explosion, social media focus will shift from the media to the social and marketers will find creative ways to meet demand for thought leadership and content. This means that the concept of consumerization will reshape business buyer expectations (Ernst et al., 2012).

However, it is known that e-commerce will continue to advance and evolve with time. The above listed are just a few trends that are being followed currently—it is possible that some of the trends might evolve more in the future or might become obsolete. Above all trends, businesses need to make sure that the quality of the product and the quality of customer support are highly competitive, as these are things which produces re-orders for e-commerce site (Cygnis Media, 2014).

Prospects of E-Commerce in Developing Countries

In its report in 1997, the Organization for Economic Co-operation and Development (OECD) stated that the arrival of the internet and web access has affected today's world in the same way that the Industrial Revolution affected the agrarian societies of countries. The internet has effectively linked all countries throughout the globe, and business no longer is limited to one's immediate town or state. Advancement in telecommunications, the flourishing of the internet and the emergence of e-commerce has helped in fostering an environment that promotes the globalization of markets throughout the world. E-commerce introduces incredible benefits, such as the diffusion of information, the development of new technologies, the promotion and sales of products and services and the collaboration between those in a supply chain (OECD, 1998).

In fact, there exists a growing consensus among development agencies and academics on the potential role of electronic commerce (e-commerce) in socio-development. Use of the internet and other related information and communication technologies (ICTs) to conduct business transactions is growing in private, public and not-for-profit sectors in both industrialized and developing countries (DCs) context. The potential value of e-commerce has received extensive coverage in research and trade publications with reports of several successful stories (Mukti, 2000; Berrill et al., 2004; Grandson & Pearson, 2003). E-commerce offers unprecedented opportunities for both developing and developed countries.

In the short-run, the gains are likely to be concentrated in developed countries but, in the long-run, developing countries have more to benefit. In the short-run, developing countries lack the infrastructure necessary to take full advantage of the internet. But in the long-run, they can leapfrog, skipping some of the stages in the development of information technology through which developed countries have had to pass (Panagariya, 2000). In other words, e-commerce arguably has a potential to add a higher value to businesses and consumers in developing countries than in developed countries (Kshetri, 2001; BBC News, 2003). E-commerce is diffusing into developing countries (DCs), and is assumed to help deliver the international development agenda (Boateng et al., 2008).

The internet is dramatically expanding the opportunities for business-to-business and business-to-consumer e-commerce transactions across borders. For business to consumer transactions especially, the internet sets up a potential revolution in global e-commerce: the individualization of trade. It gives consumers the ability to conduct a transaction directly with a foreign seller without travelling to the seller's country. The internet allows sellers to put their storefronts, in the form of web, in front of consumers all over the world. Technology has expanded the consumer marketplace to an unprecedented degree (Ham and Atkinson, 2001).

E-commerce provides multiple benefits to the consumers in form of availability of goods at lower cost, wider choice and saves time (Raghunath and Panga, 2013). However, Anckar (2003) gave a summary of the main potential drivers for consumer adoption of e-commerce. These benefits include: accessibility and convenience, global choice, online delivery, test and trial online, the real-time nature of the medium, time savings, possibilities for comparison shopping, access to extensive information, privacy and anonymity, competitive prices, availability of personalized offerings and the social nature of the purchasing process.

On the other hand, the internet and e-commerce are transforming the way firms operate by redefining how back-end operations—product design and development, procurement, production, inventory, distribution, after sales support, and even marketing—are conducted. In this process, the internet and e-commerce alter the roles and relationships of various parties, fostering new supply networks, services and business models. The end results are efficiency improvements, better asset utilization, faster time to market, reduction in total order fulfilment times and enhanced customer service (ECLAC, 2002). In fact, using the internet for business is popular now-a-days, and this provides the advantage of a variety and a new channel for commerce (Walters and Lancaster, 1999).

According to Michalski (1995), internet provides a global access at a relatively low cost. It allows firms to have a "virtual door" to customers through a home page, as well as creating useful interactions with customers, suppliers and stakeholders. In addition, it provides a simple illustration of the broad application of e-commerce. A review of the literature indicates the following as being the major benefits of the internet for e-commerce: quick response and access to global information; improvement in customer service by establishing effective lines of communication; a platform for low-cost advertising and hence for selling and buying products; low-cost entry for a network of firms for possible strategic alliances and collaborations; and the potential for a global market. In addition to this, there are intangible benefits which include strategic opportunities, a company image associated with modern technology and easy migration to the next level of technology (Gunasekaran and Ngai, 2005).

Boateng et al. (2008) summarized the contributions of e-commerce to the development of society in developing countries into three categories: Economic, socio-cultural, legal and others. Firstly, the economic contribution will result in increase in exports and trade, contribution to GDP, creation of employment opportunities, fostering of local entrepreneurs, and enlargement of sources of income at the grassroots. Secondly, the socio-cultural contributions encompass: fostering gender development, education, awareness creation, employee skill development, and impact on curriculum in tertiary institutions. Thirdly, the legal and other contributions of e-commerce include: improving e-readiness, institutional development and improvement and enactment of supporting policies. Therefore, as e-commerce sales skyrocket across the developing world, building an online presence is a low-risk way to test new markets or complement existing store footprints (Shabat et al., 2012).

Measuring National ICT Readiness in Syria

As more and more people join the global information society and high-speed communication networks become an indispensable infrastructure, the tracking and measurement of developments in information and communication technologies (ICTs) remain as relevant as ever (ITU, 2013). However, over the last decade, several attempts have been made to assess ICT developments (World Economic Forum, 2013). In his study to analyze and measure the diffusion of ICT in developing countries, Lutz (2003), used four ICT indicators. These indicators include cellular mobile subscribers per 100 inhabitants, personal computers per 100 inhabitants, internet hosts per 10,000 inhabitants and internet users per 10,000 inhabitants. The first three variables may be viewed as indicators of the state of ICT infrastructure, while the fourth indicator, viz. internet users, measures access to the internet. In addition, previous research has associated the level of a country's basic telecommunications infrastructure with its tele-density (Mbarika et al., 2002). Tele-density is defined as the number of telephone lines for every one hundred inhabitants (Mbarika, 2002).

There were 5,069,418 Internet users in Syria as of June 2012, for a 22.5 percent internet penetration rate of the Syrian population. The indicators of Internet World Stats showed that Syria ranked 12 out of 14 countries in the Middle East region, just behind Jordan (38.1 percent) and ahead of Yemen (14.9 percent) and Iraq (7.1 percent) (IWS, 2013). By the end of 2012, the updated indicators of International Telecommunication Union (ITU) revealed that the percentage of individuals using the internet in Syria was 24.3 percent (ITU, 2014). This puts Syria on the list of the less developed Arab states in terms of internet service provision (UNDP-Syria, 2004). However, growth in the number of internet users in Syria has been fairly steady since 2005 (Wikipedia, 2013), following the concerted efforts of the National ICT Strategy for Socio-Economic Development in Syria (UNDP-Syria, 2004).

In reference to internet hosts, there were 416 Syrian internet hosts in 2012, placing Syria at number 188 out of 231 in the world (The World FactBook, 2013). With a measured download speed that averages 1.68 mbps, the speed of the internet in Syria is relatively very slow compared to the world-wide average of 16.05 mbps. The data comes from Ookla, a broadband research company that "crowd sourced" research and download and upload speeds through its website SpeedTest.net, where people can test the speed of their internet connection. The Syrian Arab Republic ranks behind 180 other countries on a list of the world's fastest download speeds. Results were obtained by analyzing test data between January 7, 2014 and February 5, 2014. Tests from 127,014 unique IPs were taken in this country and of 345,621 total tests, 6,199 were used for the current Index (Net Index, 2014). On the other hand, the indicators of the World Bank in 2008 revealed that there were 18,00,000 personal computers in Syria (Trading Economics, 2013). In other words, only 8.8 percent of the Syrian population was having personal computers in 2008 (IDB, 2012). However, 43 percent of households in Syria were having computers in 2012 (ITU, 2013).

In reference to fixed-telephone market in Syria, STE is the sole fixed-service provider, providing mainline services over its own network. It is state-owned. By the end of 2010, there were 4.069 million fixed-telephone subscriptions, translating into a penetration rate of 19.9 percent. During the first six months of 2011, fixed-telephone subscriptions increased by 3.1 percent, as 128,000 subscriptions were added. By the end of June 2011, Syria's total fixed-telephone subscriptions stood at 4.197 million, corresponding to a penetration rate of 20.4 percent (ITU, 2012b). The number of fixed-line connections has increased markedly since 2000 (The World FactBook, 2013), and although penetration rates are low, they are higher than in many more wealthy Middle Eastern countries (Business Wire, 2012).

STE is investing in upgrading and extending its network and aims to gain 100 percent coverage by the end of 2013 (Hamdan, 2013). On the other hand, Syria's mobile market is served by a duopoly comprised of two operators Syriatel and MTN Syria (BuddeComm, 2013). Both companies obtained a build-operate-transfer (BOT) agreement from STE to establish a network covering the country. Syriatel is locally owned and MTN is a subsidiary of MTN of South Africa, which gained ownership through its purchase of Invest COM (Hamdan, 2013). However, there has been a talk of a third operator, with keen investors likely to enhance the mobile penetration in Syria, which is the second lowest in the Middle East (BuddeComm, 2013). In other words, mobile penetration rates are relatively low—Syria is one of the few markets in the region with room for expansion (Business Wire, 2012).

In September 2010, the Ministry of Communications and Technology announced the tender for the third mobile license. From a short list of five operators, Saudi Telecom Company (STC) and Qatar Telecom (QSC) submitted bids for the tender. The process was postponed due to political unrest in the country. By the end of 2010, total mobile-cellular subscriptions amounted to 11.8 million, translating into a penetration rate of 57.8 percent. During the first six months of 2011, 521,000 mobile-cellular subscriptions were cancelled. By the end of June 2011, Syria's total mobile-cellular subscriptions stood at 112,780 subscriptions, corresponding to a penetration rate of 54.8 percent (ITU, 2012b). However, call quality ranges from acceptable to poor. Many international calls fail or are less clear over the mobile network compared to the landline network (Wikipedia, 2013).

Mobile data services are becoming an increasingly important source of new revenue as the mobile voice market begins to mature. With 3G/HSPA networks in place, the focus for mobile data is beginning to shift to mobile broadband offerings; already mobile broadband subscriptions exceed those of fixed broadband (BuddeComm, 2013). Syriatel and MTN are the only mobile-cellular operators; they have deployed 3G mobile-broadband technology. STE announced in May 2011 that it will be working with the mobile-cellular operators to expand the 3G networks. Moreover, in April 2011, Syriatel held a trial of HSPA+ technology. The new technology enables internet speeds up to 20 mbps, compared with the current Syriatel 3G service speed of up to 7.2 mbps. As for the mobile-broadband market, by end of 2010, active mobile-broadband Internet subscriptions amounted to 256,242, corresponding to a mobile-broadband penetration rate of 1.3 percent (ITU, 2012b).

The 3G wireless internet is available in all major cities as well as cities with significant tourism. 3.5G EDGE wireless internet is available through mobile network operators, Syriatel and MTN. Wireless internet is accessed using a USB stick purchased from the mobile operators. In addition, 3G SIM cards for use on mobile phones may be purchased with a data plan. However, only W-CDMA phones support data at the moment (Wikipedia, 2013). As for other wireless-broadband technologies, VSAT services are provided by the ISP Best Italia. In March 2011, STE announced that it aims to employ technologies such as W-CDMA and that it will prepare for LTE trials according to contracts with mobile-cellular operators. Concerning fixed (wired)-broadband projects, STE is working to complete the requirements needed for FTTB technology (ITU, 2012b). To sum up, the Little Data Book on Information and Communication Technology 2014, a joint publication between the World Bank and the International Telecommunication Union (ITU), summarized the key telecom parameters in Syria (The World Bank, 2014).

However, in 2012, after two years of research and consultations with ICT practitioners, policy and industry experts, and academia, the networked readiness index (NRI) introduced a new sub-index on ICT impacts that aimed at holistically assessing the way that countries go about leveraging ICTs and benefiting from them in terms of enhanced competitiveness and well-being. This evolution ensures that the NRI framework remains at the forefront of ICT measurement. As one of the most authoritative assessments of its kind, it has been adopted by several governments as a valuable tool for informing their competitiveness and policy agendas (World Economic Forum, 2014). Its success emphasizes the importance of continuing to adapt its framework in alignment with the changing landscape of technology and its new opportunities.

The networked readiness framework translates into the NRI, comprising four sub-indexes that measure the environment for ICT; the readiness of a society to use ICT; the actual usage of all main stakeholders; and, finally, the impacts that ICT generates in the economy and society. The first three sub-indexes can be regarded as the drivers that condition the results of the fourth sub-index—that is, ICT impacts. These four sub-indexes are divided into 10 pillars and 53 variables (World Economic Forum, 2013). However, according to the Global Information Technology Report, 2012, which resulted from the collaboration between the World Economic Forum and INSEAD, Syria occupied low positions in the regional as well as in the global networked readiness index (NRI) rankings. In 2012, Syria's NRI score was 2.85, positioning the country at 129 out of 142 countries and territories. Between 2010 and 2012, Syria's NRI score decreased from 3.06 to 2.9. This means that Syria fell five ranks, from 129 to 124, in the total networked readiness index (NRI) (NCO, 2012).

Furthermore, the ICT development index (IDI) is a composite index combining 11 indicators into one benchmark measure that serves to monitor and compare developments in information and communication technology (ICT) across countries. In fact, the IDI was developed by International Telecommunication Union (ITU) in 2008 and presented at the 2009 edition of Measuring the Information Society (ITU, 2009). However, there are three stages in the evolution towards the information society. These three stages are: ICT readiness (infrastructure use), ICT use (intensity) and ICT capability (skills) (ITU, 2012). The latest IDI, which is based on the end of 2010 data, shows that ICT uptake continues to accelerate worldwide, with all countries, including those in the Arab region, improving their IDI scores. Within the Arab States region, however, Syria occupied low positions in the regional as well as in the global IDI rankings. According to IDI 2010, Syria ranked 96th globally and 11th regionally (ITU, 2012b).

However, Syria remains a market with great potential for expansion for ICT services but requires greater market liberalization to achieve that potential (Business Wire, 2012). In fact, besides understanding ICT trends in terms of such factors as infrastructure access and ICT skills, it is also important to analyze and track prices of ICT services. The cost and affordability of ICT services will influence and in some cases determine whether or not people will be able to subscribe to certain services and use ICTs. The ICT price basket (IPB) is composed of three distinct prices—for fixed-telephone, mobile-cellular and fixed-broadband services—and computed as a percentage of countries' average gross national income (GNI) per capita (ITU, 2012a).

However, an analysis of the three sub-baskets (fixed-telephony, mobile-cellular-telephony, and fixed-broadband internet) suggests that prices in Syria as a whole are relatively expensive in comparison with the rest of the Arab countries (ITU, 2012b). These finding suggests that more must be done to make ICT services and fixed-broadband services in particular, more affordable in the region, especially if the region is to achieve the target set by the Broadband Commission for Development, which is "to make sure that by 2015, entry-level broadband services should amount to less than five percent of average monthly income" (ITU, 2012a).

Conclusions

The paper has presented that the latest available ICT statistics. The new figures show that, by the end of 2014, there were more than 3 billion internet users worldwide, two-thirds of them coming from the developing world, and that the number of mobile-broadband subscriptions will reach 2.3 billion globally. Fifty-five percent of these subscriptions are expected to be in the developing world. In addition, the latest trends in e-commerce including five common, yet rapidly evolving areas are also discussed, viz. social commerce, mobile commerce, enhanced media, personalization, and segmentation. On the other hand, the paper has provided a comprehensive review on the prospects of ICT including e-commerce in developing countries as an entrepreneurial tool for socio-economic development.

In reference to the assessment of the readiness of national infrastructure, governments in developing countries are invited to adopt the networked readiness index (NRI) and the ICT development index (IDI) as they are one of the most authoritative assessments of their kind. On the other hand, the paper provides strong evidence that Syria's current ICT infrastructure is a major barrier to the process of entrepreneurship and socio-economic development, specifically, low internet penetration, mobile-cellular subscriptions, fixed (wired)-broadband subscriptions and active mobile-broadband subscriptions. It is clear that Syria has not been successful in adopting technologies. The findings indicate that Syria is on the list of the less developed Arab states in terms of ICT uptake. However, Syria remains a market with great potential for future expansion of ICT services, specifically in terms of internet penetration, mobile-cellular subscriptions and its applications including broadband services, but requires much market liberalization to achieve that potential.

The Syrian government and other ICTs related stakeholders are invited to empower and target all Syrian online users of all genders (specifically females), groups of all ages, all levels of education holders, low income internet users, married people, big-sized families, all minorities and ethnic groups, residents in rural areas and finally, the disabled persons. However, any future strategies for the development of e-commerce in Syria should achieve the objectives set by the Broadband Commission for Digital Development. In fact, this commission endorsed ambitious but achievable targets for 2015. The targets cover broadband policy, affordability and uptake. Firstly, by 2015, internet user penetration should reach 60 percent worldwide, 50 percent in developing countries and 15 percent in LDCs.

Secondly, by 2015, entry level broadband services should be made affordable in developing countries through adequate regulation and market forces (e.g. be priced at less than 5 percent of average monthly GNI per capita). In fact, any steady growth in the number of internet users will be attributed to the improvements made to the communications infrastructure, the increase in public awareness and the introduction of new regulations and legislations.

On the other hand, our findings show that mobile phones, active mobile-broadband technology, wireless applications and online social networks are currently regional and global emerging trends in ICT developments. Therefore, for the process of socio-economic development, the public and private sectors in Syria are invited to invest in these promising sectors. Finally, any successful mobile infrastructure must be supported by massive IP infrastructure; there would also be continuing growth opportunities for the fixed services. Communications' operators in the Middle East countries including the Syrian Arab Republic must be serious about investing in high-speed mobile LTE networks, including next generation mobile broadband. In other words, the Arab countries including Syria must invest in communications connectivity, especially high-speed broadband and wireless access.

References

Accenture (2012), 'Mobile Web Watch 2012: High Performance Delivered', available at: http://www.accenture.com/SiteCollectionDocuments/PDF/Accenture-Study-Mobile-Web-Watch-Germany-Austria-Switzerland-EN.pdf [Accessed 22 March 2013].

Adam, N.R., Dogramaci, O., Gangopadhyay, A. and Yesha, Y. (1998), 'Electronic Commerce: Technical, Business, and Legal Issues', 1st edition, Prentice-Hall, Upper Saddle River, NJ.

Anckar, Bill (2003), "Drivers and Inhibitors to E-commerce Adoption: Exploring the Rationality of Consumer Behaviour in the Electronic Marketplace", ECIS 2003 Proceedings, Paper 24, available at: http://aisel.aisnet.org/ecis2003/24 [Accessed 29 January 2014].

BBC News (2003), 'Poor Miss Out on Net Commerce', November 20, available at: http://news.bbc.co.uk/2/hi/technology/3223388.stm.

BBC (2013), 'PC Sales Worldwide Have Tumbled', data from IDC shows, available at: http://www.bbc.com/news/busines22103079 [Accessed 24 June 2014].

BCG (1999), 'New BCG Research Re-evaluates Size, Growth and Importance of Business-to-Business E-Commerce', Boston: Boston Consulting Group, December 21, available at: www.bcg.com [Accessed 20 June 2000].

Berrill, A., Goode, S. and Hart, D. (2004), 'Managerial Expectations of Internet Commerce Adoption After the Tech Wreck', *Journal of Global Information Technology Management*, Volume 7, No. 3, pp. 45-63.

Birnbaum, E. (2013), 'Gil Levy Presents at INSIGHT 2012: Latest Trends in Ecommerce', available at: http://www.ecommercepartners.net/blog/author/elana-birnbaum [Accessed 24 June 2014].

Boateng, R., Heeks, R., Molla, A. and Hinson, R. (2008), 'E-commerce and Socio-economic Development: Conceptualizing the Link', *Journal of Internet Research*, Volume 18, No. 5, pp. 562-594, available at:

www.emeraldinsight.com/1066-2243.htm [Accessed 28 January 2014].

BuddeComm (2013), 'Syria-Telecoms, Mobile, Broadband and Forecasts: Executive Summary', available at: http://www.budde.com.au/Research/Syria-Telecoms-Mobile-Broadband-and-Forecasts.html?r=51 [Accessed 7 August 2013].

Business Wire (2012), 'Syria: Telecoms, Mobile, Broadband and Forecasts', available at: http://www.businesswire.com/news/home/20120924005691/en/Research-Markets-Syria---Telecoms-Mobile-Broadband [Accessed 28 August 2013].

Connor, J., Galvin, E. and Evans, M. (2004), 'Electronic Marketing: Theory and Practice for the Twenty-first Century', Gosport: FT Prentice Hall.

Cygnis Media (2014), 'Possible E-Commerce Trends in the Year 2014', available at: http://www.cygnismedia.com/blog/2014-trends-for-ecommerce/ [Accessed 14 March 2014].

ECLAC: United Nations, Economic Commission for Latin America and the Caribbean, (2002), 'Electronic Commerce, International Trade and Employment: Review of the Issues', Washington Office, April 8, pp. 1-30, available at: http://www.eclac.cl/publicaciones/xml/0/10510/lcwasr22.pdf [Accessed 22 March 2014].

eMarketer (2011), 'Top Digital Trends for 2012', available at: http://creative.asiaone.com/2012/IA/a1networknews_IA120530/emarketer_digtrends2012.pdf [Accessed 25 June 2014].

eMarketer (2013), 'E-commerce Sales Topped $1 Trillion for the First Time in 2012', available at: http://www.emarketer.com/Article/Ecommerce-Sales-Topped-1-Trillion-First-Time-2012/1009649 [Accessed 24 June 2014].

Ernst, J., Cooperstein, D.M. and Dernoga, M. (2012), 'B2B Marketing Trends and Predictions for 2012', available at: http://www.forrester.com/B2B+Marketing+Trends+And+Predictions+For+2012/fulltext/-/E-RES60343 [Accessed 14 March 2014].

Goldstein, A. and O'Connor, D. (2000), 'E-Commerce for Development: Prospects and Policy Issues', OECD Development Centre, Working Paper No. 164, (formerly Technical Paper No. 164), research programme on: Globalising

Technologies and Domestic Entrepreneurship, Published by OECD: Organization for Economic and Co-operation Development, September, CD/DOC (2000)8, available at: http://www.oecd ilibrary.org/docserver/download/5lgsjhvj7b25.pdf?expires=1404832596&id=id&accname=guest&checksum=6073F1F5DBB3D3F13089EC5F9B17A6A2 [Accessed 08 July 2014].

Grandon, E. and Pearson, J.M. (2003), 'Strategic Value and Adoption of Electronic Commerce: An Empirical Study of Chilean Small and Medium Businesses', *Journal of Global Information Technology Management*, Volume 6, No. 3, pp. 22-43.

Gunasekaran, A. and Ngai, E.W.T. (2005), 'E-commerce in Hong Kong: An Empirical Perspective and Analysis', *Journal of Internet Research*, Volume 15, No. 2, pp. 141-159.

Ham, S. and Atkinson, D.R. (2001), "A Third Way Framework for Global E-commerce', Progressive Policy Institute, Technology and New Economy Project, March, pp. 1-29.

Hamdan, M. (2013), 'E-learning in Syria', available at: http://webcache.googleusercontent.com/search?q=cache:kaFvi_Kg5ucJ:hamdaneducation.com/arabic/EPeJdocs/4th6.htm+http://hamdaneducation.com/arabic/EPeJdocs/4th6.htm&cd=1&hl=en&ct=clnk [Accessed 10 August 2013].

Hariharaputhiran, S. (2012), 'Challenges and Opportunities of E-Commerce', *International Journal of Marketing, Financial Services and Management Research* (IJMFSMR), Volume 1 No. 3, Indian Institute of Technology, available at: http://indianresearchjournals.com/pdf/IJMFSMR/2012/March/10.pdf [Accessed 18 July 2014].

Human Development Report (2001), 'Making New Technologies Work for Human Development', Published for the United Nations Development Programme (UNDP) by Oxford University Press, Inc., 198 Madison Avenue, New York, New York, 10016, available at: http://hdr.undp.org/sites/default/files/reports/262/hdr_2001_en.pdf [Accessed 23 June 2014].

Information For Development Programme (2005), 'Improving Competitiveness and Increasing Economic Diversification in the Caribbean: The Role of ICT', This report was commissioned by infoDev and prepared by OTF Group, USA, available at:

http://siteresources.worldbank.org/INTLAC/Resources/Chap5_bckgr_Role_ICT.pdf [Accessed 23 June 2014].

Islamic Development Bank (2012), 'Key Socio-Economic Statistics on IDB Member Countries', Statistical Monograph No. 32, available at: http://www.isdb.org/irj/go/km/docs/documents/IDBDevelopments/Internet/English/IDB/CM/Publications/Statistical_Monograph/Monograph2012.pdf [Accessed 18 August 2013].

International Telecommunication Union (2009), 'Measuring the Information Society 2009: The ICT Development Index', available at: http://www.itu.int/ITU-D/ict/publications/idi/material/2009/MIS2009_w5.pdf [Accessed 28 August 2013].

International Telecommunication Union (2012a), 'Measuring the Information Society 2012', available at: http://www.itu.int/en/ITU-D/Statistics/Documents/publications/mis2012/MIS2012_without_Annex_4.pdf [Accessed 26 August 2013].

International Telecommunication Union (2012b), 'Connecting the Unconnected by 2015: ICT Adoption and Prospects in the Arab Region', Connect Arab Summit 2012, available at: http://www.itu.int/dms_pub/itu-d/opb/ind/D-IND-AR-2012-PDF-E.pdf [Accessed 24 August 2013].

International Telecommunication Union (2013), 'Measuring the Information Society, 2013', available at: http://www.itu.int/en/ITU-D/Statistics/Documents/publications/mis2013/MIS2013_without_Annex_4.pdf [Accessed 23 June 2014].

International Telecommunication Union (2014). 'Explore Key ICT Statistics: Percentage of Individuals Using the Internet in Syria', available at: http://www.itu.int/net4/itu-d/icteye/ [Accessed 11 February 2014].

Internet World Stats (2013), 'Middle East Internet Users: Population and Facebook Statistics', available at: http://www.internetworldstats.com/stats5.htm [Accessed 29 August 2013].

Kshetri, N. (2001), ''Determinants of the Locus of Global E-commerce', *Electronic Markets*, Volume 11. No. 4, pp. 250-257.

Kshetri, N. and Dholakia, N. (2002), 'Determinants of the Global Diffusion of B2B E-Commerce', *Electronic Markets*, Volume 12, No. 2, pp. 120-129, available at: http:///C:/Users/Asus/Downloads/SSRN-id711223%20(1).pdf [Accessed 24 June 2014].

Lutz, M. (2003), 'An Analysis of the Determinants and Effects of ICT Diffusion in Developing Countries', *Journal of Information Technology for Development*, Volume 10, pp. 151-169, IOS Press.

Marketing Online (2006), 'An Introduction to Internet Marketing', available at: http://www.marketing-online.co.uk/ch1.pdf [Accessed 19 August 2006].

Mbarika, V. (2002), 'Re-thinking Information and Communications Technology Policy Focus on Internet versus Teledensity Diffusion for Africa's Least Developed Countries', *The Electronic Journal of Information Systems in Developing Countries*, Volume 9, No. 1, pp.1-13.

Mbarika, V., Byrd, T. and Raymond, J. (2002), 'Growth of Teledensity in Least Developed Countries: Need for a Migrated Ethiopia', *Journal of Global Information Management*, Volume 10, No. 2, pp. 14-27.

Michalski, J. (1995), 'People are the Killer App', Forbes ASAP, June, pp. 120-122.

Mukti, N. (2000), 'Barriers to Putting Business on the Internet in Malaysia', *Electronic Journal on Information Systems in Developing Countries*, Volume 2, No. 6, pp. 1-6.

National Competitiveness Observatory (2012), 'Syria in the Networked Readiness Index 2012', available at: http://www.ncosyria.com/arabic/news/51.html [Accessed 12 August 2013].

Net Index (2014), 'Household Download Index: Syrian Arab Republic', available at: http://www.netindex.com/download/2,106/Syrian-Arab-Republic/[Accessed 07 February 2014].

Okoli, C. and Mbarika, V.A.W. (2003), 'A Framework Assessing E-Commerce in Sub-Saharan Africa', *Journal of Global Information Technology Management*, Volume 6, No. 3, p. 44, available at: http://chitu.okoli.org/media/pro/research/pubs/OkoliMbarika200

3JGITM.pdf [Accessed 18 July 2014].

Oracle White Paper (2012), 'E-commerce Trends for 2012: Mobile and Facebook Take Centre Stage as Online Retailers Focus on Customers' Digital Experiences', available at: http://www.oracle.com/us/products/applications/web-commerce/ecommerce-analytics-trends-2012-1504948.pdf [Accessed 14 March 2014].

Panagariya, A. (2000), 'E-commerce, and Developing Countries', Policy Issues in International Trade and Commodities, Study Series No. 2 UN, New York and Geneva, pp. 1-33.

Progressive Policy Institute (2000), 'A New Economy Task Force Report: Making the New Economy Grow, An Action Agenda', available at: http://www.dlc.org/ndol_ci09fb.html?kaid=107&subid=123&contentid=1490 [Accessed 23 June 2014].

Quibria, M.G., Ahmed, S.N., Tschang, T. and Macasaquit, M. (2003), 'Digital Divide: determinants and policies with special reference to Asia', *Journal of Asian Economics*, Volume 13, Issue 6, pp. 811-825, available at: http://ac.els-cdn.com/S1049007802001860/1-s2.0-S1049007802001860-main.pdf?_tid=c320d1a4-fbc4-11e3-bddd-00000aab0f26&acdnat=1403631005_b84d604ff99df9a28553f1b20596bf76 [Accessed 24 June 2014].

Raghunath, A. and Panga, M. (2013), 'Problems and Prospects of E-Commerce', *Medicaps Institute of Techno Management,* Volume 2, Issue 1, available at: http://www.irdindia.in/Journal_IJRDMR/PDF/Vol2_Iss1/10.pdf [Accessed 29 January 2014].

Rayport, J. and Jaworski, B. (2004), 'Introduction to E-commerce', Second edition, McGraw Hill/Irwin, New York.

Rogers, E.M. (1983), 'Diffusion of Innovations', Third Edition, New York: Free Press.

Rose, S., Hair, N. and Clark, M. (2011), 'Online Customer Experience: A Review of the Business-to-Consumer Online Purchase Context', *International Journal of Management Review*, Volume 13, pp. 24-39, available at: http://onlinelibrary.wiley.com/doi/10.1111/j.1468-2370.2010.00280.x/pdf [Accessed 24 June 2014].

Simpson, M. (2012), '2013 Global E-Commerce Trends: More Personal, More Mobile, More Channels', available at:

http://www.cmswire.com/cms/customer-experience/2013-global-ecommerce-trends-more-personal-more-mobile-more-channels-018677.php [Accessed 24 June 2014].

Simpson, M. (2013), '13 E-Commerce Trends for 2013', available at: http://www.websitemagazine.com/content/blogs/posts/archive/2013/01/02/13-e-commerce-trends-for-2013.aspx [Accessed 24 June 2014].

Smith, P. and Chaffy, D. (2002), 'E-marketing Excellence: The Heart of E-business', Great Britain: Butterworth-Heinemann.

Solomon, M.R. (2007), 'Consumer Behaviour: Buying, Having and Being', 7th edition, Eastern Economy Edition, Prentice-Hall of India Private Limited, New Delhi.

Strauss, J., El-Ansary, A. and Frost, R. (2006), 'E-marketing', Prentice-Hall of India Private Limited, New Delhi.

Tarasewich, P., Nickerson, R.C. and Wakentin, M. (2002), 'Issues in Mobile E-Commerce', *Communications of the Association for Information Systems*, Volume 8, pp. 41-64, available at: http://pdf.aminer.org/000/244/631/exploring_mobile_ecommerce_in_graphical_bound_retailing.pdf [Accessed 24 June 2014].

Trading Economics (2013), 'Personal Computers in Syria', available at: http://www.tradingeconomics.com/syria/personal-computers-wb-data.html [Accessed 29 August 2013].

Trends Watching (2012), 'Retail Revolution: E-tail is Retail', available at: http://trendwatching.com/trends/pdf/2012-05%20ETAIL%20EVOLUTION.pdf [Accessed 24 June 2014].

Turban, E. et al. (2002), 'Electronic Commerce, 2002: A Managerial Perspective', Prentice Hall, New Jersey.

Turban, E., King, D., Lee, J. and Viehland, D. (2004), 'Electronic Commerce: A Managerial Perspective', International Edition, Pearson Prentice Hall.

United Nations Development Programme-Syria, (2004), 'National ICT Strategy for Socio-Economic Development in Syria: A Study Prepared by a National Team of Experts and Consultants', available at: http://www.arab-hdr.org/publications/other/undp/hdr/2004/syria-ict-04e-strategy.pdf [Accessed 10 August 2013].

Vance, A. (2012), 'Facebook: The Making of 1 Billion Users,

available at:
http://www.businessweek.com/articles/2012-10-04/facebook-the-making-of-1-billion-users [Accessed 14 March 2014].

Walters and Lanncaster, G. (1999), 'Using the Internet as a Channel for Commerce', *Management Decision*, Volume 37, No. 10, pp.800-816.

Warkentin, M. (2001), 'The Next Big Thing in E-commerce', *Decision Line*, 32(1), pp. 7-10.

Wikipedia (2013), 'Telecommunications in Syria', available at: http://en.wikipedia.org/wiki/Telecommunications_in_Syria [Accessed 29 August 2013].

World Economic Forum (2013), 'The Global Information Technology Report: Growth and Jobs in a Hyperconnected World', available at: http://www3.weforum.org/docs/WEF_GITR_Report_2013.pdf [Accessed 12 August 2013].

World Economic Forum (2014), 'The Global Information Technology Report: Rewards and Risk of Big Data', available at: http://www3.weforum.org/docs/WEF_GlobalInformationTechnology_Report_2014.pdf [Accessed 13 August 2014].

World Trade Organization (2013), 'E-commerce in Developing Countries: Opportunities and Challenges for Small and Medium-sized Enterprises', Geneva, Switzerland, available at: http://www.wto.org/english/res_e/booksp_e/ecom_brochure_e.p [Accessed 23 June 2014].

10

Working Capital and Liquidity Management in Micro, Small and Medium Enterprises (MSMEs)

Moirangthem Biren Singh and N. Tejmani Singh

Introduction

The micro, small and medium enterprises (MSMEs) earlier known as small-scale industries (SSIs) is one of the most vital sectors of any economy. Globally, MSMEs are considered as accelerators of economic growth and development for any nation (Bihari, 2011). MSMEs have been playing a momentous role in overall economic development of a country like India where millions of people are unemployed or underemployed. This sector solves many problems viz. poverty and unemployment by providing immediate large-scale employment with lower investments and proves to be the second largest manpower employer, after agriculture (Garg and Walia, 2012). In this regard, former Prime Minister of India Dr. Manmohan Singh stated, "the key to our success in unemployment lies in the success of the manufacturing in the small-scale sector".

In India, the MSMEs play a pivotal role in the overall industrial economy of the country. It is estimated that in terms of value, the sector accounts for about 45 percent of the manufacturing output and around 40 percent of the total exports of the country. It produces over 8,000 value-added products. Further, in recent years, the MSME sector has consistently registered higher growth rate compared to the overall industrial sector (Bihari, 2011).

Micro, Small and Medium Enterprises Development (MSMED) Act, 2006 has defined and classified MSMEs into categories, depending on their investment in plant and machinery or equipments as shown in Table 10.1.

Table 10.1: Definition of MSMEs

Manufacturing Sector	
Enterprises	**Investment in Plant/Machinery**
Micro Enterprises	Does not exceed Rupees twenty five lakh.
Small Enterprises	More than Rupees twenty five lakh but does not exceed Rupees five crore.
Medium Enterprises	More than Rupees five crore but does not exceed Rupees ten crore.
Service Sector	**Investment in Equipments**
Micro Enterprises	Does not exceed Rupees ten lakh.
Small Enterprises	More than Rupees ten lakh but does not exceed Rupees two crore.
Medium Enterprises	More than Rupees two crore but does not exceed Rupees five crore.

Source: Micro, Small and Medium Enterprises Development (MSMED) Act, 2006.

Need for the Study

Working capital plays a vital role in the smooth running of a business enterprise. It is considered as the life-blood and nerve-centre for all business enterprises. The importance of working capital in any industry needs no special emphasis (Jain, 2010). No business enterprise whether manufacturing or trading can run effectively without adequate quantity of working capital. Particularly in micro, small and medium enterprises (MSMEs), the enterprise is going to collapse without adequate quantity of working capital, since the working capital requirements are of much longer duration than the requirements for fixed assets. Working capital in a business enterprise may be compared to the blood of the human body; blood gives life and strength to the business organization (Kuchhal, 1976).

It has been pointed out by RBI that a firms' profitability may be increase as more working capital is added to fixed capital provided the firm does not exceed cent percent capacity. Thus, adequate amount of working capital is maintained for the smooth running of a firm and for fulfilment of the twin objectives of liquidity and profitability (Shailaja and Rajender, 2011). In this context, efficient management of liquidity is also an important indicator of sound financial health of any business enterprise. Efficient liquidity management involves planning and controlling current assets and current liabilities in such a manner that it eliminates the risk of firm's inability to meet due short-term obligations on the one hand and avoids excessive investments in these assets on the other (Anusha, 2011).

Nevertheless, the development of MSMEs is beset with a number of problems, many of which have been analyzed and investigated into from time to time by a number of committees, commissions and researchers. But the problems of working capital in MSMEs remained an unexplored area particularly in Manipur since most of these enterprises/industries have weak financial base and limited access to financial institutions to support their scarce resources. Therefore, the study of working capital and liquidity management has assumed added significance in respect of MSMEs in India and Manipur in particular.

Literature Review

Many researchers have studied working capital from different views and perspectives in different periods to contribute valuable findings with suggestions. After reviewing some of the important studies, the following ones are remarkable and very useful for the purpose of our research.

Gangadhar's (1981) study on medium, large and small public and private limited companies in the Indian corporate sector during 1961-76 examined the statistical trends in working capital position. In his study, the application of second parabola revealed that the current assets formed a relatively higher proportion of total net assets in private limited companies than that of public limited companies. The study also revealed that in the case of medium and large public limited companies there appeared to be a lead-lag relationship between gross fixed assets and current assets over the study period.

Jain (1988) based his study among ten manufacturing, trading and service industries in the state of Rajasthan and highlighted various working capital management practices followed by the selected companies. The study found out that the companies had both over-investment and under-investment problems. The study strongly recommended for the release of excess funds in working capital and to invest the same in short-term or long-term assets.

Mohan (1995) conducted a study on various issues related to working capital management among selected private large-scale companies in the state of Andhra Pradesh during the period from 1977 to 1986. The study revealed that investment in current assets in sample companies was more than that of the fixed assets. The analysis also revealed that the liquidity position of the sample units was found to be highly unsatisfactory because the companies operated with lesser balance sheet working capital than cash working capital. Based on his findings, he concluded the dire need for improvement of liquidity and solvency position of the sample units failing which would lead to serious liquidity crunch.

Indrasena and Someswar (1996) conducted a study in Hindustan Cables Ltd. for the period from 1989-1994. They studied current ratio, quick ratio, working capital turnover ratio, debtors turnover ratio, inventory turnover ratio, and current assets turnover ratio. The authors found that liquidity position of the company was unsatisfactory. The study recommended for an effective utilization and control of current assets.

Rao (1997) conducted a study among six paper mills in the state of Andhra Pradesh to ascertain the working capital position. The study revealed that the sample companies overtraded with insufficient working capital. The sample units were compelled to under-stock raw materials for want of adequate working capital. It was found that the current ratio and liquid ratio of the sample companies were found to be very low, indicating a liquidity crunch.

Sathyamoorthi (2002) in his study attempted to ascertain how current assets were financed and also attempted to discover the relative importance of various current assets components. The study covered four years data of selected co-operative organizations in Botswana. The study revealed that the liquidity ratios played a vital role to evaluate the short-term efficiency of the organization. His study also revealed that the co-operatives had low liquidity, resulting in their weak position to pay short-term debts.

Deloof (2003) made a study of the relationship between working capital management and corporate profitability from the sample of 1,009 large Belgium non-financial firms during the period from 1992 to 1996. He found a negative relationship between gross operating income as a measure of profitability and cash conversion cycle, account receivables and inventories.

Eljelly (2004) empirically conducted a study on the relationship between profitability and liquidity for a sample firm in Saudi Arabia. The researcher took cash gap and current ratio as a measure of liquidity. Correlation and regression analysis showed a negative relationship between liquidity and profitability, where the current ratio was taken as a measure of liquidity.

Padachi (2006) made an investigation on the working capital management practices for the manufacturing firms in Mauritius by taking a sample of 58 small firms. The researcher examined the trends in working capital management and its impact on performance. Regression analysis results observed a negative relationship between inventories and receivables with profitability. The study also showed an increasing trend in short-term component of working capital financing.

Jain (2010) made a study on a sample of four oil drilling and exploration companies operating in India. The purpose of the study was to investigate the relationship between working capital management and firm's profitability. The researcher used cash conversion cycle as measure of working capital management. Results of the study found that current ratio is positively associated with profitability whereas cash conversion cycle is significantly negative when associated to the firm's profitability.

The above studies show a path and give us an idea regarding the trends in working capital and liquidity management. The findings and conclusions of those researches conducted on the same area for different industries and environment from different perspectives propelled us to develop our own methodology for research.

Objectives of the Study

Keeping in view the pragmatic importance of working capital in MSMEs, an attempt is made in this study to contribute towards a crucial element in financial management. The following are the specific objectives of the study:

- To examine the trends of working capital in the selected plastic industries in Manipur during the period of study.
- To assess the liquidity position of the sample industries during the period of study.
- To evaluate the liquidity management of the sample industries through ratio analysis.

Research Methodology and Database

The methodologies used in the present study pertain to the sampling design for collection of data and the various statistical, financial and analytical techniques used for the analysis of data and information. The database of the study covers the sources and types of data. As per the records of the District Industries Centre (DICs) and Directorate of Commerce and Industries, Government of Manipur, there were 15 plastic industries on the date of data collection for the research purpose. These industries were registered as micro and small enterprises under the MSMED Act, 2006. However, there was insufficient data in case of 6 plastic industries and hence the number of industries for the research purpose resulted in 9 (nine) for the period of 6 (six) years from 2008-09 to 2013-14.

In pursuance of the objectives, relevant data was collected that relates to the working capital trend and liquidity management in selected plastic industries in Manipur.

The sources of these data were: (i) annual audited financial statements of respective industries, (ii) Economic Survey, different issues, Government of Manipur, (iii) Annual Reports, Ministry of MSMEs, Government of India, and (iv) journals, magazines and different websites.

The collected data was processed and tabulated and the liquidity analysis was done mainly on the basis of ratio analysis such as current ratio (CR) and quick ratio (QR).

Trends in Working Capital of the Sample Industries

The direction and tendency of business can be determined by reviewing the past data relating to the problem under study. Trend analysis helps to judge the tendency of business working capital.

Trend analysis indicates the changes which have taken place from time to time in working capital and the individual component of working capital like current assets and current liabilities on the basis of any normal base year (Talekar, 2005). Table 10.2 depicts the trend in current assets, current liabilities and net working capital of the sample industries in Manipur during the period under study.

Current Assets and Current Liabilities Trend Analysis

The working capital trend can be understood by using trend percentage. To analyze the tendency of working capital in the industries under study, trend indices or trend percentages were used. Indices are constructed taking 2008-09 as the base year. Tables 10.3 and 10.4 show the current assets and current liabilities trend (in percentage) for the study period from 2008-09 to 2013-14.

Table 10.2: Current Assets, Current Liabilities and Net Working Capital in Selected Plastic Industries from 2008-09 to 2013-14

(₹ lakh)

Name of the Industry	2008-09	2009-10	2010-11
M/s AMRO Plastic Industry			
Current Assets	225.85	275.75	305.65
Current Liabilities	115.75	265.85	365.75
Net Working Capital	110.1	9.9	-60.1
M/s BISRA Polymers			
Current Assets	684.45	811.95	1068.45
Current Liabilities	439.35	546.26	690.71
Net Working Capital	245.1	265.69	377.74
M/s DEBCHAN Plastic Industry			
Current Assets	266.86	350.95	765.15
Current Liabilities	94.92	154.76	110.23
Net Working Capital	171.94	196.19	654.92
M/s KAMAL Poly Industry			
Current Assets	624.48	581.45	727.15
Current Liabilities	258.56	321.58	380.27
Net Working Capital	365.92	259.87	346.88
M/s KSHIS Plastic Industry			
Current Assets	1388.73	2226.68	3217.15
Current Liabilities	748.76	664.42	2329.51
Net Working Capital	639.97	1562.26	887.64
M/s LISMART Industries			
Current Assets	857.35	838.57	969.24
Current Liabilities	381.43	387.89	489.45
Net Working Capital	475.92	450.68	479.79
M/s MANIPUR Plastic Industry			
Current Assets	1042.45	1057.15	1339.99
Current Liabilities	603.43	641.33	624.52

Contd...

Net Working Capital	439.02	415.82	715.47
M/s RANJOY Plastic Industry			
Current Assets	224.15	255.65	291.59
Current Liabilities	95.69	82.13	110.61
Net Working Capital	128.46	173.52	180.98
M/s S.J. Plastic Enterprises			
Current Assets	550.42	654.74	769.94
Current Liabilities	384.33	439.33	556.56
Net Working Capital	166.09	215.42	213.38
Plastic Industry (Total)			
Current Assets	5864.74	7052.89	9514.31
Current Liabilities	3122.22	3503.55	5657.61
Net Working Capital	2742.52	3549.34	3856.7

Contd...

Name of the Industry	**2011-12**	**2012-13**	**2013-14**
M/s AMRO Plastic Industry			
Current Assets	485.25	395.75	675.35
Current Liabilities	495.35	390.15	450.15
Net Working Capital	-10.1	5.6	225.2
M/s BISRA Polymers			
Current Assets	1416.72	1836.25	2914.45
Current Liabilities	861.24	1255.64	1339.84
Net Working Capital	555.48	580.61	1574.61
M/s DEBCHAN Plastic Industry			
Current Assets	895.07	1042.24	1271.85
Current Liabilities	120.55	136.85	241.48
Net Working Capital	774.52	905.39	1030.37
M/s KAMAL Poly Industry			
Current Assets	981.16	1346.25	1304.15
Current Liabilities	434.35	984.56	1153.31
Net Working Capital	546.81	361.69	150.84
M/s KSHIS Plastic Industry			
Current Assets	4144.98	4669.88	5749.99
Current Liabilities	2680.25	3472.92	3957.57
Net Working Capital	1464.73	1196.96	1792.42
M/s LISMART Industries			

Contd...

Current Assets	1135.94	1280.84	1594.12
Current Liabilities	589.15	858.48	1004.75
Net Working Capital	546.79	422.36	589.37
M/s MANIPUR Plastic Industry			
Current Assets	2798.87	5066.23	5260.81
Current Liabilities	1287.75	1899.45	2779.52
Net Working Capital	1511.12	3166.78	2481.29
M/s RANJOY Plastic Industry			
Current Assets	340.31	1284.51	1103.51
Current Liabilities	240.88	500.25	500.25
Net Working Capital	99.43	784.26	603.26
M/s S.J. Plastic Enterprises			
Current Assets	917.38	1493.73	1583.25
Current Liabilities	755.65	983.15	1169.09
Net Working Capital	161.73	510.58	414.86
Plastic Industry (Total)			
Current Assets	12915.6	18415.6	21457.4
Current Liabilities	7465.17	10481.4	12595.9
Net Working Capital	5450.43	7934.23	8861.52

Source: Annual financial statements and records of respective industries.

Table 10.3: Trends in Current Assets

S. No.	Name of the Industry	2008-09	2009-10	2010-11	2011-12	2012-13	2013-14
1.	AMRO Plastic Industry	100.00	122.09	110.84	158.76	81.56	170.65
2.	BISRA Polymers	100.00	118.63	131.59	132.59	129.61	158.72
3.	DEBCHAN Plastic Industry	100.00	131.51	218.02	116.98	116.44	122.03
4.	KAMAL Poly Industry	100.00	93.11	125.06	134.93	137.21	96.87
5.	KSHIS Plastic Industry	100.00	160.34	144.48	128.84	112.66	123.13
6.	LISMART Industries	100.00	97.81	115.58	117.20	112.76	124.46

Contd...

7.	MANIPUR Plastic Industry	100.00	101.41	126.75	208.87	181.00	103.84
8.	RANJOY Plastic Industry	100.00	114.05	114.06	116.71	377.45	85.91
9.	S.J. Plastic Enterprises	100.00	118.95	117.59	119.15	162.83	105.99
10.	**Industry Average**	**100.00**	**117.54**	**133.77**	**137.11**	**156.84**	**121.29**

Source: Annual financial statements and records of respective industries.

Table 10.4: Trends in Current Liabilities

S. No.	Name of the Industry	2008-09	2009-10	2010-11	2011-12	2012-13	2013-14
1.	AMRO Plastic Industry	100.00	229.68	137.58	135.43	78.76	115.38
2.	BISRA Polymers	100.00	124.33	126.44	124.69	145.79	106.71
3.	DEBCHAN Plastic Industry	100.00	163.04	71.23	109.36	113.52	176.45
4.	KAMAL Poly Industry	100.00	124.37	118.25	114.22	226.67	117.14
5.	KSHIS Plastic Industry	100.00	88.74	350.61	115.58	129.57	113.95
6.	LISMART Industries	100.00	97.81	115.58	120.37	145.71	117.04
7.	MANIPUR Plastic Industry	100.00	106.28	97.38	206.20	147.50	146.33
8.	RANJOY Plastic Industry	100.00	85.83	134.68	217.77	207.67	100.00
9.	S.J. Plastic Enterprises	100.00	118.95	117.59	119.15	162.82	105.99
10.	**Industry Average**	**100.00**	**126.56**	**141.04**	**140.31**	**150.89**	**122.11**

Source: Annual financial statements and records of respective industries.

Liquidity Analysis of the Sample Industries

This section presents the liquidity management in the

selected plastic industries focusing on examining the components of working capital and liquidity position using different liquidity ratios for the study period. Tables 10.5 and 10.6 depict the current ratio and quick ratio as a measure of liquidity.

Table 10.5: Current Liquidity Ratios

S. No.	Name of the Industry	2008-09	2009-10	2010-11	2011-12	2012-13	2013-14
1.	AMRO Plastic Industry	1.95	1.04	0.84	0.98	1.01	1.50
2.	BISRA Polymers	1.56	1.49	1.55	1.64	1.46	2.17
3.	DEBCHAN Plastic Industry	2.81	2.27	6.94	7.42	7.61	5.27
4.	KAMAL Poly Industry	2.41	1.81	1.91	2.26	1.37	1.13
5.	KSHIS Plastic Industry	1.85	3.35	1.38	1.55	1.34	1.45
6.	LISMART Industries	2.25	2.16	1.98	1.93	1.49	1.59
7.	MANIPUR Plastic Industry	1.73	1.65	2.14	2.17	2.67	1.89
8.	RANJOY Plastic Industry	2.34	3.11	2.64	1.41	2.57	2.20
9.	S.J. Plastic Enterprises	1.43	1.49	1.38	1.21	1.52	1.35
10.	**Overall Plastic Industry**	**2.04**	**2.04**	**2.31**	**2.28**	**2.34**	**2.06**

Source: Annual financial statements and records of respective industries.

Results, Interpretations and Conclusions

It is observed in the present study that size of the current assets is continuously growing in all the plastic industries sampled during the study period from 2008-09 to 2013-14. The average annual trend of current assets ranges from 117.54 percent in 2009-10 to 156.84 percent in 2012-13 but it decreases to 121.29 percent in 2013-14. This shows that there is a fluctuating trend in current assets among the plastic industries during the period of study.

It is also found that the magnitude of current liabilities shows an increasing trend among the sampled industries during the period of study but some of the industries depict a fluctuating trend. Due to increase or decrease in the current liabilities, the net working capital position of some industries also fluctuated. The average annual trend of current liabilities ranges from 122.11 percent in 2013-14 to 150.89 percent in 2012-13.

Table 10.6: Quick Ratio/Acid Test Ratio

S. No.	Name of the Industry	2008-09	2009-10	2010-11	2011-12	2012-13	2013-14
1.	AMRO Plastic Industry	0.43	0.28	0.22	0.18	0.24	0.26
2.	BISRA Polymers	0.52	0.39	0.32	0.44	0.42	0.53
3.	DEBCHAN Plastic Industry	1.17	0.97	1.94	2.08	2.43	1.75
4.	KAMAL Poly Industry	1.25	1.19	1.06	1.34	0.81	0.91
5.	KSHIS Plastic Industry	0.83	0.77	1.07	0.98	0.99	1.02
6.	LISMART Industries	1.20	1.13	1.26	0.91	0.91	1.14
7.	MANIPUR Plastic Industry	0.95	0.72	1.05	0.61	0.47	0.33
8.	RANJOY Plastic Industry	0.82	1.13	0.54	0.66	0.37	0.90
9.	S.J. Plastic Enterprises	1.16	0.97	0.95	0.68	1.36	0.98
10.	**Overall Plastic Industry**	**0.92**	**1.04**	**0.93**	**0.87**	**0.89**	**0.96**

Source: Annual financial statements and records of respective industries.

The liquidity position of the sampled industries is measured by the twin ratios of current ratio and quick ratio. The current ratio measures the ability of the industries to pay off its short-term liabilities. The ideal or standard current ratio 2:1 is recommended for every enterprise. In the present study, two industries did not touch this figure during the study period. It is also observed that the highest current ratio 7.61:1 was shown by Debchan Plastic Industry and lowest ratio 0.84:1

was shown by Amro Plastic Industry. It reveals that liquidity position of the Debchan Plastic Industry is higher than the ideal ratio which means too much holding of current assets and poor liquidity position of Amro Plastic Industry which means shortage of current assets to meet its short-term debts.

The quick ratio or acid test ratio is important device to test the short-term financial strength of the business enterprises. It is an improved device of assessing liquidity position of the enterprise than current ratio. The rule of thumb is 1:1 for quick ratio which is the ideal or standard for every enterprise. In this study, most of the industries touched this level except two industries during the period of study. It shows a very poor liquidity for the two industries and position of other industries in maintaining their liquidity position during the study period. It was also found that the highest quick ratio of 2.43:1 was shown by Debchan Plastic Industry and lowest of 0.22:1 by Amro Plastic Industry.

References

Agarwal, Anusha (2011), 'How to Manage Working Capital?: An Empirical Study of Maruti Suzuki India Limited', *Journal of Accounting and Finance*, Volume 25, No. 2, pp. 85-92.

Bihari, Suresh Chandra (2011), 'Redefining MSME with CRM Practices', *IJMBS*, Volume 1, Issue 2, pp. 49-55.

Deloof, Marc (2000), 'Does Working Capital Management Affect Profitability of the Belgian Firms?', *Journal of Business Finance and Accounting*, Volume 30, Issues 3-4, pp. 573-588.

Eljelly Abuzar, M.A. (2004), 'Liquidity-Profitability Trade-off: An Empirical Investigation in an Emerging Market', *IJCM,* Volume 14, No. 2, p. 48.

Garg, Ishu and Suraj Walia (2012), 'Micro, Small and Medium Enterprises (MSMEs) in Post-Reform India: Status and Performance', *International Journal of Latest Trends in Engineering and Technology (IJLTET),* Volume 1, Issue 3, pp. 134-141.

Gangadhar, V. (1981), "Trends in Working Capital in India", *The Management Accountant,* March 1981, pp. 111-112.

Indrasena, Reddy P. and K. Someswar (1996), "Working Capital Management in Public Sector Undertakings: A Case Study', *The*

Management Accountant, September, pp. 643-645.

Jain, Anupam (2010), 'Effect of Working Capital Management on Profitability of Firms: A Study of the Indian Oil Drilling and Exploration Industry', *Global Journal of Business Management*, Volume 4, No. 1, pp. 42-49.

Jain, R.K. (1988), 'Working Capital Management of State Enterprises in India', National Publishing House, Jaipur.

Kuchhal, S.C. (1976), 'Corporate Finance: Principles and Problems', Chaitannya Publishing House, Allahabad.

Mohan, Reddy P. (1995), 'Management of Working Capital', Printwell Publishers, Jaipur.

Padachi, Kesseven (1996), 'Trends in Working Capital Management and its Impact on Firm's Performance: An Analysis of Mauritius Small Manufacturing Firms', *International Review of Business Research Papers*, Volume 2, No. 2, pp. 45-58.

Rao, Subba O. (1997), "Financial Analysis of Small Paper Mills in Andhra Pradesh', *Finance India*, Volume XI, No. 3, pp. 689-696.

Sathyamoorthi, C.R. (2002), 'Management of Working Capital in Selected Co-operatives in Botswana', *Finance India*, New Delhi, Volume 16, No. 3, pp. 105-125.

Shailaja, G. and K. Rajender (2011), 'Liquidity Management in APGENCO Ltd.", *The Journal of Institute of Public Enterprise,* Volume 34, Nos. 3 and 4, pp. 93-106.

11

Role of Corporate Houses in Developing Entrepreneurship

Bidhu Kanti Das

Introduction

Corporate houses have been played a vital role for developing entrepreneurship at micro level. This action may be taken as a corporate social responsibility (CSR) initiative or by any other name, which has played a huge role for the development of entrepreneurial activity in India as well as in North-Eastern part of India. But much of the studies in the field of entrepreneurship have not highlighted this phenomenon which is growing slowly for boosting up the entrepreneurial activity in the region and the proactive role of corporate houses in this regard. It can be construed that entrepreneurship cannot be developed in isolation—it needs some kind of help or support from others. For example, John D. Rockefeller's Standard Oil Company developed because he was able to control the distribution network, which at that time, relied on the railroad infrastructure. Henry Ford's assembly lines were feasible only when there was enough of a mass market for automobiles. The fortunes of Bill Gates rose along with the fledgling personal computer industry. None of these individuals invented the technology that made them wealthy, but they had the foresight to take advantage of an entrepreneurial opportunity. When entrepreneurs take advantage of profit opportunities, they create new entrepreneurial opportunities that others can act upon. Entrepreneurship creates an environment that results in further entrepreneurial activities.

In this paper, the researcher tries to find out the entrepreneurial development in North-East India and the role of corporate houses in the development of entrepreneurial activity in the region.

Objective of the Study

It can be seen that in India and abroad, corporate houses have been played a vital role in the development of entrepreneurship at micro level. This action may be taken as a step towards corporate social responsibility (CSR) to depict their commitment towards the society. In this paper, the researcher has identified two objectives: first to study the public sector enterprises which are promoting entrepreneurship at micro level in the North-Eastern States of India, and second to study the initiatives undertaken by the corporate houses to promote entrepreneurship.

The present paper is explorative in its nature and scope. Researcher has used both the primary and secondary data. Data was collected from different locations of North-Eastern states of India especially from Assam and Tripura. Under this study, four public sector undertakings in the field of oil and natural gas sector were studied. The time period of the study was from 2005 to 2010.

Literature Review

When available literature was analyzed, it was found that the entrepreneurship has been studied in different dimensions including social entrepreneurs, young entrepreneurs, women entrepreneurs, minority entrepreneurs, immigrant entrepreneurs and corporate entrepreneurs. But literature pertaining to corporates which are promoting entrepreneurship at the micro level is not available in a desired manner. However, the researcher studied the available literature and presented it for the understanding of the concept of entrepreneurship and how corporate houses are promoting entrepreneurship at micro level.

The first edition of the Oxford English Dictionary (OED)

1897) defined entrepreneur as 'the director of a public musical institution'. Only in a later edition was the word used in its more modern sense, as the editors acknowledged that the control and direction of capital labour in a modern economy might be so difficult and different from past experience that a new class of person was needed and with it a new word, adopted from the French. In present edition of the same dictionary, entrepreneur has been defined as 'a person who undertakes a commercial venture'.

Kirzner (1973) depicts entrepreneurs as people who are alert enough to spot previously unseen profit opportunities and then act on them. As Kirzner describes it, 'entrepreneurship involves noticing something that nobody has noticed before'.

Zammerer and Scarborough (2011) defined entrepreneur as, "an entrepreneur is one who creates a new business in the face of risk and uncertainty for the purpose of achieving profit and growth by identifying significant opportunities and assembling the necessary resources to capitalize on them. Although many people come up with great business ideas, most of them never act on their ideas. Entrepreneurs do. The process of creative destruction, in which entrepreneurs create new ideas and new businesses that make existing ones obsolete, is a sign of vibrant economy".

One of the most comprehensive studies of global entrepreneurship, conducted by the Global Entrepreneurship Monitor (GEM 2004), shows a significant variation in the rate of new business formation among the nations of the world when measured by total entrepreneurial activity, or total entrepreneurial activity (TEA) index. The study found that 11.3 percent of the adult population in the United States, roughly one in nine people was working to start a new business. Nations in the Americas—North, South and Latin—led the world to an entrepreneurial activity, with Asian countries posting the lowest level of entrepreneurship. The study also concluded that these different rates of entrepreneurial activity may account for as much as one-third of the variation in the rates of economic growth among these nations. The GEM study also reports that globally men are twice as likely to start a business as women and that the majority of the entrepreneurs turn to family members and informal investors for external capital, and that nearly one-third of global entrepreneurs are in the age bracket of 25-44 years.

Drucker opined, "starting a business is neither necessary nor sufficient for entrepreneurship". He explicitly comments that "not every new small business is entrepreneurial or represents entrepreneurship". He cites the example of a husband and wife who open another delicatessen store or another Mexican restaurant in the American suburb as a case in point. There is nothing especially innovative or change-oriented in this. The same would be true of new not-for-profit organizations. Not every new organization would be entrepreneurial. Drucker also makes it clear that entrepreneurship does not require a profit motive. Early in his book on 'Innovation and Entrepreneurship', Drucker asserts, "no better text for a history of entrepreneurship could be found than the creation of the modern university, and especially the modern American university". He then explains what a major innovation this was at the time. Later in the book, he devotes a chapter to entrepreneurship in public service institutions which basically talks about social entrepreneurship. In this book, he explained that entrepreneurship in public service institution can provide goods and services to the poor people at affordable prices.

Analysis and Findings

After analyzing the literature on CSR policy of the documents, we found that that following PSU Companies operating in North-East India are working towards promoting entrepreneurship for quite long. A brief about them is depicted in Table 11.1.

According to CSR policy of the company, ONGC is

actively involved in promoting education, healthcare and entrepreneurship and is supporting water management in the community, in and around its areas of operations. ONGC is also providing calamity relief throughout the country.

Table 11.1: Public Sector Companies Promoting Entrepreneurship in North-East India

Company	ONGC	OIL	IOC	GAIL
Major entrepreneurial activity	PURA–Project, Yuva Samridhi and Guwahati Rickshow Bank	Rupanthar, Handicrafts Training and Production Centre, Duliajan	Established Handloom Training Centre in the State of Manipur	Small and Micro entrepreneurship development programme

CSR activities being implemented by oil PSUs in North-East India—especially for entrepreneurship development, women empowerment, promoting self-help groups—is creating employment opportunities for the people. Special initiatives include equipments given to fishermen of both SC and ST community, driving training, training for poultry, piggery, goattery, electric wiring, cane and bamboo crafting, mushroom cultivation, tailoring etc. This has resultantly generated a lot of employment for the local people. Also, beneficiaries can start up their own ventures from the initial grant given by the oil PSUs.

Every year, at least one hundred people get different types of training from ONGC and other companies in the field. This apart, ONGC is distributing bicycles, tri-cycle rickshaws, fishing nets, drum sets, sewing machines and other equipments to the poor people for their self-employment and livelihood. Apart from this, all the PSUs are offering regular employment to the local people and few at all-India level, depending on the merit and education qualifications.

ONGC is also conducting entrepreneurial development programmes (EDPs)—training programmes for the people in its operational areas, namely tailoring, piggery, goattery, dairy development and beauty parlours on a regular basis. It is also providing initial grants for starting new ventures by the beneficiaries.

Another public sector undertaking GAIL has done remarkable work for the employment generation of local people at different places in Tripura. Few of them are: composite scheme on semi-intensive fish culture for Putia self-help group of Putia Gram Panchayt under Boxanagar block in the year 2003-04; a contribution of ₹ 1,21,024 towards supporting the composite scheme on pig fattery unit for the group 'Milam Badal' self-help group and 'Khumtia Badal' self-help group of Dayal Para under the Boxanagar block in the year 2003-04. At present, both these self-help groups are performing well. Their business has increased manifold and every member of the respective group is earning a good amount every month.

A massive entrepreneurship scheme by way of developing and supporting genuine self-help groups has been undertaken by the ONGC in the Sivasagar District in collaboration with the district administration and the State Institute of Rural Development (SIRD), Government of Assam. To cite an example, ONGC contributed ₹ 20 lakh for the purchase of milk van, deep freezer and cycles for distribution of milk to Sundar Pukhuri Milk Co-operative Society which in collaboration with State Veterinary Department is supplying milk to individual consumers in Nazira and has been able to provide employment to many unemployed youth of the area.

'Yuva Samridhi' is a project undertaken by ONGC for the promotion of self-help groups and creation of self-employment opportunities in Sivasagar district. Developed by the district administration, it proposes to establish integrated efforts between the district administration, banks and ONGC to create approximately 4,000 direct employment for the unemployed youth of the district. It is proposed that self-help groups will be promoted for taking up projects under fishery, dairy, poultry and related activities. ONGC would be sharing 30 percent of the cost of the project (₹ 6.38 lakh) and infrastructure cost of ₹ 15 lakh bringing the total outlay to ₹ 21.38 lakh. It has been estimated by district authorities that 4,000 families of the district will benefit out of this project.

'Project Sampark' is another ambitious project by the district administration to empower the community through e-literacy and e-governance in which ONGC has invested ₹ 40 lakh. About 100 kiosks would be set up in rural and urban areas. Apart from it, facilities for internet browsing, DTP, scanning, CD writing, photocopier, other government services like issue of certificates, information about government schemes of all the departments, market rate of local produces, expert opinion about scientific cultivation, health-care etc. would be provided online through the 'Sampark' kendra. Different training modules would also be introduced to educate people in computer applications. It is expected that initially 200 unemployed educated youth will get the direct benefit.

ONGC has also contributed ₹ 15 lakh towards Centre for Rural Development (CRD) for its innovative project "Rickshaw Bank Guwahati". Under this project, it provides rickshaws to participants and in turn the rickshaw pullers have to refund a daily minimum amount of ₹ 20 towards the cost of the rickshaw. In one year, the participants would become the owners of their rickshaws. For this, the addressed persons would have to take the membership and start saving with the Rickshaw Bank. Apart from ensuring the livelihood of the rickshaw pullers, the project also aims to create a bank to provide accidental and life insurance for pullers and their families, and to enable them to borrow and save regularly. In case of funding, a single sponsorship of ₹ 7,000 covers the purchase of a rickshaw and extended expenses like insurance, license, uniform etc. Each sponsor has its advertisement or name on the back of the rickshaw for five years. The puller is able to pay the cost within a year and own the rickshaw thereafter.

Established in 1984, OIL's Handicrafts Training and Production Centre located at Duliajan, imparts training to women in handicraft, weaving, embroidery and tailoring on a monthly stipend for a 9 month period.

A growth centre with modern handlooms has been installed for training and production in diversified handloom products in Eri and Muga (the world famous golden silk of Assam) under the 'Project Rupantar Scheme'.

112 mushroom units have been provided spawn under the action research project of SIRD. 115 shops have been allocated to unemployed youth in the Indian Oil Corporation's, Assam oil division's market at Digboi and about 650 persons have been employed in these shops. A trade apprentice course has been conducted since 1962 for imparting skills to local youth in various trades. 423 youngsters have been trained under this programme in the last ten years.

Indian Oil Corporation's, Assam oil division, has assisted in setting up of a handloom training centre in the State of Manipur, which is giving training to hundreds of people and making them self-employed.

Conclusion

From the above facts and findings, it was observed that the corporate houses have been actively working to encourage and develop entrepreneurial skills and activity in the North-Eastern states of India. Though, it is only PSUs at present, gradually it may happen that private organizations may join hands for the development of entrepreneurship in the region. The initiative or contribution may be very small, but it may lead to greater economic growth and create an environment that encourages markets and rewards productive activity.

References

Drucker, P.F. (1985), 'Innovation and Enterepreneurship', New York: Harper and Collins.

Global Entrepreneurship Monitor (2004), 'Global Entrepreneurship

Monitor, 2004, Executive Report', Babson Park, MA: Ewing Marison Kauffman Foundation and London Business School.

Indian Oil (2011), 'Indian Oil News', *Journal of Indian Oil Corporation Limited,* XLVIII(10).

IOCL (2010), 'Corporate Social Responsibility', available at: www.iocl.com/aboutus/corporatesocialresponsibility.aspx: http:www.iocl.com/aboutus/corporatesocialresponsibility.aspx.

Oil India Ltd. (2011), 'Looking Beyond Business', Duliajan: Public Relation Department, Oil India Limited.

ONGC (2005-2012), 'ONGC-Tripura Utkarsha', Journal of Tripura Assets, Agartala.

Schumpter, J.A. (1934), 'The Theory of Economic Development', Cambridge, Mass: Harvard University Press.

Zammerer, T.W. and Scarborough, N.M. (2011), 'Essentials of Entrepreneurship and Small Business Management', Fifth edition, New Delhi: PHI Learning Private Ltd.

12

Remittances and Micro Enterprises

Sultana B.A. Mazumder

Introduction

A micro enterprise is considered a small business employing 10 people or less. Internationally, most micro enterprises are family businesses employing one or two persons. The entrepreneurs operate micro enterprises by choice. Most micro enterprise owners are primarily interested in earning a living to support themselves and their families. They only grow the business when something in their lives change and they need to generate a larger income.

The households in many developing countries cannot rely on the financial system when borrowing money due to corruption and inappropriate financial system, thereby limiting the access to capital. However, the problems mentioned above can be solved with remittances from family or friends who are living abroad or in different regions in their own country. The access to remittances can change the households' decisions to invest more and thereby achieve asset accumulation (Adams, 1998). Self-employment can be a way out of the poor life for many individuals in low and middle-income countries as it has been recognized as an effective tool in increasing employment, economic development and decreasing poverty levels. A micro firm is usually self-financed by an entrepreneur. In the part of the world where self-financing is impossible for a majority of the population, money lenders are restrictive with their loans and charge unreasonably high interest rates (Azad, 2005).

Remittance is defined as transfer of money by a foreign worker to an individual in his or her home country. More than 215 million people or 3 percent of the world's population live outside their home countries. Adams found in 2005 that households that receive international remittances spend 2.2 percent more on household expenditures than the households that do not receive any remittances. This increase in household expenditure is mostly spent on consumption from a world standpoint. However, from the individual immigrant's viewpoint, this increase in household expenditure can be seen as an investment whereby the individual can expect some financial returns in the future. The increased remittances are important for an economy as it affects wages, employment and business opportunities. Adams also states that remittances have a positive effect on the area of the recipient in terms of health care, education and poverty. A small proportion of the remittances goes to savings and investments in houses, land and buildings (Adams, 2005).

The individual that is remitting money tends to have problems controlling how the money is used by the receiver. If the money is used in a process of starting up a SME, it can be a way for the individual that is transferring money to have a larger control over how the money is invested. It can also be a more desirable way for the entrepreneurs in the developing countries to receive money through their families and friends to be able to overcome the capital constraints that (Anderson, 2009).

Review of Literature

An enterprise is an economic initiative to produce or provide a service which involves undertaking of risk. It creates job and income opportunities for people involved in it. A micro enterprise is considered a small business employing 10 people or less. Internationally, most micro enterprises are family businesses employing one or two persons. These micro entrepreneurs operate micro enterprises by choice. Most micro enterprise owners are primarily interested in earning a living to support themselves and their families. According to Maleko, G.C. (2005), the term micro enterprise is used to mean very small business that produces goods or services for cash income. Different countries use various measures of size depending on their level of development. The commonly used yardsticks are: total number of employees, total investment and sales turnover. SME's all over the world are known to play a major role in socio-economic development. Successful small businesses are the primary engines of economic development, income growth and poverty reduction in much of the developing world.

Since 1960s, efforts have been made to train and motivate people to be entrepreneurs. Attitudes could be developed, capacities and skills could be built to develop and promote entrepreneurship, and these were the assumptions in the approaches of the time. Considerable emphasis was placed on developing the entrepreneurial spirit in many developing countries. Special initiatives were taken by the International Labour Organization (ILO) in collaboration with national governments. Governments formulated policies and programmes and also established institutions to promote entrepreneurship amongst its citizens.

In the study 'Micro Enterprise and the Poor', Clarg, Peggy and Kays, Amy (1995, 1999) found that training and technical assistance in development of MEs is a critical service component. Effectiveness of training is a very important factor, and the quality and frequency of technical assistance to MEs was also seen as importantly.

Micro enterprises are also commonly described as businesses with limited capital operated by owner and having a few, if any, employees and not a major share in their market (Tezler, 1992).

Servon (1997, 2000) mentions that micro enterprise is a business of a low income people. Thus, emphasis on training and technical assistance is a must as it has a complementary role in poverty alleviation.

In the MSMED Act of India, 2006, MSMEs, micro small and medium enterprises are broadly classified into two categories viz., manufacturing and those engaged in providing services. The Act defines micro enterprises as those businesses that have invested a maximum of ₹ 10,00,000 in plant and equipment for services and a maximum of ₹ 25,00,000 for a production set up. In India, various efforts are in the progress for development of entrepreneurial environment and motivation for it like training, policies and programmes etc. Earlier published literature, referred to micro enterprises as self-employment promotional activities. The focus was mostly on an individual's self-employment. However, since 1990s, the group approach towards the building up of enterprises is being extensively promoted and implemented to help the poor and the underprivileged (Morduch, Jonathan, 1999).

Literature reviews revealed a few constraints in the promotion and development of micro enterprises. These constraints emerged from various studies and reviews on entrepreneurship efforts in general. Availability of credit to the small enterprises was found be the most crucial constraint in the development of enterprises (Reddy, T.K., 2008).

A remittance is a transfer of money by a foreign worker to an individual in his or her home country. The standard definitions for compilation of statistics on remittances by countries currently follow the International Monetary Fund's Balance of Payments Manual (BPM5) where remittances have the following components.

Worker's remittances are defined as 'current transfers by migrants who are employed in other economies and considered residents there. A migrant is a person who comes to an economy and stays there, or is expected to stay for a year or more'.

Compensation of employees **is** defined as 'wages, salaries, and other benefits earned by individuals in economies other than those in which they are residents, for work performed for and paid for by residents of those economies'.

Migrant transfers are defined as 'contra entries to the flow of goods and changes in financial items that arise from the migration of the individuals from one economy to another'.

Contemporary studies on remittances by migrants—sending as well as receiving—at both macro as well as micro level have generally displayed more optimism about its developmental impacts.

At the macro level, remittances have been found to have a positive impact on a country's long-run economic performance by not only increasing foreign exchange reserves, but also by financing trade deficit in certain countries (Rapoport and Docquier, 2005) and also increasing the credit ratings of a country (Newland, 2007). In case of labour surplus economies especially, remittances have offset the loss of human capital and have increased the per capita income of the countries (Jadhav, 2003).

However, whether labour depletion or even 'brain drain' is compensated by remittance flows, depends on the skill composition of labour supplied by sending countries and that demanded by the host countries. This is because many developing countries do not have a control on the skill composition of their labour supplies as it is mainly determined by the host countries (Newland, 2007). Hence, this leads to a skill mismatch in the labour surplus economies. According to Taylor (1999), developmental impact of remittances lies between two extremes. One, where remittances instigate reduction of production constraints of the poor in developing countries, and the other where migration opportunities elsewhere cause labour depletion in sending areas and also cause 'brain drain'.

At the micro level, issues revolve around elimination of credit constraints of households and scope for enhancement of investment opportunities and savings mobilization. A host of country specific micro level studies on impact of remittances can be observed in literature. These studies explore impact on various aspects such as consumption and savings pattern of households (Parinduri and Thangavelu, 2008; Zhu, Wu, Wang,

Du and Cai, 2009), household welfare (Quartey, 2006), labour supply and school attendance (Andersen, Christensen and Molina, 2005; Acosta, 2006, Binzel and Assaad, 2009), precautionary saving and asset accumulation (Adams, 1996 and 2002), rural factors like agricultural expenditure and insurance (Azam and Gubert, 2006) and gender (Guzmán, Morrison and Sjöblom, 2008).

Commonalities between these studies include indications of positive impacts of remittances on household welfare through consumption smoothing and positive insurance role. Also the fact that most of the remittances are used up for subsistence with less percentage used for investment or other productive purposes, Andersen, Christensen and Molina (2006) found that remittances lead to an increase in schooling of children in migrant households and upward mobility of the families. However, they also find that remittances also lead to 'moral hazard problems'. Evidence was also found by some others like Chami, Fullenkamp and Jahjah (2003) where members of the migrant households receiving remittances from abroad who are in their working ages do not engage themselves voluntarily into any economic activity.

A common finding amongst these studies has been that remittances lead to an increased welfare of the households in general and increase in human capital investments, entrepreneurship, healthcare and consumption smoothing in particular. However, a huge percentage of the remittances received by the households go into conspicuous consumption and household expenditure whereas a very little amount goes to investment and entrepreneurial activity.

Objectives of the Study

1. To understand how remittances result in micro enterprise development in various developing countries.
2. To understand the Indian scenario in terms of remittances and micro enterprise.
3. To suggest some policy proposals for better and enhanced

micro enterprise development in India.

Remittance and Micro Enterprise Development

In poorer societies, money lenders do not lend money to entrepreneurs because of the fear of being repaid and they fail to accumulate even tiny amounts of start-up capital. In spite of these difficulties, the micro enterprise sector is overlooked by the formal financial system even though it has tremendous power for poverty alleviation in the impoverished societies. Interest in this sector grew with the emergence of micro financial institutions that targeted micro enterprises as potential mechanisms of poverty alleviation. Unfortunately, most of these micro financial institutions are non-governmental organizations, poorly funded by donor agencies. Hence, they provide very little credit to the entrepreneurs who are mostly insufficient to meet their capital needs, let alone help the budding entrepreneurs to help establish their enterprises.

Micro finance was conceived as a sustainable tool for poverty alleviation. Since becoming popular in Bangladesh in the 1970s, it now reaches millions of people all over the world. Micro finance helps dampen poverty by raising incomes and human capital stock. It also reduces the vulnerability of the poor to internal and external shocks. Livelihoods financed through micro finance boost income, which, in turn, is spent to increase food consumption, attain better education, maintain good health, improve housing conditions, and acquire durable goods and assets. The biggest impact of micro finance has been in helping the poor smooth their consumption.

Micro enterprises are said to add value to a country's economy by creating jobs, enhancing income, strengthening purchasing power, lowering costs and adding business convenience (Munoz, 2010). Because micro enterprises typically have little to no access to the commercial banking sector, they often rely on "micro loans" or micro credit in order to be financed. Micro finance institutions often finance these small loans, particularly in the third world. Micro loans are a way for organizations and entrepreneurs to make small loans to those in poverty, often in third world countries. The term micro loans is more commonly referred to as micro credit.

In India like elsewhere, micro enterprises are a subset of the informal economy with common elements of ease of entry, lack of organized markets, lack of access to credit, high cost of borrowing etc. Financing has always been a major problem for the small and medium industries in India. The MSMEs mostly depend on internal sources of finance like personal savings, loans from relatives, and loans from local money lenders than that of institutional financing by banks and other financing institutions because of their reluctance towards providing loans.

The scheduled banks do not consider MSMEs as their preferred areas of investment. Traditionally, banking sector considers small industries a risky field of investment due to reasonably low growth rate of the small firms, firms following informal business practices, inability of the MSME entrepreneurs to maintain collateral securities, lack of creditworthiness, relatively high processing cost, and poor flow of information. Moreover, incidence of non-performing assets (NPAs) in small and medium sector is about 15 percent compared to about 9 percent in large business houses (Lahiri, 2012).

The micro enterprises face ruthless competition from the large domestic firms and multinationals armed with improved technology, managerial ability, skilled workers, marketing skills, better product quality, and wide range of products. A small percentage of firms operate with sophisticated technology base whereas majority of firms use outdated technology. They suffer from low productivity and poor product quality. They also face lack of several infrastructural necessities including inadequate power supply, transportation, water supply etc. Other problems include lack of skilled manpower and marketing and distributional problems. With a more liberalized economy they also are very much prone to several changes in the global market.

The escalating volume of international migrants' remittances has emerged as a potential source of funds for development activities, including micro enterprises, which are now part of the development strategy of many developing countries. Remittances which is a portion of the wages of migrant workers earned in foreign countries and sent back to their home country to their families are a strong source of foreign exchange for labour sending countries, used for paying import liabilities, improving the balance of payments, building foreign exchange reserves, servicing external debt, and enhancing the viability of the recipient countries' external sector.

On the domestic front, remittances increase the household incomes of migrants' families, improve living standards, enhancing savings, and generally contributing to national economic growth. However, against the backdrop of rural poverty, inefficient and insufficient credit delivery, and poor public services in many developing countries, development seems a difficult task. Despite difficulties, some receiving countries like El Salvador, Guatemala, Mexico, Philippines etc. have succeeded in establishing remittance-backed enterprises and various community development projects. The following examples provide some useful insights into the beneficial links between migrant remittances and micro enterprise development.

Micro Enterprise Development in Mexico

Remittances channelled through so-called hometown associations (HTAs) and other self-help groups are responsible for almost 20 percent of the capital invested in micro enterprises in urban Mexico. These types of investments on the part of remitters can reduce poverty significantly by expanding businesses in their home communities and generating jobs and income that would not otherwise exist. While the actual number of jobs created and the overall earnings will vary with the market environment, such investments can help provide economic momentum in struggling local economies (Azad, 2005).

National Financeria (NAFIN), a development bank, has provided financial and technical support to more than 80,000 micro entrepreneurs since 1994. It supports productive projects in Mexico using migrant workers' remittances. The NAFIN program offers several advantages to migrants interested in establishing or expanding an enterprise in their home country, including financial training and technical and marketing assistance. NAFIN has developed community investment funds that can be adapted to mobilize remittances for community-managed investments in micro enterprises. Mexican government has initiated economic projects to attract and use collective remittances. Mexico's most successful program is a three-for-one matching fund to encourage emigrant investments in small-scale infrastructure and other community projects and programs.

Woodruff (2004) found using a survey of more than 6,000 self-employed workers and small firm owners located in 44 urban areas of Mexico, estimated the impact of access to remittances on capital investment in micro enterprises. The impact was identified from the geographic pattern of migration from Mexico, a pattern with long historical roots. The analysis indicates that remittances were responsible for more than one-quarter of the capital invested in micro enterprises throughout urban Mexico. Within the ten states with the highest rates of migration to the United States, it was estimated that more than 40 percent of the capital invested in micro enterprises was associated with remittances.

The results also suggested that the impacts spread well beyond the rural areas from which migrants have traditionally come. Previous research has focused on the impacts of remittances on agricultural development in rural areas. The data used here suggests that investments in productive activities may be larger in urban areas (Zenteno, 2004).

Micro Enterprise Development in Ecuador

Ecuador has experienced a massive emigration which is mainly motivated by economic factors. After several crises, and high poverty, unemployment, and few economic prospects, the emigration rate increased strongly since the end of the 1980s. Main motivation for most of the Ecuadorian migrants was thus not the prospect of a better life in another country, but the possibility to provide financial support for relatives in the home country (Pew Hispanic Centre and Benedixen and Associates, 2003). In 2006, remittances accounted for 7 percent of the GDP.

The inflows have the potential to reduce poverty, liquidity constraints, and income volatility. Moreover, they can increase household expenditures on education and health, categories which are considered as especially important for economic development. Women form an increasing part of the migratory movement, whether as migrants, who send remittances, or as head of the households, who receive international transfers (Zur Erlangung, 2013).

In Ecuador, MIF has been working with the Banco Solidario to support micro enterprises through lines of credit. One of the main objectives of the project is to facilitate the flow of remittances and make it easier for Ecuadorian migrants and their families to gain access to services, maintain savings, and engage in productive investments. In addition, the project is extending coverage of the formal financial system in Ecuador to the micro enterprise sector, especially in rural areas, inducing more people, including remittance recipients, to use financial instruments, while demonstrating to financial institutions the feasibility of achieving attractive financial returns through medium- and long term lending (Azad, 2005).

Micro Enterprise Development in El Salvador

The smallest country in Central America geographically,

El Salvador has the fourth largest economy in the region. During the global recession, real GDP contracted in 2009 and economic growth has since remained low, averaging less than 2 percent from 2010 to 2013. Remittances accounted for 16 percent of the GDP in 2013 and were received by about a third of all households.

Huneycutt (2003) used a large survey containing household-level data on both remittances and micro enterprises. The data came from El Salvador, a country defined economically by its migrants and micro entrepreneurs. The paper demonstrated the following: (i) urban households with access to remittances were 42 percent more likely to own small businesses than those without remittances; and (ii) remittance receiving micro enterprises benefit 190 percent more than firms without such income.

Micro Enterprise Development in Philippines

According to the Bangko Sentral ng Pilipinas, remittances from Filipinos working and living abroad grew faster than expected in 2013, hitting a new record high of US$ 22.76 billion from US$ 21.391 billion in 2012. Last year's figure represented a growth rate of 6.4 percent from a year ago, surpassing the BSP's five-percent growth target. It also accounted for 8.4 percent of the country's total economic output for 2013. The solid growth of remittances from OFs (overseas Filipinos) remained supportive of the economic activity, with cash remittances accounting for 8.4 percent of the country's gross domestic product in 2013.

Unlad is one of the few organizations in the Philippines that aims to mobilize migrant-worker resources for productive use and community's overall development. It has mobilized pooled migrant remittances, helped to identify the apt investments, and facilitated credit applications with the motto of creating employment through sustainable businesses. Services available to migrants include the following:

- Savings accounts;

- Investments in existing businesses;
- Special start-up funds; and
- Skills training, logistical support and networking.

In addition to these services, Unlad has implemented a social support program to educate and organize migrant workers (Azad, 2005).

Micro Enterprise Development in Lesotho

Lesotho is one of the most migration dependent countries in the world. Migrant remittances are the country's major source of foreign exchange, accounting for 25 percent of the GDP in 2006. Lesotho is also one of the poorest countries in the world. The majority of households and rural communities are dependent on remittances for their livelihood. Households without access to migrant remittances are significantly worse off than those that do have such access (Jonathan Crush, 2011).

More than 60 percent of Lesotho's working population works in South African mines. The Association of Mine Workers established a deferred pay scheme in 1974 to ensure that more money earned by Lesotho workers was invested or spent in the domestic economy. The scheme was also meant to raise an appreciation among migrant workers for savings. A board of trustees—chaired by the principal Secretary of Labour and Employment and including representatives from Lesotho's central bank and Ministries of Employment and Labour, Agriculture, and Finance; and from South Africa's Ministry of Labour—administers the fund (Azad, 2005).

The Indian Scenario

India received foreign exchange remittances worth US$ 70 billion in 2013 from its migratory workforce to retain the top spot in the world amid a broad slowdown caused by regulatory hindrances on both movement of people and capital. China (US$ 60 billion), Philippines (US$ 25 billion), Mexico (US$ 22 billion), Nigeria (US$ 21 billion), Egypt (US$ 17 billion),

Pakistan (US$ 15 billion), Bangladesh (US$ 14 billion), Vietnam (US$ 11 billion) and Ukraine (US$ 10 billion), rounded up the top 10 remittance recipient nations, according to a World Bank study.

As per the Ministry of Overseas Indian Affairs (MOIA), remittances were received from the approximately 25 million members of the Indian diaspora.

India is the destination of nearly 40 percent of the inflow of worker's remittances to South Asia and nearly 10 percent of the global remittances (OIFC, 2009). The buoyancy of remittances has helped to substantially reduce the country's current account deficit. The inward remittances to India have been steadily increasing and were close to US$ 45 billion in 2008. Beginning 1991, when economic and financial reforms were initiated, the inward remittances have been recording a steady increase, suggesting a possible linkage between inward remittances and migrants' perception of the Indian economy and its future.

Since the beginning of the liberalization era in the early 1990s, these transfers have become an important component of India's overall balance of payments. NRI deposits have become a stable source of financing the current account deficit. With a share of nearly 10 percent in the global remittances, India has been at the top of the list of major recipients of inward remittances.

The issue of whether remittances are used for consumption or investment has been widely debated in literature. RBI survey (2010) attempted to find out the possible end-use of the funds remitted by overseas Indians to their families back home. The survey found that 61 percent of the remittances received are utilized for family maintenance and a small proportion goes into investment.

Policy Proposals

To mobilize remittances to micro enterprise development might be a difficult task. Our government might adopt nationwide micro enterprise development programme which might be financed through remittances. The government might also introduce financial instruments to mobilize micro enterprise development.

The members of the Indian diaspora communities have resources like money, time and intellect which can be used to help reduce poverty and micro enterprise development. Establishing and maintaining strong links and relationship with them will help enormously in micro enterprise development.

Our government can also come up with several investment vehicles that can become part of the diaspora portfolio through which they can earn reasonable returns and suffice their financial goals as well.

Several micro financial institutions can also play an important role in tapping remittances received through informal channels. They might be able to devote their attention towards estimating and exploiting the volume of informal remittances and eventually replacing them with formal channels.

Banks could engage NGOs and MFIs as partners in tapping the potential of the micro credit market and leverage their infrastructure and relationships toward delivering micro finance services.

Remittance-backed bonds permit countries to leverage diaspora funds to raise external financing for development. Introduction of such bonds may be beneficial in improving investment.

Nationalized and private commercial banks may be allowed and encouraged to issue special bonds or saving schemes for migrants. The banks could lend these funds to micro enterprise initiatives through their own networks of branches and improve access to financial services for migrants and their beneficiaries, thereby creating formal banking relationships to provide greater financial security, reasonable returns, liquidity, and a greater capacity to utilize funds for productive activities.

Financial institutions are sometimes more comfortable

lending to remitters who use their services because a regular stream of remittance payments can represent a form of collateral. In some cases, recipients could use future remittances as collateral for lower lending rates.

Conclusion

This paper tries to link remittances with micro enterprise development. This approach has already been used in many developing countries receiving a good share of foreign remittances.

Micro enterprises are usually small business enterprises operated by few entrepreneurs. These entrepreneurs suffer a lot in the developing countries when it comes to access of capital because of poor financial infrastructure.

Remittances are a good source of foreign exchange earnings for India. But the remittance receivers are mostly risk averse when it comes to investment. Most of them are even ignorant about the sources of investment. Pooling and mobilizing these investments becomes a further problem because of the lack of infrastructure in channelling them. Even though the Government of India continues to provide enhanced facilities for sending remittances by the migrants to India, still a huge portion of it moves through the informal channels. These remittances carry enormous opportunities to be invested in various entrepreneurial activities.

References

Adams, R. H. Jr. and J. Page (2005), 'Do International Migration and Remittances Reduce Poverty in Developing Countries?, *World Development*, Volume 33, pp. 1645-1669.

Adams, R. Jr., (1998), 'Remittances, Investments and Rule Asset Accumulation in Pakistan', *Economic Development and Cultural Change*, 47(1), pp. 155-173.

Adams, R. Jr., (2005), 'Remittances, Household Expenditure and Investment in Guatemala', World Bank, Policy Research, Working Paper #3532.

Andersen, L.E., E. Christensen and O. Molina (2005), 'The Impact of Aid on Recipient Behaviour: A Micro Level Dynamic

Analysis of Remittances, Schooling, Work, Consumption, Investment and Social Mobility in Nicaragua', Institute of Advanced Development Studies, Development Research Working Paper No.02/2005.

Azad, A.K. (2005), 'Migrant Workers' Remittances: A Source of Finance for Micro Enterprise Development in Bangladesh?', in S.M. Maimbo, Remittances: Development Impact and Future Prospects, World Bank.

Azam, J.P. and F. Gubert (2006), 'Migrants' Remittances and the Household in Africa: A Review of Evidence', *Journal of African Economies*, Volume 15(2), pp. 426-462.

Bhavani, T.A. (2011), 'Dynamic Business Environments: What These Mean for Indian Small Enterprises', in K. Das (ed.), *Micro and Small Enterprises in India: Era of Reforms,* pp. 27-45.

Binzel, C. and R. Assaad (2009), 'The Impact of International Migration and Remittances on the Labour-Supply Behaviour of Those Left Behind: Evidence from Egypt', German Institute of Economic Research, Discussion Paper No. 954.

Blanchflower, David G. and Andrew J. Oswald (1998), 'What Makes an Entrepreneur?', *Journal cf Labour Economics,* 16(1), pp. 26-35.

Chami, R., C. Fullenkamp and S. Jahjah (2003), 'Are Migrant Remittance Flows a Source of Capital for Development?', International Monetary Fund, Working Paper No. WP/03/189.

Clark, P. and Amy, J.K. (1995), 'Enabling Entrepreneurship: Micro-Enterprise Development in the United States', Washington DC: Aspen Institute.

Clark, P. and Amy, J.K. (1999), Micro Enterprise and the Poor, Washington: Aspen Institute.

Guzmán, J.C., A.R. Morrison and M. Sjöblom (2008), 'The Impact of Remittances and Gender on Household Expenditure Pattern: Evidence from Ghana', A.R. Morrison, M. Schiff and M. Sjöblom (eds.), The International Migration of Women, World Bank and Palgrave Macmillan Co. publication.

Jadhav, N. (2003), 'Maximising Developmental Benefits of Remittances: The Indian Experience', Paper Presented on International Conference on Migration and Remittances, DFID and World Bank, London, October 9-10.

Jonathan Crush, B.D. (2011), 'Migration, Remittances and

Development in Lesotho', Retrieved, November 11, 2014, from africa portal library: http://www.africaportal.org/dspace/articles/migration-remittances-and-development-lesotho.

Lucas, Robert E. Jr. (1978), 'On the Size Distribution of Business Firms', *Bell Journal of Economics,* 9(2):508-523.

Maleko, G. (2005), 'The Impact of Electricity on Enterprise', Enshade: University of Twente.

Morduch, J. (1999), The Microfinance Promise, *Journal of the Economic Literature,* Volume XXXVII, pp. 1569-1614.

Munoz, J. (2010), 'Contemporary Microenterprise: Concepts and Cases', Cheltenham: Edward Elgar Publishing.

Newland, K. (2007), 'Migrant Networks as a Development Resource: Remittances and Beyond in Migrations', Observation and Analysis of Contemporary Trends, available at: http://www.ikuspegi.org/documentos/ponencias/nuevas/k_newland.pdf.

Parinduri, R.A. and S.M. Thangavelu (2008), 'Remittances and Migrant Household's Consumption and Saving Patterns: Evidence from Indonesia', Nottingham University Business School Research Paper No. 2008-02.

Quartey, P. and T. Blankson (2004), 'Do Migrant Remittances Minimize the Impact of Macro Volatility on the Poor in Ghana', Global Development Network Report, available at: http://www.imf.org/external/np/res/seminars/2005/macro/pdf/quarte.pdf.

Rajeev, S.A. (2009), 'Globalisation and its Impact on Small-Scale Industries in India', *PCMA Journal of Business,* 1, pp. 135-146.

Rapoport, H. and F. Docquier (2005), 'The Economics of Migrant's Remittances', IZA Discussion Paper No. 1531.

Reddy, T.K. (2008), Problems and Prospectus of Small-Scale Industries in India', *Man and Development,* Volume XXX(3), pp. 23-40.

Servon, L.J. (1997), 'Micro Enterprise Programs in US Inner Cities: Economic Development or Social Welfare', *Economic Development Quarterly*, 11(2), pp. 166-180.

Servon, L.J. (1999), 'Bootstrap Capital: Micro Enterprises and the American Poor', Washington, DC: Brookings Institution Press.

Taylor, J.E. (1999), 'The New Economics of Labour Migration and the Role of Remittances in Migration Process', *International*

Migration, Volume 37(1), pp. 63-88.

Tezler, R. (1992), 'Small-scale Industry's Contribution to Economic Development', in Baud, I., de Bruijine, G. (eds.), Gender, Small-Scale Industry and Development Policy, IT Publications, London, pp. 24-32.

Zhu, Y., Z. Wu, M. Wang and F. Cai (2009), 'Do Migrants Really Save More? Understanding the Impact of Remittances in Rural China', University of Kent, Department of Economics, Discussion Paper No. KDPE-0923.

13

Tourism Industry and Entrepreneurship Development

Hedayatullah Choudhury

Introduction

Tourism is the world's largest industry and is one of the fastest growing segments. The concept of tourism is not new with tremendous potentiality for sustainable development of nature-based tourist attractions including beautiful forests, wildlife and landscapes.

North-East India with both physical and human diversities is one of the most promising regions of the country in respect of tourism promotion. Among the North-Eastern states, Assam took the pioneering step to recognize tourism as a booming sector way back in 1958.

When the British declared Kaziranga a game reserve in 1916 and wildlife sanctuary in 1950, Assam was projected as an attractive destination for tourists, particularly those who are interested in nature and wildlife observation.

Entrepreneurs are persons, who organize, manage and take the risk of running a business or an enterprise. This paper pertains to tourism industry with special reference to entrepreneurship development in the sector in the North-Eastern states. The dynamic element of the tourism system is its historical potential for development and the resultant benefits.

However, the system operates within a global economic environment along with national priorities. Entrepreneurial success depends on management issues. For this, the entrepreneur requires certain traits, qualities or behavioural competencies like, risk taking, self-motivation, creativity and innovation, initiative, information seeking aptitude, problem solving qualities, quality assurance and monitoring etc.

Prospects of Tourism Industry in North-East (NE) India

Although North-East India is considered a very backward region in the country, yet it has the greatest potentiality to become a potent force in tourism development. These states share their international borders with China, Myanmar, Bhutan and Bangladesh and have an unusually rich diversity of ethnic groups, languages, religions, climates and landscapes. Let us explore its potentiality from various angles. Tourism is one of the enormous service industries in India with its contribution of 6.23 percent to national GDP and 8.78 percent to total employment.

During the year 2013, the country witnessed the arrival of foreign tourists at 6.97 million with foreign exchange earnings of US$ 18.45 billion.

According to WTTCR 2007, India ranked 6th in terms of price competitiveness and 39th in terms of safety and security. North-East India is well blessed by nature and lies at the centre of one of the worlds richest bio-geographic areas. It is the treasure house of various economic resources. It has a rich cultural and ethnic heritage that can easily make it a tourist-spot.

Tourism has the greatest potential for generating income and employment opportunities in the North-East Indian states because the region is not only characterized by the blending of flora and fauna, it is also exceptionally rich in bio-diversity. Moreover, the wildlife sanctuaries at various places of NE India can attract tourists from all over the world. For example, the national park of Kaziranga in the district of Golaghat is a gift of nature which covers approximately an area of 429.93 sq. km. and is situated on the southern bank of the river Brahmaputra and has been declared a World Heritage site by UNESCO. It is a heavenly place for the tourists because of its world famous one-horned rhinoceros. Herds of rhinoceros, vast grassy and green forests of the park can easily enamour any tourist of the world.

Besides Kaziranga, there is the Manas riverine situated towards the western part of the district of Baksa. It is extended on both the banks of the river Manas and covers almost an area of 519 sq. km. It is especially famous for its wild buffaloes and also for other animals and birds.

Besides Kaziranga and Manas sanctuaries, the wildlife sanctuaries of Pobitora and Orang can attract the tourists from all over the world. Moreover, the golden languor pygmy hog and other endangered species can easily enchant the minds of the tourists. Besides the animals and the birds of various kinds roaming singing and playing in the vast green forest, the region has many ornamental fishes, rare plants, medicinal herbs and exotic orchids.

It has many tranquil lagoons and reverie locations like Bhalukpung, Loktok, etc. that will attract the tourists for angling and boating. There are many other wonders and important things for the tourists in the region.

For example, even today, when science and technology have achieved miraculous success in unearthing the hidden things of the world it has totally failed to unearth the mystery of the Jatinga Hill where thousands and thousands of birds commit suicide every year. This mysterious Jatinga Hill is a great source of attraction for the tourists from all over the world.

Moreover, the world's largest river island 'Majuli' will encourage tourism industry in NE India to a great extent. Majuli covers an area of 929 sq. km. This amorphous land mass is constantly being sculpted into new dimensions and shapes by the Brahmaputra. Sibsagar, heart of Assam's tea and oil producing region, is also the state's most historic city encompassing the seat of Ahom dynasty which ruled Assam for 600 years. The various historical monuments and places like 'Rangghar', 'Karengghar', 'Joysagar', 'Joydoul', etc. can encourage tourism in NE India. Besides these, the various historical places like Sonitpur (at present Tezpur), the capital of Ban Raja, Garhgaon, the capital of the Ahoms, Jerangapathar, a place where Joymati sacrificed her life for her husband , etc. are potential tourists attractions.

Moreover, the various religious places and temples like Kamakhya temple, the Umananda temple, the Agnigarh and the Mahabhairavi temples of Sonitpur etc. can foster tourism industry in NE India. Besides this, there are wooded hill stations like Haflong, Shillong, Gangtok, etc. in the region. Additionally, the region is home to Tawang Monastery, the largest Buddhist monastery in India. Twang is situated in Arunachal Pradesh at an altitude of 3,050 metres (10,007 ft.) and attracts tourists for hiking, trekking and camping. Further, tea tourism and golf tourism of NE India also hold good potential. Guwahati, the capital of Assam is also known as the gateway to North-East India; Tezpur meaning, "City of Blood" derived its name from its legendary past as the capital of the Hindu demon kings. Itanagar, the capital of Arunachal Pradesh in 1971, was a settlement of the Nishi tribe, one of the largest among the 26 major tribes that inhabit the state.

Besides this, the Namdapha National Park, which is located in remote eastern Arunachal Pradesh, bordering Mayanmar, covers an area of 1,985 sq. km. This is the only reserve in India where all the four big cats of the Himalayas can be noticed viz., tiger, leopard, clouded leopard and rare snow leopard. Shillong, capital of the tiny state of Meghalaya, with its mist-shrouded hills, pine forests, lakes and waterfalls, is described as the "Scotland of the East". Kohima, the capital of Nagaland, is a pleasant town surrounded by hills which are dotted with villages.

Kohima is famous in World War II history for the decisive battle, fought on the tennis court of the British deputy commissioner's house that finally stopped the Japanese advancement into India in April 1944. Imphal, the capital of Manipur is addressed as the "Jewelled land". Imphal lies in a broad oval valley enclosed by forested hills. Its inhabitants mostly belong to the Meitei tribe. The North-East India is also very rich in cultural heritage. It is a heavenly abode of various tribes, castes and communities having their religious and cultural festivals— 'Bihu' of the Assamese, 'Bathou' of the Bodos, 'Cheraw' of the Mizos, etc.

Role of Small and Medium Enterprises (SMEs)

The role of SMEs becomes more significant in the case of tourism industry, because of its very nature i.e., being a service industry. Leaving aside a few big companies, most of the travel agencies or tour operators come under the category of SMEs. Travel agency, as the name suggests, is responsible for organizing travel. At the same time, it provides a link for the supply of services for tourists/travellers. A travel agency books air tickets, arranges for pick up from the airport, books hotels and so on. While providing all these services, a travel agency supports and supplements the business of the suppliers of services while serving the tourists at the same time.

An opportunity is identified by one who wishes to set up his/her own enterprise. The process by which an opportunity is identified is at times described as opportunity scanning or sensing and identification. An opportunity is identified and established so that the person who carries out all the operations is self-employed, earns some income and also profit. This whole activity is at times covered under one term, namely "entrepreneurship". In a developing economy like India, there is no dearth of opportunities. One reads about innovative devices being conceived and manufactured by engineers and technicians. One also comes across interesting success stories of entrepreneurs and businessmen describing a life span from rags to riches. Presently, in our country several schemes of promotion and assistance for setting up small-scale units or small businesses, by new or first generation entrepreneurs are being implemented by the central and state governments. New product lines, new processes, new services and new technologies have come to the fore in the last 2 decades.

Entrepreneurial Leadership in Tourism Industry

The tourism industry has been identified as one of the key industries for driving economic development and economic transformation in developing countries. The marketing challenges facing tourism businesses are unique in that these businesses cannot be promoted in isolation from their competing and complementary products. Entrepreneurship quality, entrepreneurial leadership, market and marketing orientation, have been identified as having a positive influence on the business performance of a tourism enterprise. Also, it is important to identify the specific factors that influence success in small tourism businesses mentioned above.

The relationship between entrepreneurial leadership, market orientation and marketing orientation could be explored with their common elements—the skills and characteristics of the owner-manager and owner-manager knowledge and alliances. These elements of entrepreneurship on one hand, and innovation orientation on other hand, are positively linked to various measures of organizational performance. Actually, the performance of a small tourism enterprise could be determined by the personality of its entrepreneur. Hence, owner-managers are the people who recognize the potential of a particular project. The importance of the owner-manager is essential in small tourism businesses because of the inseparability of production and consumption.

Government Policies

The knowledge of entrepreneurial competencies has sharpened over the last four decades. Earlier, there used to be a firm belief that persons with business family background could become successful entrepreneurs. After attaining Independence in 1947, India adopted economic planning as a method to achieve economic development. The pattern of planning that came to be accepted was of a mixed type meaning thereby that industrial units both in the public and private sector would be operating in the country.

The mixed nature of the economy meant that on crucial areas, the policy of the government was decisive and changes therein were of great relevance to industrial units. In the field of industry, government's objectives and intentions were announced through industrial policy resolutions (IPRs). These resolutions were announced in 1948, 1956, 1977, 1980 and 1990. Government policy resolution and programmes needed a proper administrative and institutional set up. Right from the time of IPR, 1948, the institutional set up pertaining to small-scale industries comprised of two major groups, viz., The Small Industry Development Organisation (SIDO) and the non-SIDO. The SIDO is centralized in the Office of the Development Commissioner, Small-Scale Industry (DCSSI). At the local or state level, there is Director of Industry (DI) or Industries Commissioner (IC). In the states again, District Industry Centre (DIC) is an important extension in this field.

For any individual intending to obtain information and help in district-based towns or villages, DIC is easily the best office. DIC has managers to help small entrepreneurs in areas like procurement of raw material, marketing and infrastructure needs etc.

In case of small units in the unorganized sector, there are autonomous boards, such as Khadi and Village Industries Commission, Handloom Board, Powerloom Board, Silk Board, Coir Board and all-India SSI Board. These boards provide assistance in spheres like establishment of enterprises, sourcing of raw materials, technical know-how and marketing help.

Resource Mobilization

An entrepreneur, besides having the idea has also to mobilize different resources for establishing a business. Firstly, finance, that is, initial funds required to set and run an enterprise. Working capital requirements and financial planning is important to run an enterprise. Secondly, the manpower requirement, which entails appropriate labour requirements with desired skills. Finally, the technology, which plays a major role in smooth conduct of business operations.

Role of Private Shops and Co-operative Outlets

The entrepreneurial instinct of India's communities has been fine tuned over centuries and generations. The survival instinct of those who have to find their place in an increasingly commercialized and consumerist society creates clever business people out of pavement dwellers as well as high society womenfolk.

Dull shops transform into glittering boutiques overnight if "fashion" and "demand" is in the air, on placement in Mumbai young boys do a brisk trade in selling crisp sizzling *dosas*, fried in butter before your very eyes.

A few attractive objectives, whether they are rag puppets, handkerchiefs, brass elephants, paper snakes, richly embroidered clothes or a pile of fresh guavas, will invite customers of a suitable category.

Shops catering to selling of souvenirs often put government approved status on their display boards to assure customers of their honesty and quality. Many shops at high-end tourist destinations like Agra, Jaipur, Srinagar and Varanasi in North India and in the same way in Tezpur, Sibsagar, Itanagar, Shillong, Agartala, Aizawal, Kohima, Dimapur etc., are fiercely competitive and employ touts or agents to bring tourists.

The co-operative societies, as an important organization for the unified marketing of rural products have been quite successful in some states, especially for the handloom sector. Each state has its own co-operative laws. In states such as Arunachal Pradesh, Tripura, Manipur, Meghalaya, Sikkim etc., there are many societies which form federations and their goods are brought by the apex body and sold through co-operative shops all over the North-East India. Today, there are a variety of services that constitute the tourism mix or are directly and indirectly related to tourism viz., shops and emporiums, handicrafts and souvenirs shops, taxi operators, hawkers and coolies, advertising agencies, artists, performers, musicians etc., Above all, an organized development of tourism in rural areas will give rise to many new job opportunities. These new opportunities can be in the form of information assistants, drivers, guides, escorts, security staff, food service staff etc. which can all provide the rural community with a continuous source of income.

Problems of Tourism Industry in North-East

From the above discussion, it is clear that tourism has a great potential for generating income and employment opportunities in NE India. But even then, no noticeable change has been seen in this sector due to various problems associated with it. The main constraints that are coming in the way of its development are self-explanatory and can be identified as under:

- Lack of infrastructure.
- Ethnic clashes leading to political instability.
- Geographical isolation.
- Lack of a proper tourism development policy of the Government for the region.
- Lack of investment-friendly atmosphere.
- Lack of funds.
- Absence of leadership and entrepreneurship ability.
- Indifferent attitude of the governments both at the State and the Central level.
- Defective socio-economic and political set up.
- Communication bottlenecks.
- Lack of people's co-operation and consciousness.
- Growth of insurgent activities.
- Absence of congenial atmosphere to attract the tourists.

Suggestions to Improve the Scenario

In spite of the problems pointed out above, NE India still holds a bright prospect for economic development in terms of tourism industry. However, for this, some immediate as well as long-term measures need to be adopted, which can be summarised as:

- A strong political for the restoration of peace and political stability in the area with whole hearted efforts including political dialogue with the various insurgent groups working in NE India to redress their grievances within the framework of Indian constitution in a democratic manner.
- Planned, sustained and well-thought long-term efforts have to be made by the Government to improve the socio-economic and political set up of NE India.
- Planned efforts are required to be made by the Government to build up the required infrastructure for the region.
- In short, restoration of peace and tranquillity to attract the foreign tourists is of utmost importance for the development of trade and tourism in NE India.
- Moreover, maintenance of a friendly investment atmosphere is very important for attracting foreign investors as well as the tourists. International and national confidence has to be restored for attracting the national and foreign tourists.
- Government should make huge investments to break the geographical isolation and remove communication-bottlenecks from the NE Indian states.
- People's consciousness to develop their own area through the development of tourism-industry is a great need of the hour.
- Proper tourism development policy is the need of the hour and for this Government should make a thorough survey in the region.

Conclusion

India is a secular country, having a number of states, with different religious sects, number of languages, number of caste groups, related to different cultural heritages. There is a need to promote the country as a cultural destination in international tourism offering historical destinations and museums as travel packages thereby helping with the growth of special interest tourism in the context of history. For example, those interested in paintings can be attracted to Ajanta Caves or Bhimbhetka, for forts and palaces Rajasthan and Madhya Pradesh should be promoted, for festivals like Losar, Rongali Bihu, Weiking dance, Lai Haraoba tourism should be promoted in North-East India.

The consideration of the needs of the tourists and the preservation of the natural environment are essential factors which will bring larger benefits for small tourism businesses in North-East India. Since locals are better equipped to assist in the maintenance of an atmosphere conductive to tourism, promotion of entrepreneurial activities should be given priority in the region.

In order to underline the importance of discussion for the essential meaning of entrepreneurial leadership, marketing orientation and tourism destination development should be fostered to understand their stronger influence upon the development of new products/services.

References

Fayissa, B.C. Naish, and B. Tadasse (2012), 'The Impact of Tourism on Economic Growth and Development in India', JNU, Department of Economics, Working Paper No. 8.

Government of Assam (2013), 'Profile on Forest and Wildlife'.

Iyer, K.H. (2006), 'Tourism Development in India', Vista International Publishing House, New Delhi.

Jocab, Robert (2005), 'New Facets of Tourism Management", New Delhi.

Kreishan, F.M. (2008), 'Tourism and Economic Development: The Case of India', *European Journal of Social Sciences,* Volume 34, No. 8.

Mishra, P.K. and Himansu, B. (2010), 'Casuality between Tourism and Economic Development: Empirical Evidence from India', *International Journal of Tourism Research,* Volume 12, pp. 201-205.

Sharma, Shashi Prabha (2013), 'Tourism Education: Principles, Theories and Practices', New Delhi.

14

Tourism Entrepreneurship

R.R. Blesson Hrangao and Robita Sorokhaibam

Introduction

Senapati District is located in the northern part of Manipur. It is bound on the east by Ukhrul District, on the west by Tamenglong District, on the north by the state of Nagaland and on the south by Imphal East District and Imphal West District. The district is at an altitude varying from 1061 metres to 1788 metres above the sea level. The hills run along the north-south direction and gradually slope down towards south and meet the Imphal valley.

Senapati district was earlier known as Manipur North District which came into existence w.e.f. November 14, 1969 with its headquarters at Karong. Later the district headquarter was shifted to Senapati on December 13, 1976. The district came to be known as Senapati District w.e.f. July 15, 1983.

The District is endowed with kaleidoscopic landscape of blue hills, green valleys, serpentine streams and rivers flowing through mountains and deep gorges. Rich varieties of flora and fauna adorn the land. Agriculture is the main occupation of the people and terrace cultivation is generally practiced by the people. Paddy, maize, cabbage, potato and cereals are the main crops of the district. 80 percent of the area is covered by forest and the remaining 20 percent is arable land having a total land area of 3271 sq. km. with an altitude of 2500 metres lying in the latitude of 24.37°N and longitude of 93.29°E to 94.15°E.

A new township and district headquarters, Senapati is 62 km. from Imphal. More than 30 government offices are located in the district headquarters. People of various ethnic communities are enjoying harmonious life in the town.

Overview of Tourism Industry in Manipur

In August 1972, as a publicity wing of the IPR Department, Tourism Department of Manipur came into existence. In later years it has vibrantly evolved as one of the independent tourism department in India. Manipur is geographically segregated to the extreme eastern part of the country and this little nestled Shangri-La (Jewelled land) has a legendary belief that it was discovered as a result of the delight the Gods took in dancing. Today, Manipur's mythological concept of creation is revealed in her famous folk dances. It is also a mosaic of traditions and distinctive cultural patterns.

Rich in its natural beauty, art and traditions, it has given sufficient insights to many a great minds who have inspired them to make such magnificent description like the "Switzerland of the East" and "Jewel of India". The people of Manipur include Nagas, Meitei, Kuki-Chin-Mizo and Gorkhas and Muslims and other colourful communities which have lived in complete harmony for centuries.

The tourist traffic toll in Manipur both foreign and domestic tourists during the year 2008-09 was 271 and 1,15,300 thousands respectively wherein, in the year 2009-10 it increased to 1,27,929 as against 1,15,571 in 2008-09, with an increase of 12,358 over 2008-09.

The dances of the tribal people have a high artistic and aesthetic value. The folk dances of tribal people captivate the beholders with their exotic costumes and simple but graceful rhythm. Their folklore is quite rich in quality. The dances of the tribal people are ritualistic and recreational, religious and temporal. The ritual dances are performed at a particular rite or ceremony or sacrifice and these dances naturally have a spiritual and religious basis. The dances of the tribal people have a high artistic and aesthetic value.

The colourful tribesmen are the dwellers of the 'Blue Mountains' which surround the green and fertile valley in the centre. Each of these tribes has their own distinct culture and tradition which find expression in their dance, music, dress, customary practices and pastimes. A tribesman represents a tradition, a way of life, a cultural heritage and love for life and beauty. The culture of tribesmen, their love and need for leisure and creation find eloquent expression in their various dances and music. Dance and music have been part and parcel of the tribal life. They are very simple and their way of life is gay.

Role of Entrepreneurs in the Growth of Tourism Industry

Tourism entrepreneurship basically encompasses individuals or group of persons, industry, government, government aided-NGOs and local bodies, engaged with the activities of creation, development and promotion of tourism avenues.

Seeking, finding and the unending exploration activities is basically done by the entrepreneurs, both in nature and in character. The district is endowed with natural beauty and many opportunities have remained hidden, untouched and unexplored with the failure of state intervention and vis-à-vis. Therefore, in these aspects, the importance of entrepreneurs and their role in grabbing the opportunities of tourism destination which has been hidden since time immemorial and if so taken up appropriately could lift the tourism industry of the state to a higher level and may even stand out as the most demanding tourist destination across the country and the world in particular.

Failures of entrepreneurship education and entrepreneurship development programmes in the district have dismayed the entrepreneurs. This sorry state of affairs could have been avoided if the responsible authorities had taken the right decision in due course of time. To rectify such needless shortcomings, it becomes pertinent for the timely and rightful intervention of the responsible authorities of the state.

Some of the important roles which have been played and being playing by the entrepreneurs in the development of tourism industry can be briefly stated below:

1. Maintenance and funding.
2. Carrying out sanitation programs.
3. Imparting tourism education to the younger generation through awareness programmes.
4. Creation of job opportunities.

Need for the Study

Senapati is a land of culture, flora and fauna blessed with peace loving population, forming the north-eastern district of Manipur. Manipur is agglomerated to the north-eastern states of India called as the seven sisters. The resident groups in Senapati include, The Poumai Naga, Mao Naga, Maram Naga, Zeliangrong Naga and other tribes of Manipur nagas. Also, Meitei, Kuki-Chin-Mizo, Gorkhas, Muslims and other colourful communities share the population of the district. Together, these ethnic tribes and communities have been living in complete harmony for centuries.

Though Tourism Department of Manipur came into existence in August 1972 under the IPR Department, it is no doubt, the tourism industry of the state particularly Senapati, is still in its infancy. Many efforts would be required to make the district one of the most focused tourist destination in the state and in the country at large.

Manipur is geographically segregated to the extreme eastern part of the country and this little nestled Shangri-La (Jewelled land) has a legendary belief that it was discovered as a result of the delight the Gods took in dancing. Today Manipur's mythological concept of creation is revealed in her famous folk dances.

Senapati which is also the district headquarters of the northern hill district of Manipur on National Highway No. 2 is indeed a land of rich culture and traditions. Varieties of flora and fauna are found in the district despite its geographical rough topography. It can be noted that Senapati has remained hidden and unexplored for too many decades though in this present era of fast and dynamic changing world, the government has done exceptionally well to some extent with the rapid increasing tourist incoming in the state in the recent decades. However, the attempts of the tourism department of the state and the Government has left undone in so many pros and cons of tourism opportunities in the district of Senapati. Therefore, this paper, attempts to arrive at a picturesque and amicable outlay of the opportunities of the tourism industry in the district in accordance with the entrepreneurial perspective in making Senapati a world class tourist destination.

This research paper specifically deals with the three unexplored caves in Senapati district. The area which is minutely undertaken into strict consideration in the present study has been elaborately studied in the later parts of the paper.

Review of Literature

Mohammad Saleem Mir (2012), 'Emerging Trends of International Tourism in India: Response of Tourism Industry to Globalization'—Globalization and tourism reinforce each other. Travel has been given full reign to develop throughout the world as globalization has made the world barrier-less, with fewer restrictions. In turn, tourism has led to globalization process in the areas of transportation, communication and financial systems and in far and inaccessible areas.

Established destinations and the major sources of international tourism are slowly, but steadily, losing their importance while the new ones are coming into the scene. But how fast is Indian tourism industry growing in this age of globalization and what trends is it following? What impacts does economic globalization had on the changing trends of international tourism in India? And what can be done to make India more prominent on the map of global travel? To such basic questions the author has attempted to achieve an answer relying basically on the government policies and not realizing the important contributions and responsibilities of the entrepreneurs in the country.

Pepita Seth (2012), 'Heaven on Earth'—Described the popularity of Gunvyur temple of Kerala in the tourism realms of the country locally known as Guruvayurappan, a deity whose precious idol was, according to myth, originally worshipped by Lord Vishnu and presents its relative significance amongst the generation. Even after a long period of the study, the researcher comes to the conclusion in which she has collectively omitted or neglected the importance of management approach/behaviours of the temple.

White Flag Media and Communications (2011), 'Hotels and Resorts in India'—A coffee table book that accounts the transformation as well as the engineering of the 20 enchanting palaces and resorts into hotels. Crafted with beautiful pictures and descriptions, the work showcases the splendid artistry behind each of these and necessarily not the man/entrepreneur behind the scene.

Erberto Lo Bue (ed.) (2010), 'Wonder of Lo: The Artistic Heritage of Mustang'—Showcases a special introduction to the cultural history of Lo (Mustang): a Tibetan architecture; the traditional building of Lo; cave hermitages and chapels in Eastern Lo; early cave paintings rediscovered in Upper Lo; early wall paintings in Lo wonders of Montang; Portable Buddhist sculptures of Lo: A Chronological Selection, 15th through 17th Centuries; the restoration of Murals in the Maitreya Temple of Montang; the restoration of Murals in the Mahamuni Temple of Montang; Bono and Buddhist Art in the 20th century Lo; reviving a sacred place: the hermitage of Samdrupling. Nevertheless, it would be wrong to say that he has at large, failed to cover up the other side of Lo.

Matt Brandon and Marryam H. Reshii (2008), 'Kashmir: The Mystery'—Kashmiris call their land 'Reshver' on the land of the sages. They just may have a point. From the earliest times, the valley of Kashmir has been a playground of gods and goddesses.

Multiple faiths, namely Buddhism, Shaivite Hinduism, Islam flourished in this land. Brandon's camera has captured the abundance of nature, the cold blue mountains, the tall trees, the flower laden *shikaras*, the wooden houses dotting a misty shore, the embroidered rugs, portraits and touchingly human. The author believed that the collection of photographs will rekindle the beauty and essence of Kashmir that we hold dear.

Urmi Popat (2008), 'Dream Destinations'—Presents a coffee table book on exotic travel destinations, UNESCO world heritage sites and structures designed by renowned architects, titled 'Dream Destinations' by Urmi Popat. It is a travelogue on 11 global destinations (Israel, Iceland, Russia, China, Tibet, Japan, Spain, Portugal, Turkey, Greece and Brazil).

It covers art, architecture, culture, destinations/places, food, shopping, politics, and archaeology, history of these destinations and much more; from the dense rain forests of the Amazon to the horrors of war-ripped Israel to the beauty of the largest glacial formation in Europe in Iceland. The book with over 350 images helps glean information on various UNESCO recognised sites, structures designed by world renowned architects as well as the New Seven Wonders of the World.

Himanshu Joshi (2008), 'Unknown Himalayas'—In this book, the author exhibits a clear and beautiful picture of the snow-clad peaks rising majestically in the horizon, mysterious lakes reflecting the mountains ringing them, massive glaciers and fast-flowing rivers, a world stamped by divinity.

The author also mentioned that the mountain trails winding up to far-flung corners where people in remote villages pursue age-old lifestyles are almost untouched by the contemporary world. Lavishly illustrated with vibrant colour photographs, this book takes you on a journey through these sublime heights, capturing the drama, diversity and mystic beauty of the Himalayas, up pristine tracks leading to rarely explored places.

Nafees A. Khan (2008), 'Human Resource Development in Tourism Industry in India: A Case Study of Air India Ltd.'—States that the purpose of human resource development is to improve the capacity of the human resource through learning and performance at the individual and organizational levels. The author lamented that certain threats endangering the organizations could be solved by applying a well-ordered and professional HRD approach to work in the protected areas of the field.

The skills, knowledge and attitudes of personnel will be enriched and the overall quality of work performed will improve. His study was an attempt to analyze the HRD initiatives of tourism industry with special reference to Air India Ltd. to enhance and sharpen the capabilities of its employees. The study also identified the need of Air India to incorporate the spirit of HRD in day to day functioning by utilizing all possible human resource systems and mechanisms of the organization.

Gulia, K.S. (ed.) (2007), 'Discovering Himalaya: Tourism of Himalayan Region'—The author deals with ecotourism and travelogues by introducing the readers to mountaineering in the snow-capped peaks of Everest, Nanda Devi, Kanchenjunga, Nanga Parbat, etc.

The book also deals with the inclement weather and other climatic conditions of the mountainous regions, including, snowfall, rainfall, glaciers, ecosystems, and river systems of Nepal, Uttarakhand, Jammu & Kashmir, Himachal Pradesh and Assam, etc. It also deals with various river gorges and valley. The book is specially meant to serve well for the students of tourism, environment and ecology.

Dai, Mamang (2002), 'Arunachal Pradesh: The Hidden Land'—The author attempts to present a view of the tribal world in the context of the environment that surrounds them. Even today very little is known about Arunachal Pradesh. Very little is known about the explorers and adventurers who travelled here and provide the first glimpses of this hidden land.

The purpose of this book was to record images, myths and some of the customary practices of life in these hills that seemingly are changeless, but may be changed forever in the fast paced world of today.

The above reviews have directly or indirectly left blank on the rcle of entrepreneurs who have been responsible for the success or failure of such magnificent works. Therefore, the objective of this paper is to elaborately discuss the role of entrepreneurs in the field of tourism industry in the state of Manipur and to bring about some desirable solutions.

Objectives and Methodology of the Study

Based on the above literature reviews, the following objectives have been adopted and sought to be achieved:

1. To specifically study the opportunities and challenges of the three unexplored caves.
2. To explore a wider campus of tourism destinations in the district (state).
3. To suggest remedial measures and draw concrete conclusions.

Research methodology involves the systematic process of solving the research problems not necessarily through the methods alone but also through the logic behind the use of methods to draw a satisfactory result by the researcher himself or by others. The methodology thus adopted, is systematically elaborated below.

The proposed research work is purely descriptive and exploratory in nature as it is data-based. In accordance with the data collected, conclusions are drawn unanimously using reliable statistical tools and techniques.

The type of data which the researcher used in this research paper is basically the primary data. Consequently, secondary data has also been referred, so as to draw a meaningful research for achieving the aim and objectives. Further, to light up the dark side of tourism and to explore its immense opportunities in the district which have been left unheard and untouched by the society and the outside world.

The study is of direct personal interview with the

respondents of the selected villages/areas. Hence, the use of questionnaires and schedules has been neglected in the process of collecting the desired information from the informants.

A pilot survey study was conducted for the research study. However, while realizing the need for accurate information for a successful research, the researcher adopted the technique of direct personal interview with the residents of the particular site of the study and the old persons whom the researcher thought of interviewing for getting the desired information comprising both the genders. Apparently, the researcher also interviewed some of the local organizations and union executives so as to draw a meaningful conclusion.

In the process of collecting the secondary data the researcher also referred to books, journals, magazines, periodicals, articles, papers, etc.

Non-random sampling was used for the collection of data samples and for the generalization of ideas of the research work. The study was carried out extensively in the two villages of Kodom and Lakhamai. A sample size of 20 persons from each from these villages was used. The data so collected comprised both the village and the union executive records. In order to serve the desired outcome of the research study, a sample size of 100 was designed.

Pertinent and most reliable statistical tools were used by the researcher for attaining the desired outcome of the research work. Other relevant tools were also applied for the purpose of summarization, generalization and analysis of the stated objectives.

Unexplored Shipao Deikulu (Shipao Cave) in Lakhamai

Most excitingly, the Shipao cave in Lakhamai has remained unexplored till date. It is interesting to know that the cave was a home to a dragon which resembles half human and half wild beast (tiger) called Shipao (local name). His lady-wife was killed by the legendary warrior (a knight) called Prou-pou-ziio who was then the great forefather of the

Proumais. Now it is settled in four different areas (villages), namely Kodom (original Place of the Proumais), Kodom Khavii, Lakhamai and Sirong. The Shipao Deikulu is located in the Peiri River stretching 10 kms. from the Lakhamai village. Apart from Shipao cave, there are 6 (six) other identical caves in the same particular location extending their height to approximately 20 feet from the ground. Lakhamai is located in the extreme eastern part of Senapati District (60 kms. from the district headquarters) bordering Ukhrul in the east and Nagaland in the north.

Another interesting fact of this cave is also complimented by the numerous and permanent existence of huge bee hives in around the cliffs. These bees are locally called as the '*Laihchie*'. This peculiar bee has its time old fact and belief that when angered, it dares not even the fire and the water.

Khrou-Chi (Moon Hill) of Kodom

The Khrou-chi (moon hill/mountain) is located in the Kodom and Phuba Thapham areas standing as the border mark between the two villages. It stretches for almost 15 kms. from Kodom village.

It is the highest mountain in the range. The cave which lies in this mountain peak was used by the forefathers of the Proumais known as '*Prou-Pou- Ziio*' who on his expedition into the thick of the forest came across a wild cock (Rei) carrying a *Moon like Pearl*. Chasing against all odds, he finally held captive of the pearl and hid it in the mountain cave.

One may find interesting to take the risk of climbing the cliff to have a clear view of the cave where the moon like pearl was kept hidden by *Prou-pou-ziio*. The pearl shines and dims its radiant light according to the movement of the moon.

This mountain was famous and explored by many adventure lovers; the wondrous feature of the mountain is also largely added by the age old belief that the small meadow (plain) at the mountain peak gives sufficient accommodation to all the pilgrims. This pilgrimage practice is carried on even in today's time by many a neighbouring villages and by the people of Proumais (Kodom, Lakhamai and Sirong). At the top of Khrou-chi, one can have a bird's eye view across the eastern part of Manipur exceeding even to some parts of south-eastern part of Nagaland and major western part of Myanmar.

Siiya-Chu (Siiya stone cave) of Kodom

The Siiya-Chu Stone cave is located to the western part of the Kodom village. One distinguishing feature of the cave is held by its huge room inside the cave, sufficient enough to accommodate 15-20 persons.

It is believed that any person who wishes to enter the cave has to bring with him/her a walking stick and place it at the entrance of this huge boulder and ask for the permission for the rest. Else, the person could be shut forever inside the cave.

Unexplored Tourist Centres

The age old caves which have been studied in the above passage of the study have tremendous strength in the light of the tourism realms and archaeological field.

These caves were not just caves; the wondrous beauty and the myth can have a significant impact on both the above mentioned areas.

It is believed that no one has ever trodden down the Shipao cave rather than *Proupouzii-o* who slained the lady of *Shipao*. No one could say what wondrous facts lies inside this very particular cave.

However, on the contrary, the immense importance behind the other two caves is closely associated with the legendary literature facts which was and is still believed by the natives and pilgrims who have taken the journey and have shared its beauty and wonder.

The story behind all these caves could add a significant impact even in the field of literature.

Some of the opportunities behind the three caves are briefly inked below:

1. Attraction of more tourists if due importance is given by the Government.
2. Useful in archaeological and literature studies.
3. Useful contribution to the field of art and culture.

Apparently, opportunities are closely associated by such distinct hindrances which are clearly stated below:

1. No road connectivity and poor cellular connectivity.
2. Absence of rest house and canteens.
3. Absence of medical facilities.
4. Negligence by both the parties (Government and locals).

Outcome Issues of the Analysis

The three caves which were minutely studied in the above paragraphs provide us with both positive and the negative impacts as regards tourism industry in the state. Therefore, it is necessary to ink the key outcome issues of the study for prompt revival measures.

Some of the key issues are briefly highlighted below:

1. Not just the beauty but the awe to its magnificent cravings.
2. The caves are not just ordinary caves, they have a story worth to be told and to be learnt.
3. This extraordinary beauty is completely shut to the outside world due to less social awareness.
4. The dark and thick forests have made human interference more negligible.
5. Lack of discovery, research and development activities has left such beauties untouched, unheard and unknown to the outside world.
6. The potentials of these caves can be richly yielded to its fullest only when the responsible authorities initiate the needful steps.

Senapati is a situated 60 kms. from the mainland valley to the north-eastern part of the state. National Highway No. 2 cuts through the middle of the district headquarters, bordering the state of Nagaland.

Senapati is generally populated by the tribals, wherein

some of the mainland Indian populace has started residing in the recent decades due to their business activities also. Some of the major ethnic communities of Senapati district are: Poumai, Mao, Maram, Thangal, Zemai, Liangmai, Rongmei, Tangkhul, Meetei, Kuki, Nepalese, Vaiphei, Chothe, Chiru, Maring.

Dominated by the tribes with difference in culture and dialects it contributed largely to the shortfalls of the researcher during the course of research study. The social structure and taboos of the tribes and particularly the villages has kept some restraining impact on the detailed analysis of the research work.

Despite such significant hindrances the researcher aimed at stressing people's needs towards the maintenance of tourism spirit and conservatism in the district. This study could well be a first step towards sensitizing governmental agencies to the special needs of the valley-hill tribes of Manipur and evoking better appreciation of the unique features of the state tourism and the varied tourism opportunities available in the state in general.

The researcher also regretted in the time lapse of the research study by which many more hidden opportunities of tourism in the district were held unexplored and undiscovered. The absence of road connectivity and communication system has all the more added the researcher a brainstorming hurdle in the smooth and successful conduct of the research work.

Findings

With the extensive coverage of the research study and the experience thus acquired during the course of research work, the study has certain realistic findings which could serve the objective of the tourism industry of the state. Some of the major findings are listed below:

1. Less initiation for new discoveries in the field of tourism.
2. Funding for maintaining and conserving of these sites are almost neglected.

3. Poor road connectivity.
4. Failure of means of communications.
5. Reluctant approach of the villagers to make it popular due to their culture and taboos.
6. Minimal intervention of Government and the agencies.
7. Absence of rest houses and canteens.
8. Less research and development (R&D) activities.

Suggestions

Based on the above studies and findings achieved, the researcher hints out the following optimistic suggestions which could drastically contribute in achieving the desired purpose or aims of tourism industry in the district/state of Manipur.

1. The government should take up immediate and remedial measures for its revival.
2. Funding schemes should be adopted.
3. Better connectivity of roadways and communication systems should be initiated.
4. Tourism education should to be imparted among the younger generations.
5. Construction of rest houses and canteens should be initiated.
6. Free trespassing and loitering of domestic animals should be avoided with proper fencing.
7. Research and development strategies should be initiated for newer explorations and discoveries.

Conclusion

Mother nature has been extra generous in her bounty for the district of Senapati. Least touched and least discovered, Senapati promises to be a great tourist discovery of the 21st century. The district is surrounded by blue green hills and rich art and traditions.

The district is eminently surrounded by its cascading rapids, tripling rivers, varieties of flowers, exotic blooms and stone caves. The district of Senapati is largely dominated by the Nagas. However, small groups of other communities also share the pride and beauty of the district. Some of them are Meitei, Kuki-Chin-Mizo, Gorkhas, Muslims and other colourful communities which have lived in complete harmony for centuries.

From the above research study, we can conclude that opportunities of tourism in the district are bounty and can be explored and discovered to add more nerves in the realms of tourism industry and to make the district/state tourism industry rich and one of the world's best tourist destinations.

By giving the desired education and training to the entrepreneurs of the district, the researcher believes, opportunities which are hidden and unexplored in parts of the district particularly the above studied caves could vibrantly contribute to the field of archaeological and literature studies in the district which in turn would befittingly contribute to a large in achieving the aims and objectives of making and creating Manipur one of the best tourist destinations in the country. Thus, the needful and realistic intervention of the responsible authorities should not be delayed.

References

Brandon, Matt and Marryam H. Reshii (2008), 'Kashmir: The Mystery'.

Dai, Mamang (2002), 'Arunachal Pradesh: The Hidden Land'.

Erberto, Lo Bue (ed.) (2010), 'Wonder of Lo: The Artistic Heritage of Mustang'.

Gulia, K.S. (ed.) (2007), 'Discovering Himalaya: Tourism of Himalayan Region'.

Khan, Nafees A. (2008), 'Human Resource Development in Tourism Industry in India: A Case Study of Air India Ltd.', New Delhi.

Mir, (2012), 'Emerging Trends of International Tourism in India: Response of Tourism Industry to Globalization', LAP LAMBERT Academic Publishing, April.

Popat, Urmi (2008), 'Dream Destinations'.

Seth, Pepita (2009), 'Heaven on Earth'.

Sinha, Juhi (2007), 'Beyond the Dunes: Journeys in Rajasthan'.

Warikoo, K. (2009), 'Cultural Heritage of Jammu and Kashmir'.

White Flag Media and Communications (2011), 'Hotel and Resorts in India'.

15

Ecopreneurship Development through Ecotourism

A. Ibemcha Chanu and Hunasing Engti

Ecopreneurship and Environment

In today's world, human economy has grown so large that there is no longer room for all species in the ark. Growing population and uncontrolled urbanisation with technological advancement is putting a strain on the environment and on countries' natural resources. According to the IPCC (2007), the global average temperature increase in the 21st century would vary between 1.8 degree Celsius and 4.0 degree Celsius. And some of the effect of this can be observed with rise in sea level due to melting ice caps and glaciers, more extreme weather patterns like storms, heat waves, floods and droughts, changes in fresh water availability and loss of biodiversity. In Goodland (1991) report, it has mentioned that, the world's richest habitat, the tropical forests have already been destroyed to the extent of 55 percent and the current rate of loss exceeds 1,68,000 square kilometre per year.

Many authors and researchers from different nations of the world believe that the main cause of this global warming is because of the present business paradigm. In fact, entrepreneurship is widely acknowledged to be an engine of economic growth.

Increasing pollution levels, loss of biodiversity, land degradation and climate change have been experienced in the past few decades. It is therefore, rightly said that the growth of entrepreneurial activities does not grow hand in hand with the preservation of nature. Hence, entrepreneurship development has to be nurtured against the background of today's increasing environmental problems.

To prevent the risk of becoming such a subject of a green washing, a new management system known as green management has been adopted. With this new management policy, a new field of entrepreneurship has emerged, called ecopreneurship. This type of entrepreneurship can contribute to solving environmental problems by creating new and more environmentally sustainable products and services.

The term 'ecopreneurship' is relatively young and fragmented in the literature of entrepreneurship. The term is referred to as a portmanteau to ecology and entrepreneurship. It means ecopreneurs are individuals who carry out ecology and ecopreneurial activities for sustainable growth.

Sustainable growth means the growth of meeting today's need without sacrificing the need of future (Glenn Croston, 2010). The author of "75 Green Businesses You Can Start to Make Money and Make a Difference" too believes that ecopreneurship is a combination of business savvy techniques with a commitment to the environmental protection.

Many authors have defined the term from their own views and understanding. There is no specified or generally accepted definition of the term. Some of the common definitions, which have been taken out from the existing literature are listed below.

According to Shaltegger (2005), ecopreneurship is referred to as entrepreneurship through environmental lens.

Volery (2002), defined it as environmental responsibility in entrepreneurship. According to Pastakia, (1998), ecopreneurs are referred to as a new breed of eco-conscious change agents who are redefining the way business is conducted and are introducing eco-friendly ideas and innovations in the market place.

With a view to address the term 'ecopreneurship' in a more coherent way in the field of entrepreneurship, the working definition has been developed by the researcher. It is presented as, 'ecopreneurs are those who try to seek opportunities and undertake the risk there in, for sustaining the growth of the triple bottom line, viz. economic, social and environmental'. Ecopreneurship is a dynamic process of identifying opportunities and organising and mobilizing various factors of production for economic, environmental and social gains.

Ecotourism as a Means to Ecopreneurship Development

The concept of ecotourism came into prominence in the late 1980s as a strategy for reconciling conservation with development in ecologically rich areas. In fact, it is a new form of tourism which is based on the idea of sustainability. According to the concise Oxford English Dictionary, 'ecotourism is a tourism directed towards unspoiled natural environments and intended to support conservation efforts'. Hector Ceballos Lascurian in 1983 described the term as a nature-based travel.

In 1987, he defined it as 'travelling to relatively undisturbed or uncontaminated natural areas with specific objectives of studying, admiring, enjoying the scenery and its wild plants and animals as well as the existing cultural manifestations (both past and present) found in the areas'. According to Valentine (1993), ecotourism characteristic is restricted to the kind of tourism which is based on relatively undisturbed natural areas which are:

- Non-damaging, non-degrading, ecologically sustainable;
- A direct contributor to the continuous protection and management of natural areas; and
- Subject to an adequate and appropriate management regime.

Today, ecotourism has received global importance. It has become an important economic activity in natural areas around the world. Besides generating employment opportunities and earning large amount of foreign exchange, ecotourism too, conserves natural resources and prevents environment from its degradation.

It also provides opportunities for visitors to experience

powerful manifestations of nature and culture and to learn about the importance of biodiversity conservation and local culture. With a view to bring the term's relevance and its recognition locally and globally, year 2002 was declared as the 'International Year of Ecotourism'. Since then, a huge number of players with varying interests and goals have participated in the field.

The attributes of ecotourism makes it a valuable tool for increasing ecopreneurial activities. Its implementation can:

- Give economic value of scenic beauty of nature.
- Enrich the cultural beauty of the local people.
- Increase ecopreneurial activities and bring sustainable growth.
- Convert backward but beautiful areas into developed areas.
- Lead to the growth of business and environment hand in hand.

Profile of Karbi Anglong District

The United Mikir (Karbi Anglong at present) and North Cachar Hills (Dima Hasao at present) district saw the birth of a new district on November 17, 1951, which was formally created on the aforesaid date vide a government notification on November 3, 1951. This was followed by the bifurcation of the erstwhile district of United Mikir and North Cachar Hills district in the year 1970.

The Mikir Hill district was again rechristened as 'Karbi Anglong district' on October 14, 1976. Thus, the Karbi Anglong came to be recognised as a full-fledged separate district in the map of Assam with its headquarters at Diphu. It covers an area of 10,434 sq. km. which makes it the largest administrative district in Assam and also enjoys the autonomy under the provision of the Sixth Schedule of the Indian Constitution. It shares border with Nagaon, Golaghat and Nagaland in the east and Nagaon, Dima Hasao, Morigaon and Meghalaya in the West.

The population of the district is predominantly tribal. The major tribal ethnic groups of this district include Karbis, Dimasas, Bodos, Kukis, Garos, Rengma Nagas and Hmars. Besides, a large number of non-tribals also live together in this hill region. With multi-coloured cultures and traditions, Karbi Anglong is an extremely beautiful hill destination right within the lap of an unexploited virgin nature. There are numerous rivers and tributaries in the district. The forest area covered is approximately 4,922.01 sq. km.

The present study is basically focused on ecotourism which is accepted as a means to develop ecopreneurial activities for sustaining the growth of the triple bottom line.

The purpose of the present study is to contribute to the growth of ecopreneurial activities in the field of business. With this view, the present study has been undertaken to find out:

- The problems of ecotourism for ecopreneurship development in the district, and
- The future prospects of ecotourism for ecopreneurship development.

The type of research is descriptive in nature. The study is based on both primary and secondary data. Primary data has been collected through informal conversations with some renowned authors and politicians in the district and secondary data from books, journals, websites and newspapers.

Need for Ecopreneurship Development

Environmental degradation, which has become a serious threat to the lives of people, plants and animals have started diminishing the vitality of a sustainable economy and shortened our time on earth too and has also destroyed the heritage. With this growing issue of climate change and depletion of natural resources, it has become pertinent for the countries to adopt resilient measures that will contribute towards attainment of economic, social and environmental gains. In other words, this translates into a healthy ecosystem with an established economic progress.

With a view to solve these warning issues, many managerial experts from different nations of the world have adopted a green management system. Ecopreneurship, which is considered as a product of green management has been accepted to be the panacea for economic, environmental and social gains. In this context, promoting ecopreneurship as a development strategy is what the countries across the globe are striving for.

According to Robert Issak (2002), 'businesses that are not designed to be sustainable decrease our health, shorten our time on earth and destroy the heritage we leave for our children, no matter where we are located globally'. The nature with its 'healthy ecology is the basis for a healthy economy' as Claudine Schneider says. There is a wide scope for attaining the growth of the triple bottom line and it is never too late.

The term 'ecotourism' is a relatively new concept, and it is still often misunderstood. The term was first heard in the year 1980. The first widely accepted definition was established by the International Ecotourism Society in 1990 as, "responsible travel to natural areas that conserves the environment and improves the well-being of local people".

In fact, it generally deals with living parts of the natural environment, which focuses on socially responsible travel, personal growth and environmental sustainability. It typically involves travel to destination where flora, fauna and cultural heritage are the primary attractions. So, the term whether called nature tourism or ecotourism is a recreational and educational travel based on natural attractions and is a promising means of advancing social, economic and environmental objectives in developing countries.

Ecotourism, which is considered as a smokeless industry is one and an important avenue for increasing ecopreneurial activities in the field of entrepreneurship. Saving the environment around and preserving the natural luxuries and forest life, that's what eco-tourism is all about. It mainly focuses on local cultures, wilderness adventures, volunteering, personal growth and learning new ways to live on our vulnerable planet. Therefore, the logic behind the origin of these two concepts is meant to be the same. Hence, it is rightly said that ecotourism is a means to increase ecopreneurial activities.

Prospect of Ecotourism for Ecopreneurship Development

Karbi Anglong, in spite of its enchanting natural green forests and picturesque hills, is still relatively unknown to the tourists. Ecotourism in Karbi Anglong is still at a very nascent stage, but there are for sure conscious efforts to save the fragile ecosystem, culture and heritage of the indigenous people.

The district has rolling hills, dense forest, waterfalls, paddy, green hills interspersed with blue meandering rivers which can attract visitors from all over the world. Ecotourism has emerged as an important instrument for sustainable human development including poverty alleviation, employment generation, environment regeneration and development of remote areas and advancement of women in the district.

The district is economically poor and backward but beautiful. Hence, if Karbi Anglong with its beauty is commercialised, the results would have the potential to be truly fascinating and rewarding and may also convert the district into an economically sound and strong entity. Though Karbi Anglong is isolated from the rest of the districts of Assam; yet it is famous for its unique physiological beauty with rich flora and fauna, rolling hills, multi-colour culture and naturally blended cultural centre called Taralangso.

A brief review of some of the prospects of ecotourism and the attractive destinations in the district are as follows.

Adventure Tourism: The stunning variety of terrain, splendid landscapes and sparkling rivers offer adventure sports lovers' a vast choice of activities. The popular adventure activities include angling, river rafting, mountaineering, trekking, mountain biking and golf as well as a river cruise in some of the rivers. Some of these different forms of adventure tourism are briefly discussed below:

- Safari: Safari means an expedition to observe animals in their natural habitat. This tourist attraction is an excellent way to explore the remote areas of the district.
- Trekking: It is an exciting adventure for the tourists. Karbi Anglong district favourably facilitates trekking.
- River rafting: One of the thrilling adventures for tourists is river rafting. This facility is available in some of the rivers in the district. It attracts a lot of international tourists.
- Handloom and handicraft: These products are highly praiseworthy and are very often purchased by the tourists. Recently, the Tourism Department of Karbi Anglong Autonomous Council has undertaken schemes for their promotion at Langhin and Rongmongve.

Pilgrimage: Karbis are nature worshipers. The pilgrimage in Karbi Anglong district is unique and is different from pilgrimage in other districts or states. Harlongpuru, Longchap Sarpo, Donka Sarpo, Bichikri, Deopani etc. are among the most common pilgrimages in the district. These are briefly discussed below:

- Harlongpuru: Located in Umcheret under Hamren sub-division, it is basically a cave where people pray for solving their problems and difficulties and also to cure away sickness.
- Donka Sarpo: Generally, Donka Sarpo is the name of a river that flows in the whole of Donkamukam area. It is naturally blended, where people take rice bear, bitternut and leaves for praying Donka Sarpo.
- Bichikri: It is basically a lake, located on top of the hill in Chinthong, under Hamren sub-division. One surprise feature of this lake is that, it has more water during the dry season (winters) and lesser water during summers and has not dried up till today.
- Arnampharo (100 Goddess) Alongpak: According to Karbis' belief, it is a place of hundreds of goddesses assembled together for discussion.

- Deopani Temple: The temple is located in the eastern side of Karbi Anglong under the Bokajan sub-division. The temple is dedicated to an *avatar* of goddess Durga. People from different corners of India come to worship and sacrifice (if required) some animals (goats, hens, pigeons etc.) for achieving their needs.

There are many other such type of destinations which have unique features and can attract tourists. Some others which are not incorporated above include Ronghang Rongbong, Teronpi Alanghe, Langhemphi and many others.

Wildlife Sanctuary: Karbi Anglong is one of the best destinations for a truly memorable wildlife adventure. The wildlife sanctuaries in this district are a home to some of the rare species like hoolock gibbon, great Indian pied hornbill and many others. At present, there are three wildlife sanctuaries in the district, namely East Karbi Anglong Wildlife Sanctuary, Garampani Wildlife Sanctuary and Nambor Wildlife Sanctuary.

Tourist Spots: More and more new tourist spots have been identified and developed by the tourism department to provide adequate facilities for tourists. Some of the newly identified tourist spots are Longsokangthu, Langvoku, Horhoti, Kathilangso and Sapanalla.

Ethnic Cultural Heritage: Karbi Anglong has a rich cultural heritage since times immemorial. Every work or events of the Karbis are associated with some rituals or festival. Some of the prominent festivals are briefly mentioned below:

- **Chojun:** It is a ritual puja, performed mostly during the winters. It is observed by the Karbis for having a propitiate family and relatives. The main deities in these rituals are Barithe, Urmi, Sar Arnam, Birne, He-i and Arni. And others like Ar-e (Hemphu) and Lamki are also observed during the rituals.
- **Rongker:** It is basically a spring time festival and is performed at the beginning of a new year. It is celebrated

to propitiate different gods and goddesses for the well-being of the entire village and also to have a good harvest in that particular year.

- **Hacha-Kekan:** The Hacha-Kekan is a harvesting festival. There is no specific deity that is observed. It is simply a post-harvest rejoicing festival.
- **Chomkan:** The Chomkan (also known as 'thi-karhi' and Chomangkan) is a death ritual of the Karbis. It is actually a ceremony performed by a family for the peace and the safe passage of the soul of family members who had died.

Problems of Ecotourism for Ecopreneurship Development

Karbi Anglong, not only rich in its natural resources and biodiversity, but is also well known for its hospitality. Even though the district has been hospitable to visitors from an ancient era, it is seen that the number of tourists visiting the place has been fluctuating in recent years. This can be clearly seen from the record of tourists visit during the period 2008-2012, which is depicted in Table 15.1.

It is important for both the tourism department and other organisations in the district to find out the various causes and problems for such a diminishing pattern of tourists visiting the district. The district has been a hot spot but the ultras of each and every kind of hue are presently active and have added to the political turmoil that has seen many riots and *bandhs*.

Table 15.1: Number of Tourist Visits: 2008-2012

S. No.	Year	Domestic	Foreign	Total
1.	2008	18,217	53	18,270
2.	2009	14,237	21	14,258
3.	2010	9,369	10	9,379
4.	2011	8,708	09	8,717
5.	2012	8,234	08	8,242

Source: 'Tourism and Environment: Its Problems and Opportunities in Karbi Anglong District of Assam', by B. Rongpipi, M. Terangpi and H. Engti.

Some of the problems associated are mentioned as follows:

- Unfavourable situation due to frequent insurgency and terrorism.
- Frequent *bandh* called by different organisations and extremists.
- Inadequate infrastructure, such as poor transport and communication system.
- Lack of proper planning and policies.
- Lack of efficient and dynamic leader.
- Easily accessibility of information regarding lodging, boarding, hiring of vehicle, etc. is absent.
- No sincerity in utilisation of funds.
- Inability of the tourism department of the district to bring awareness about the benefits and importance of ecotourism.
- Lack of sound medical and healthy drinking water facility.
- Non-availability of good accommodation facilities near eco-tourist spots.

All these problems are man-made and hence solvable. Most of them have arisen because of the irresponsible attitude of the tourism department.

Therefore, the department has to take some necessary steps as soon as possible to tackle these issues.

Suggestions

All problems, which have been mentioned above are man-made and controllable in nature. The only need is some sort of sincerity towards utilisation of funds by the tourism department of the district. Besides sincere utilisation of funds, proper planning and policies are also required to make the situation favourable. Some suggestions to reduce the problems are presented below:

- Planning and framing of policies should be made keeping in mind the local and regional issues.
- More funds need to be invested for decent accommodation

and transportation facilities.

- Easily accessible information should be provided.
- More facilities like trekking, rafting, etc. should be introduced and provided to the visitors.
- Need to set up eco-resorts.
- The local people should be well aware about the benefits and importance of ecotourism. This can be achieved by conducting awareness programmes.
- Tourist guides and maps should also be provided.
- The favourable image for ecotourism should have to be re-generated.
- Well educated and dynamic managers should be engaged for proper planning.
- Local populace needs to understand the importance of hospitality to attract more tourists.
- Need to earn cultural popularity.

If all the suggested steps are undertaken, ecotourism in the district will be on positive track. Therefore, the tourism department along with NGOs and other social organisations can solve the problems.

Conclusion

While capitalizing on the natural beauty and turning it into a commercialised venture with innovative ideas for promoting ecotourism, will ultimately help in promoting ecopreneurship in the district.

Evidently, saving the environment around you and preserving the natural luxuries and forest life, that's what eco-tourism is all about.

Whether it is about a nature camp or organizing trekking trips towards the unspoilt and inaccessible regions, one should always keep in mind not to create any mishap or disturbance in the life cycle of nature. This is what every ecopreneur should keep in mind while implementing their innovative ideas.

References

Chawla, Romila (2003), 'Ecotourism and Development', New Delhi: Sonali Publication.

Gale, T. and Hill, J. (2012), 'Ecotourism and Environmental Sustainability: An Introduction'.

Kainrath, David (2009), 'Ecopreneurship in Theory and Practice: A Proposes Emerging Framework for Ecopreneurship'.

Kumari Devi, Meena (2012), 'Ecotourism in Assam: A Promising Opportunity for Development', *SAJTH*, January, Volume 5, No. 1.

McEwen, Thaddeus (2013), 'Ecopreneurship as a Solution to Environmental Problems: Implications for College Level Entrepreneurship Education', *International Journal of Academic Research in Business and Social Sciences,* available at: www.hrmars.com/journals, Retrieved May 6, 2014.

Pastakia, A. (1998), 'Assessing Ecopreneurship in the Context of a Developing Country: The Case for India', *Greener Management International.*

Sheltegger, S. (2005), 'The Framework and Typology of Ecopreneurship: Leading Pioneers and Environmental Managers to Ecopreneurship'.

Urlaud, Julie (2010), 'Breathing Live into Social Communication for Business', *Indian Streams Research Journal,* Volume II, Issue X.

Volery, T. (2002), 'Ecopreneurship: Rationale, Current Issues and Future Challenges'.

Websites:

http://timesofindiatimes.com/city/guwahati/karbi-anglong-gets-itsdue/articleshow/2850642.com, Retrieved June 6, 2014.

http://www.greenprof.org/wp-content/uploads/2010/06/The-of-the-Ecopreneur.pdf, Retrieved June 6, 2014.

http://www.divaportal.org/smash/get/diva2:280302/FULLTEXT01.pdf, Retrieved May 6, 2014.

http://www.springerreference.com/docs/html/chapterdbid/349624.html, Retrieved June 10, 2014.

http://www.greenprof.org/wp-content/uploads/2010/06/AFramework-for-Ecopreneurship.pdf, Retrieved May 10, 2014.

http://blog.taigacompany.com/blog/sustainability-business-life-

evvironment/ecopreneurship-is-it-for-you-
Ecopreneurship-Entrepreneurs and Ecology, Retrieved January 11, 2011.

16

Entrepreneurship, Employment Generation and Tourism

Thrinadha Rao B. and Venkata Rao Y.

Introduction

History has revealed that the economic imbalances are the major causes for social disputes in a society or a region. Nature has solutions to these imbalances, problems or gaps before their existence. As a human our duty is to identify the right source to fulfil the gaps. Here, the person or persons who are identifying these resources and trying to fill the gaps are known as entrepreneurs. Entrepreneurs for economic development have emerged in the last couple of decades. In developing countries, the primary barrier to economic growth is often not so much a scarcity of capital, labour or land as it is the scarcity of the dynamic entrepreneurs. For some countries or even regions, such as rural areas or declining industrial areas or where industrial establishments are not possible due to geographical nature of the region, tourism may offer an opportunity to diversify the economy, increasing the variety of empowerment opportunities available for the local population. In addition to this, any downturn in one particular sector may be offset by an increase or stability in other sectors (Holloway, J. Christopher, 2009).

Concepts

Entrepreneurship can be defined as the process of using private initiative to transform a business concept into a new venture or to grow and diversify an existing venture or enterprise with high growth potential. Entrepreneurs identify an innovation to seize an opportunity, mobilize money and management skills, and take calculated risks to open markets for new products, processes and services (UNDP, Evaluation Office, 1999).

Tourism is a collection of activities, services and industries that delivers a travel experience, including transportation, accommodation, eating and drinking establishments, retail shops, entertainment businesses, activity facilities and other hospitality services provided for individuals or groups travelling away from home (Lori Langone, 2006). According to Macintosh and Goeldner (1986) tourism is "the sum of the phenomena and relationships arising from the interaction of tourists, business suppliers, host governments and host communities in the process of attracting and hosting these tourists and other visitors".

Significance of Tourism for Employment Generation

The World Tourism Organization (WTO) claims that tourism is currently the world's largest industry with annual revenues of over US$ 3 trillion. Tourism is the fastest growing sector with more employment generation. In the year 2013, 265,745,000 total jobs were generated in the tourism sector and the estimates put the figure at 337,819,000 jobs by the year 2023. As a leading international organization in the field of tourism, United Nations World Tourism Organisation (UNWTO) has been promoting tourism as a driver of economic growth, inclusive development and environmental sustainability.

Tourism has a direct impact on the national revenue of all touristic countries—it creates work opportunities, industries, and several investments to serve and raise nation's performance and cultures, also distributes their history, civilization, and traditions. After implementing the LPG model (liberalization, privatization and globalization) in India, tourism was completely recognized as an industry which is providing more employment opportunities to the skilled and unskilled labour. Tourism is an industry that currently affects the livelihoods of many of the world's poor, both positively and negatively. It transforms economic growth rate from low to high. Tourism was one of the third largest net earners of foreign exchange for the country (IL&FS, 2007) after gems, jewellery and readymade garments (Kurukshetra, 2012). The importance of tourism as a creator of job opportunities can be understood from the fact that in India, every one million invested in tourism creates 47.5 jobs directly and around 85-90 jobs indirectly. In comparison, agriculture creates only 44.6 jobs and manufacturing a mere 12.6 jobs (Kurukshetra, 2012, p. 1).

Tourism development in India has passed through many phases. The Sixth Five Year Plan marked the beginning of a new era when tourism began to be considered a major instrument for social integration and economic development. However, it was only after the 1980s that tourism activity gained momentum. As per the working strategy for the 12th Five Year Plan, the Ministry of Tourism has adopted a "pro-poor tourism" approach which could contribute significantly to poverty reduction. More than half of Tourism Ministry's Plan budget is channelized for funding the development of destinations, circuits, mega projects as also rural tourism infrastructure projects (LARRDIS, 2013).

The role of the Government in tourism development has been redefined from that of a regulator to that of a catalyst. Apart from marketing and promotion, the focus of tourism development plans is now on integrated development of enabling infrastructure through effective partnership with various stakeholders (LARRDIS, 2013).

Tourism in North-East India

As discussed earlier, an entrepreneur seizes an opportunity and converts it into products and services. North-East India is a paradise, unexplored. The North-East offers a wide array of products in the form of its pristine natural beauty, forests and wildlife, rivers and mountains, and a unique multi-ethnic cultural heritage for the tourist (Assam Tribune, July 12, 2011). The region is endowed with diverse tourist attractions and each state has its own distinct features. For the development and promotion of North-East Region, the Ministry of Tourism ensured that 10 percent and 2.5 percent of its total Annual Plan (2012-13) outlay went towards the tourism projects in the North-Eastern region and the tribal areas respectively. An amount of ₹ 100 crore was earmarked in the Budget Estimate 2012-13, for the region.

In order to develop and promote tourism in the region, Ministry of Tourism has identified seven major tourism projects in six states and funds were allotted to three projects in the states of Manipur, Nagaland and Sikkim. During the 11th Five Year Plan (2007-2012), 289 tourism projects were sanctioned in the North-East region (Ministry of Tourism, 2012-13). The tourism policy recognizes the roles of Central and State Governments, public sector undertakings and the private sector in the development of tourism (LARRDIS, 2013). The need for involvement of Panchayati Raj Institutions (PRIs), local bodies, non-governmental organizations and the local youth in the creation of tourism facilities has also been recognized. Now let us discuss the unique characteristics of North-East India for entrepreneurial development in tourism.

North-East India

Geographical: The North-East region can be physiographically categorized into the Eastern Himalayas, North-East Hills (Patkai-Naga Hills and Lushai Hills) and the Brahmaputra and the Barak Valley Plains. North-East India has a predominantly humid sub-tropical climate with hot, humid summers, severe monsoons and mild winters. Along with the west coast of India, this region has some of the Indian sub-continent's last remaining rain forests which supports diverse flora and fauna and several crop species. Similarly, reserves of petroleum and natural gas in the region constitute a fifth of India's total potential. The region is covered by the mighty Brahmaputra-Barak river systems and their tributaries. Geographically, apart from the Brahmaputra, Barak and Imphal valleys and some flat lands in between the hills of Meghalaya and Tripura, the remaining two-thirds of the area is a hilly terrain interspersed with valleys and plains. The altitude varies from almost sea-level to over 7,000 meters above MSL. The region's high rainfall averages around 10,000 millimetres and above. The states of Arunachal Pradesh and Sikkim have a montane climate with cold, snowy winters and mild summers.

Wildlife, Flora and Fauna: World Wildlife Fund (WWF) has identified all the eight states of North-East India as a priority 'Global 200 Ecoregion'. The richness of the region's avifauna largely reflects the diversity of habitats associated with a wide altitudinal range. North-East India supports some of the highest bird diversities with about 850 bird species. The Eastern Himalaya and the Assam plains have been identified as an 'Endemic Bird Area' by the Royal Society for Protection of Birds (ICBP, 1992). The global distribution of 24 restricted-range species is limited to the region. The region's lowland and moist-to-wet tropical evergreen forests are considered to be the northernmost limit of true tropical rainforests in the world. The region is rich in medicinal plants and many other rare and endangered taxa. Its high endemism in both higher plants, vertebrates and avian diversity has qualified it to be a biodiversity 'hotspot'. WWF has identified the following priority ecoregions in North-East India:

- Brahmaputra Valley Semi Evergreen Forests.
- The Eastern Himalayan Broadleaved Forests.
- The Eastern Himalayan Sub-alpine Coniferous Forests.
- India-Myanmar Pine Forests.

Forest Reserves of North-East: These include the Namdapha National Park, Manas National Park, Kaziranga National Park, Orang National Park, Pobitora Wildlife Sanctuary and Keibul Lamjao National Park.

Demographics: The North-East India with over 220

ethnic groups and equal number of dialects makes it a hugely diverse region. The economy of North-East India is agrarian in nature. The inaccessible terrain has made rapid industrialisation, difficult in the region.

Entrepreneurial Opportunities in North-East

Beginning from the early 1970s, there have been planned and systematic efforts to promote entrepreneurship in the North-East, initially by the Government of Assam and later on by the North-Eastern Council. There will be more opportunities for small entrepreneurs in business and service sectors than in the industry sector in future partly because of economic liberalisation and partly due to development of information technology (D.D. Mali, 2013). Now we see the opportunities for entrepreneurial development in the tourism sector in North-East India.

Ecotourism and Adventure Tourism: Ecotourism means making as little environmental impact as possible and helping to sustain the indigenous populace, thereby encouraging the preservation of wildlife and habitats when visiting a place. This is a responsible form of tourism and tourism development, which encourages going back to natural products in every aspect of life. It is also the key to sustainable ecological development. Ecotourism focuses on local cultures, wilderness adventures, volunteering, personal growth and learning new ways to live on our vulnerable planet. It is considered the fastest growing market in the tourism industry. According to the World Tourism Organization, ecotourism is witnessing an annual growth rate of 5 percent worldwide and contributes 6 percent to the world gross domestic product.

Ecotourism in India is still at a very nascent stage, but there are conscious efforts to save the fragile Himalayan ecosystem and culture and heritage of the indigenous people, which probably has the largest concentration in the world.

The entire North-East India is recognized as ecoregion. This region contains of six national parks with diversified flora and fauna. Most of this region is covered by hills with dense forests. These type of places are suitable for adventure tourism activities like trekking and attracts tourists from different parts of the world.

Cultural Tourism: Culture is the collective programming of the mind which distinguishes the members of one human group from another (Hofstede, 1980). According to Edward Taylor, culture includes knowledge, beliefs, art, morals, law, customs and other capabilities acquired by human beings as a member of the society. Nearly 220 ethnic groups are present in North-East India. Along with a few similarities, all these groups differ by some unique characteristics like art, customs, traditions etc. Each ethnic group has its own folk dances and folk songs and these are performed by different group of people on different occasions. Some of the popular folk dances including, Bihu, Khamba Lim, Aku, Nongkrem, Dhol-Cholam, Thang-ta and etc. are performed at various locations. If these cultural attributes are marketed in a proper way, it will attract more tourists to the region.

Agricultural/Farm Tourism: Some people consider agri-tourism as a part of ecotourism due to its larger interaction with the nature. Due to the hilly region (geographical conditions), terrace cultivation is famous in most parts of North-East India. The way of performing terrace cultivation activities differ from the cultivation activities in the plain area. This diversity also attracts tourists.

Food Tourism (Culinary Tours): Culinary tourism or food tourism basically means experiencing the food of a country, region or an area, and is now considered a vital component of the tourism experience. Dining out is common among tourists and food is believed to rank alongside climate, accommodation, and scenery as important to tourists. In North-East India, one can identify the food items which are not available in rest of India. This region is famous for food prepared with bamboo suit, some chicken varieties like "kappa chicken" and food items prepared with pork. This region is famous for fruits like pineapple, citrus fruits, strawberry's etc.

Rural Tourism: Rural tourism is essentially an activity which takes place in the country side. It is multifaceted and may entail farm/agricultural tourism, cultural tourism, nature tourism, adventure tourism, and ecotourism. As against conventional tourism, rural tourism has certain typical characteristics. It is experience-oriented, locations are less populated, predominantly in natural environments and it is based on the preservation of culture, heritage and traditions (Kurukshetra, May 2012, pp. 3-4).

The scheme of rural tourism was started by the Ministry of Tourism in 2002-03 with the objective of highlighting rural life, art, culture and heritage at rural locations and in villages which have core competence in art, craft, handloom, textiles and natural environment. The intention was to benefit the local community economically and socially as well as to enable interaction between tourists and local population for a mutually enriching experience. The promotion of village tourism was also aimed towards generating revenue for rural communities through tourist visits, which may stop exodus from rural to urban areas.

In North-East India, a majority of the accommodation facilities like hotels and restaurants are located in very few places and that too in cities. This is an opportunity for the rural people to start small restaurants or accepting the tourists as paying guests. It would be mutually beneficial for both the tourists and the local people. The tourists will get a chance to participate in local food preparation and the local people will get the economic benefit from the tourists.

Conclusion

For some countries or even regions, such as rural areas or declining industrial areas or where industrial establishments are not possible due to geographical nature of the region, tourism may offer an opportunity to diversify the economy, thereby increasing the variety of empowerment opportunities available for the local population. In addition to this, any downturn in one particular sector may be offset by an increase or stability in other sectors.

North-East region has huge potential towards tourism and would be helpful in creating empowerment opportunities for the local population. The local people are the best ambassadors to market their culture, art, festivals, beliefs etc., to the tourists. For this, the entire community should participate in the tourism development activities directly or indirectly and should accept the tourists to see and participate in their culture. The locals of the North-East region can frame each tourism opportunity or combinations of tourism opportunities into a tourism project. Central government, state governments and many NGOs are ready to give finance to start business, help in marketing of the service products and help in management activities. The only one thing is as an entrepreneur, the local people will have to take the initiatives towards entrepreneurial activities.

References

Government of India, Ministry of Tourism, 'Annual Report, 2012-13'.

Hofstede, G. (1980), 'Culture's Consequences: International Differences in Work-related Values', CA, Sage Publications.

Holloway, J. Christopher (2009), 'The Business of Tourism', Pearson Education Limited, p. 102.

Lori, Langone (2006), 'Tourism as an Economic Development Tool in Montcalm County', Travel, Tourism and Recreation Resource Centre, Michigan State University Board of Trustees.

Mali, D.D. (2013), 'Entrepreneurship Development in North-East', available at: http://www.cosidici.com/newlettmay/entrepreneurship.html, accessed on August 20, 2013.

Mcintosh, R.W. and Goeldner, C.R. (1986), 'Tourism: Principles, Practices and Philosophies', John Wiley & Sons, New York.

Parliament Library and Reference, Research, Documentation and Information Service (LARRDIS) (2013), 'Tourism Sector in India', Lok Sabha Secretariat, No. 13, August.

UNDP Evaluation Office (1999), 'Entrepreneurship Development

Essentials', *Entrepreneurship,* No. 2, December.

UNWTO (2009), 'Tourism and Community Development: Asian Practices'.

Wolf, Erik (2006), 'Culinary Tourism: The Hidden Harvest', Kendall/Hunt Publishing.

17

Entrepreneurship Development in the Indian Rice Mill Sector

Amir Jafar, Partha Sarar and Anjan Kumar Ghosh

Introduction

In this world, everything one does, calls for innovation. Every age old technique needs to be revamped and old things need to be done in a new way. Where competition gets severe, survival strategies comprise more and more complex ways of dealing with the situation. Thinking differently and looking into a matter from a different perspective brings forth interesting solutions to problems. In thc highly unpredictable domain of entrepreneurship, innovative ideas and a confident self give the entrepreneur the courage to cruise through a sea of uncertainties. Entrepreneurship is an aspect of human behaviour. It is just hidden in a bud and needs to be blossomed. Desirable entrepreneurial qualities are already present in a person albeit his unawareness. Initiatives are required to bring out the entrepreneurial qualities to full potential. It is a challenge for an entrepreneur to keep himself grounded and focused towards the achievement of his goals.

The entrepreneurship process takes place when a potential entrepreneur expresses the intention to start a new business in near future (GEM, 2014). Many studies have been carried out on entrepreneurship during the last century and the entrepreneurship concept has been enriched with the pace of time. Previous studies considered entrepreneur as those business executives who are associated with the group of new business units or extensions of established units or have given active efforts to adapt established units to a changing environment (Evans, 1942). However, the present studies view entrepreneurship as professional application of knowledge, skills and competencies, new ideas by individual(s) by lunching an enterprise for the purpose of generating wealth, employment and social development (NKC, GOI, 2008).

Entrepreneurship can be considered as an economic agent for the development of a nation as it leads to economic development of a country. For developing economies like India, setting up of more number of small-scale businesses (SSBs) is advantageous since it leads to employment generation and capital productivity (Panda, 2000). India is in the forefront of developing countries, committing enormous resources to small business enterprises (Kamalanabhan et al., 2006). In India, the small-scale industries (SSIs) contribute to 50 percent of total industrial production and 80 percent of total industrial employment (Hussain, 2004). The unemployment rate of India was 8.5 percent in 2012 and was ranked 97th in the world. But noticeably more than half of the total population (52 percent) in India is self-employed, while 18 percent is working as regular wage/salaried employees and 30 percent as casual labourers.

The share of self-employment in total workforce is 55 percent for rural men and 59 percent for rural women, while it is 42 percent for urban men and 43 percent for urban women (Central Investigation Agency, 2012, NSSO, 2013). India's entrepreneurship and innovation rank stood at 74th and 62nd respectively, which is very poor compared to China (58th, 29th), Japan (28th, 20th), UK (13th, 10th) and US (1st, 7th) respectively (GEDI, 2012 and GOI).

However, from the entrepreneurship and innovation ranks of India, we can infer that the Indians are innovative but they are not capable enough to translate their business ideas into reality. In this backdrop, it is very significant to identify the hindering factors behind the starting and growth of entrepreneurship. In this study, we have considered the rice mills operating in Burdwan district, West Bengal, India, since it is a major sector in the SSI segment and it contributes immensely towards the economic development and employment generation of this state. This study has identified different challenges faced by the new as well as the existing rice millers. After analyzing all the pertinent data, we have proposed certain remedies, which may be useful to the rice millers, government and other stakeholders for better operations in the future.

Review of Literature

Entrepreneurship is becoming an extremely interesting topic among the academicians, researchers, businessmen and governments across the globe. Many researchers in the field of entrepreneurship have focused on two major areas—one is established organisations, and other are large multinational companies and small and medium-sized businesses within the national context (McDougall and Oviatt, 2000). Previous studies on entrepreneurship have showed that SSBs have a very significant impact in the society of developing countries. In the study of entrepreneurship, the researchers have specially concentrated on role of entrepreneurs in economic development of developing countries like India, Malaysia, Singapore, etc. Presently, the researchers in this field are focusing on SSBs as they create more employment and thus improve economic conditions of the people.

On the other hand, the SSIs are viewed as inefficient, highly capital intensive and outdated in terms of production technology and consequently, products compared to large-scale sectors of the industry (Singh, 2001). Panda (2000) pointed out that the SSIs also reduce productivity of the employees. Though setting up of small business is viewed as 'decentralization of industrialization', but it is imperative for the developing nations like India and China where enormous size of the population is an issue. The development of SSIs becomes possible when cooperation exists between the economic and political structures at local level with support from the government side (Singh, 1999). Medhora (1965) also pointed out that failure of industrialization cannot be credited to lack of entrepreneurship and this failure happened due to political influence at the early stages of industrialization. Since Independence, the entrepreneurial activities were found smooth in the first two decades but later on, the sequence was lost due to populism, bureaucracy, etc. (Manjunatha, 1998).

There are a number of problems faced by the existing as well as new entrepreneurs. Market competition, change in regulatory affairs, technology, getting resources on time are becoming severe challenges for them. Price of raw materials, lack of marketing information and marketing of products are becoming issues for the small industries (Latha and Murthy, 2009). Previous studies identified that majority of the SSIs have been closed due to high financial and marketing problems faced by them. Problems like unavailability of raw materials, labour problems, natural disaster, ownership conflict, have also compelled the small business owners to close down their units (Panda, 2002). All these factors have made the environment more challenging for the new or potential entrepreneurs. Kristiansen (2007) has pointed out that limited information and knowledge about the overall business, uncertainties due to the concentration and market dominance by powerful business groups, etc. act as hindering factors for the growth of small-scale entrepreneurship.

Amidst these challenges, entrepreneurs need to carry on their business. The comparative success of an enterprise depends a lot upon the entrepreneur or owner of the business. This ownership can be obtained through starting a new business or by purchasing an existing business or through inheritance from the family. The success of entrepreneurship or the 'degrees of entrepreneurship' also varies according to ownership of the business (Cooper and Dunkelberg, 1986). The authors have remarked that the individuals who have started new firms are more entrepreneurial than the inheritors and the persons who have purchased the existing businesses, and it is least for those who have been promoted or brought in to become an owner or a manager.

The relative success of entrepreneurship at times depends on factors like time of establishment, goal orientation, and direct supervision with managerial responsibility and sales promotion (Panda, 2000). The author also pointed out that the large-scale investment without own managerial responsibility sometimes results in failure of the entrepreneurship. Managerial skill plays a vital role behind the success of an entrepreneur.

According to Schwartz and Malach-Pines (2007), some characteristics of an entrepreneur like involvement in business, optimism, energy level, independence and initiatives are same for high technology entrepreneurs and small business owners, but educational level and leadership quality creates considerable differences in the performance of the entrepreneurs. Factors like economic status of the family, age, technical education and training, and work experience also have a positive linkage with entrepreneurship (Nair and Pandey, 2006, Sandhu et al., 2012). Information technology (IT) also plays a vital role in modern enterprises. Effective uses of IT can foster the growth of entrepreneurship in international market (Todd and Javalgi, 2007). Thus, we can see that several issues relevant for the growth of entrepreneurship have been identified by several empirical researches. In our study, we have made an attempt to understand the factors retarding the growth of entrepreneurship in the Indian rice mill sector.

Objectives of the Study

Today, entrepreneurship is considered to be one of the most critical factors contributing towards an economy's growth and development. But for the proper development of entrepreneurship, it is essential to understand the factors hindering its growth. The main aims of this study are:

- To comprehend the deterring factors for entrepreneurship development in Indian rice mill sector.
- To identify the ways to overcome the obstacles to

entrepreneurship development.

Methodology of the Study

For this study, a questionnaire entitled 'Obstacles to Entrepreneurship Development' was designed. The items of the questionnaire were identified after a thorough review of the extant literature on entrepreneurship. The empirical and research based articles on entrepreneurship were obtained from several databases, including, Academic Search Premier, JSTOR, EBSCO, SAGE Online Journal and Business Source Premier. Resources for this study were also obtained from the websites of different bodies engaged in the promulgation of knowledge and research on entrepreneurship.

In this paper, the deterring factors for entrepreneurship development have been identified on the basis of an empirical study carried out in the district of Burdwan. This study is a perceptual study and the data have been collected through self-administered questionnaire. The questionnaire was filled in by several entrepreneurs in West Bengal and we have focused mainly on the rice mill sector. We considered the responses of eleven would-be-entrepreneurs and eighteen existing entrepreneurs.

Rice Mill Sector in West Bengal

In India, West Bengal is the highest producer of rice. The district of Burdwan is considered as the granary of West Bengal. Presently, there are 430 rice mills in Burdwan district and the average production capacity is 500 sacks per day. This sector is labour intensive and it has been observed that majority of the rice millers have partly automated their operations. The workers need to perform a wide array of activities, ranging from soaking of rice in water, pumping it into large tanks for boiling, drying it by spreading it in the sun, and beating the dried rice in machine. These activities can also be performed through a fully automated or semi-automated business process. The rice mill sector has been subject to competitive pressure and is largely privately operated by the mill owners.

In India, the rice mill sector encompasses a variety of mills with different capacities in terms of capital employment and technological advancement. In order to meet the competitive pressure in this sector, there is an increasing preference of entrepreneurs towards technological up-gradation combined with cost reduction. There has been a considerable impact on the strategic action orientation and on the practices adopted by the entrepreneurs in this sector. Nevertheless, the degree of modernization depends on the financial strength of the entrepreneur and this act as a determinant of the degree of automation and has an impact on the usage of factor inputs in the business process. Despite variation in business process, there are certain activities in the basic business process of a rice mill that are largely common to all rice mills.

In this regard, the significant activities are pre-cleaning and de-stoning (elimination of external particles from paddy), husking (removing husk from paddy), paddy separation (taking apart the unhusked paddy from rice), whitening (removing the bran layer and germ from brown rice), polishing (developing the look of milled rice), blending (amalgamation of unbroken rice with amount of brokens) and bagging (sacking the milled rice for transport to the market). The basic strategic action orientation revolves around cost minimization for which the entrepreneur has to identify different ways of cost minimization that would give him a competitive advantage.

Although, technology is an important consideration, the rice mill sector is still a labour intensive sector. A rice mill of generic type employs five categories of workers which include clerical staff, managers, cashiers and go-down keepers. The second category comprises of fire-men, helpers, machine-men and courtyard/ground supervisors. In the third category they have the contractual labour involved in the loading/unloading and stem boiling activities. The fourth category of workers encompasses the daily wage workers who work as machine coolies, broken rice cleaners and courtyard/ground workers. There are many female workers under this category and it is a source of employment for the rural females.

Modernization exercise in the rice mill sector has a considerable impact on the nature of workforce employed. While modernization has led to the reduction of workers, there is need for specific type of skills to work with the updated technology. The financial involvement in establishing a rice mill is quite large. For a small rice mill with semi-automatic machines, the cost involvement is around ₹ 6 crore besides the cost of land. An individual needs to have his land along with 40 percent of the proposed cost of the project. That is the minimum with which he can apply for a bank loan. Subsequently, the issue of collateral securities becomes crucial. Hence, in all, we can conclude that establishment of rice mill for an individual is a very expensive issue. The present regulations of the bank regarding the loan are quite rigorous.

Major Findings of the Study

On the basis of the survey carried out with the questionnaire containing items which have been identified from the extant literature on entrepreneurship, we have been able to identify the factors retarding the growth of entrepreneurship in the rice mill sector. We have then classified the factors under seven different groups—governmental factors, environmental factors, socio-cultural factors, financial factors, entrepreneurial factors, infrastructural factors, institutional factors and assorted factors.

Under the *governmental factors,* we have considered variables like excessive and complex regulations, reservation of certain sectors, government policies related to entrepreneurship and government programmes on entrepreneurship development. The *environmental factors* include the economic position of the country, attractiveness of the country to foreign experts, education level of the populace, diversity of ideas, the control of corporations in hands of few and opportunities for new venture. Social attitudes, culture that rewards self-made success, social stigma, cultural facilitation and supportiveness of cultural and social norms have been considered under the *socio-cultural factors*. *Financial factors* like progressive marginal tax rates, lack of capital, lack of well-developed financial system, discrimination in credit markets, availability of financial support, business loans, and lack of venture capital or angel investors have been considered in our study.

Entrepreneurial factors depict the basic characteristics/qualities of an entrepreneur which are very important for success. We have considered items like leadership skills, managerial skills, risk-taking ability, other skills like information processing, risk assessment, preparing business plan, alertness to opportunities, innovation, identifying opportunities in the environment, non-scientific estimation and biases in entrepreneurial decision-making, overconfidence in individual behaviour, over-optimistic judgments about the business, psychological factors, lack proper social networks, personality traits of the entrepreneurs, capacity for utilizing opportunities and ability to organise resources.

Infrastructural factors include lack of capital, physical infrastructure like land, built up space, electricity, communication etc., corruption in the legal and regulatory environment and in various systems, political influences, political and economic environment, efficiency of the judicial system, bureaucracy, quality and accessibility of physical infrastructure, commercial, legal and professional infrastructure, entry barrier by the established firms, opportunity to use technology etc. Under *institutional factors*, we have considered lack of information on entrepreneurial activities and opportunities, research and development, proper education and training, and the role of universities and other institutes in the promotion of entrepreneurship and small business development centres.

Other varied factors have been labelled as *assorted factors*. It includes cost of establishment, management of small businesses by experts or qualified employees, market concentration, partnership problem, labour supply and other labour issues and labour unionism, spurious products or low cost substitutes, business ethics, market selectivity, entry barriers, market environment, increasing cost of employee benefits, networking with the various bodies etc.

We have observed that the set of challenges faced by the existing and would be millers are quite different. Thus, we have discussed the challenges and the remedial measures separately for the potential and existing entrepreneurs in the rice mill sector.

Future Rice Millers: Challenges and Remedial Measures

We self-administered the questionnaire to eleven people who were trying to establish a rice mill. Unstructured interviews were also conducted to gain better insights about their problems and aspirations. Based on the inputs received from the would-be rice millers through questionnaire and interviews we were able to identify the following problems:

- **Creating the Profile:** The would-be entrepreneurs need to create a profile so that they can apply to the banks for loan. This process is very rigorous and time consuming. Many fail to do it and that brings an end to their dream to be an entrepreneur.
- **Government Regulations:** They perceive that the government regulations are excessive and complying with them is a challenging task. They have a strong demand for liberalizing the government regulations.
- **Lack of Capital:** Many researchers have pointed out that capital procurement is not as challenging as it used to be in the earlier days. The would-be millers agree to this but since rice mill is a capital intensive venture, procurement of capital is a serious issue for them. The financial

involvement in establishing a rice mill is quite large. For a small rice-mill with semi-automatic machines the funds required are around ₹ 6 crore besides the cost of land. An individual needs to have his land along with 40 percent of the proposed cost of the project. That's the minimum with which he can apply for a bank loan. Later on comes the issue of collateral securities. Hence, in all we can conclude that establishment of a rice mill for an individual is a very expensive issue.

- **Cost of Infrastructure:** The cost of land and building materials is escalating at an unprecedented rate. The cost involved in setting up the infrastructure for a rice mill is very high. Procurement of the requisite land at a reasonable price in a convenient location is a very difficult issue. The machinery cost is also very high. Hence, the entrepreneurs are keen in establishing a semi-automatic mill as setting up a fully automatic mill is too expensive.
- **Bank Loans:** Banks are not much interested to give loans to the new entrants. The Banks are very meticulous about the loan sanctioning process. The previous experiences and escalating non-performing assets have compelled the bankers to be very cautious while sanctioning a loan. The provision of collateral assets is very difficult for many to adhere to.
- **Market/Product Selectivity:** This is a major challenge for many of the would-be entrepreneurs. This is many due to the lack of information. The existing entrepreneurs do not share much, neither there is any institutional support for information dissemination for the potential entrepreneurs.
- **Co-operation from the Present Millers:** The indifferent attitude of the existing millers definitely retards the growth of entrepreneurship in the rice mill sector. Most of the time the potential millers are discouraged and misguided. The present millers project this sector to be unattractive and mainly talks about the market problems, government interventions, labour problems, etc. It has also been

observed that a majority of the mills are in hand of few families.

- **Locational Disadvantage:** Since the price of the land near to the city is very high, the would-be millers have to opt for land which is far from the market or main road. This definitely reduces their project cost but the operational cost increases.
- **Political Influences:** Almost all the respondents believe that political influences are essential to get the formalities done. Some of them have admitted that their work is progressing well because of the political references.

We have also identified certain *remedial measures* which may reduce the impeding factors for new entrepreneurship. Single window system for all mandates can reduce time and hurdles for getting all the necessary formalities done. Other governmental initiatives like creating awareness, providing guidance, etc. can foster new entrepreneurship. When technology is involved, rice mill sector becomes capital intensive. It is essential that the individuals desiring to be rice-millers should have a sound financial background. Besides that, it is imperative to have a sound educational background. Without requisite education and training it is very difficult to sustain in this highly competitive and technology-driven sector. The entrepreneurs should educate themselves regarding the business process, technology and the procedural aspects. Formal training, skill development and self-assessment can be fruitful to the new players. Formation of partnership can reduce the financial burden. It can also provide scope for innovation. The new comers need to develop good networks with the banks, political people and the existing millers.

Existing Rice Millers: Challenges and Remedial Measures

Responses from eighteen established rice millers were elicited for our study. Gainful insights from the follow up of unstructured interviews were also observed. The set of challenges faced by the existing rice millers in the district of

Burdwan have been identified as follows:

- **Government Regulations:** According to them, the government regulations are excessive but they think it is essential. Presently, the millers are lacking government support for domestic as well as international marketing of their products. Supplying rice at the government rate (₹ 19.65/kg.) is becoming a challenge—they cannot even reach the break-even.
- **Financial Return:** There is a mismatch between investment and return. Due to high competition in this industry, earning normal profit and sustaining is becoming a serious challenge for the present millers. The rate of interest on the loans has also gone up.
- **Competitive Market:** The market is becoming very competitive, and they think that there are too many players in the market. Getting sufficient raw materials and labour is becoming a serious concern for the millers. The attractiveness of this sector is diminishing day by day. Earning the normal profit is even a big issue today.
- **Labour Issues:** The labour problem is a grave concern for the rice millers. The high degree of politicization has worsened the situation. Complete technological upgradation has not been allowed due to the labour issue. Only semi-automation is permissible.
- **Political Persuasion:** Political influences are becoming a major concern. Donations to the political parties, employment of political referred candidates, union practices are becoming a pressure for the present rice millers. They also admitted that the situation has improved a bit during the recent past.

We have identified certain remedies which may reduce the deterring factors for existing rice millers. As most of the present millers have inherited the business, they need to upgrade their knowledge, attitude, mode of operation, etc. for better performance. They need to realize gone are the good golden days of doing business. They should tap newer locations to combat the problems relating to market, labour and insufficiency of raw material. Rapport building with the other stakeholders, viz. trade union leaders, traders, banks, local government, etc. may be productive for better understanding and operation. Their profit-driven motive should be reduced. They should think about sustainability and not resort to unethical business practices. Loan repayment to the banks should be done properly; otherwise many will suffer in terms getting financial assistance from those banks. Adopting fair labour practices may improve the work efficiency.

Owners of the organisation should emphasize on health, abolition of child labour, ensuring different provisions of labour laws (minimum wages, social security, health and safety) to ensure a decent work environment for the workers. They should emphasize on quality to compete in the international market. Product innovation, alternative use of rice and the by-products can enhance their span of production and profit margin. The present millers need to strengthen their relationships with the allied industries in order to ensure continuous production. Effective use of IT like computerized accounting system and inventory can reduce the total cost. Launching own website, advertising on external sites can be effective tools for promotional activities. Introduction of 'Mandi' system and strong vigil from the government side are essential. The institutional mechanism needs to be strengthened in the right perspective.

Conclusion

Entrepreneurship plays a vital role for the economic development of developing countries. The rice mill sector plays a vital role for economic and social development especially in the eastern part of Burdwan district and its sourroundings. Since Independence, it has been a very profitable and attractive sector. But in last two decades, this industry is losing its magnetism due to several problems.

Financial, political, technological and marketing problems are at the forefront. These challenges can only be dealt with through proper interventions from the government, rice millers, political parties, financial institutions and the society. Active and cognizant participation of all the stakeholders is essential. This sector has immense potential for contributing towards revenue generation, employment creation, and social development. Issues of national importance like eradiction of poverty, women empowerment, development of rural areas, etc. can be addressed well with the active contribution of the rice mills. We can expect that if the challenges are dealt with due assiduousness, this sector can reemerge with its magnetism and vigour and positively contribute towards the welfare of the state.

References

Bouckenooghe, D., Clercq, D.D., Willem, A. and Buelens, M. (2007), 'An Assessment of Validity in Entrepreneurship Research', *Journal of Entrepreneurship,* 16(147), 147-171.

Cooper, A.C. and Dunkelberg, W.C. (1986), 'Entrepreneurship and Paths to Business Ownership', *Management Journal,* 7(1), 53-68.

Evans, G.H. (1942), 'A Theory of Entrepreneurship', *The Journal of Economic History,* 2, 142-146.

GEDI (2014), The Global Entrepreneurship and Development Institute, available at: http://www.thegedi.org.

Hussain, S.V. (2004), 'Performance of Small-scale Industries in India and the Challenges Ahead', *Indian Journal of Industrial Relations,* 39(3), 391-401.

Kamalanabhan, T.J., Sunder, D.L. and Manshor, A.T. (2006), 'Evaluation of Entrepreneurial Risk-taking Using Magnitude of Loss Scale', *Journal of Entrepreneurship,* 15(1), 37-46.

Kristiansen, S. (2007), 'Entry Barriers in Rural Business: The Case of Egg Production in Eastern Indonesia', *Journal of Entrepreneurship,* 16(1), 53-76.

Kumar, N.S. (2013), 'Unemployment Rate Increases in India', Retrieved February 19, 2014, from The Times of India: http://articles.timesofindia.indiatimes.com/2013-06-

23/india/40146190_1_urban-india-urban-women-rural-women.

Latha, K.L. and Murthy, B.E. (2009), 'Problems of Small-scale Entrepreneurs in Nellore District', *Journal of Chinese Entrepreneurship,* 1(3), 268-278.

Manjunatha, M.S. (1998), 'India and Indonesia: After 50 Years of Independence', *Economic and Political Weekly,* 33(5), 214-218.

McDougall, P.P. and Oviatt, B.M. (2000), 'International Entrepreneurship: The Intersection of Two Research Paths', *The Academy of Management Journal,* 43(5), 902-906.

Medhora, B.P. (1965), 'Entrepreneurship in India', *Political Science Quarterly,* 80(4), 558-580.

Nair, K. R. and Pandey, A. (2006), 'Characteristics of Entrepreneurs: An Empirical Analysis', *Journal of Entrepreneurship,* 15(47), 47-61.

National Sample Survey Office, Government of India, (2013), 'Key Indicators of Employment and Unemployment in India, 2011-12', Retrieved February 19, 2014, from Ministry of Statistics and Programme Implementation:
http://mospi.nic.in/mospi_new/upload/press%20release-68th-E%26U.pdf.

National Knowledge Commission (2008), 'Entrepreneurship in India'.

Panda, N.M. (2000), 'What Brings Entrepreneurial Success in a Developing Region?', *Journal of Entrepreneurship,* 9(2), 199-212.

Panda, T.K. (2002), 'Entrepreneurial Success and Risk Perception among Small-scale Entrepreneurs of Eastern India', *Journal of Entrepreneurship,* 11(2), 173-190.

Planning Commission, Government of India (2011), 'Creating a Vibrant Entrepreneurial Ecosystem in India', Retrieved February 19, 2014, from:
http://planningcommission.nic.in/
reports/genrep/rep_eco2708.pdf.

Sandhu, N., Hussain, J. and Matlay, H. (2012), 'Entrepreneurship Education and Training Needs of Family Businesses Operating in the Agricultural Sector of India', *Education+Training,* 54(8/9), 727-743.

Schwartz, D. and Malach-Pines, A. (2007), 'High Technology Entrepreneurs versus Small Business Owners in Israel', *Journal of Entreprenzurship,* 16(1), 1-17.

Singh, S. (2001), 'Employment, Efficiency and Entrepreneurship in Small Industry: A Study of the Baking Industry in Punjab, India', *Journal of Entrepreneurship,* 10(1), 71-88.

Singh, S.K. (1999), 'Panchayat Udyogs in Uttar Pradesh: A Democratic Experiment in Micro Enterprise Development', *Journal of Entrepreneurship,* 8(2), 207-217.

The Global Innovation Index, 2013, Retrieved February 20, 2014, from: http://www.globalinnovationindex.org/userfiles/file/reportpdf/rankings.pdf.

The World Factbook, Retrieved February 19, 2014, from: Central Intelligence Agency: https://www.cia.gov/library/publications/the-world-factbook/geos/in.html.

Todd, P. R. and Javalgi, R.G. (2007), 'Internationalization of SMEs in India: Fostering Entrepreneurship by Leveraging Information Technology', *International Journal of Emerging Markets,* 2(2), 166-180.

18

Entrepreneurship: Global Opportunities and Challenges

Trailokya Deka

Introduction

Job opportunities either in government or in the private sector has become tough off late. After the introduction of New Economic Policy in 1991, the new generation is in a big fix to decide whether it is better to accept the traditional opportunities provide by the governments or to establish business ventures through a good entrepreneurial process. Traditional system gives a constant but secured incentive and the other though competitive gives dynamic opportunities and dynamic challenges. In recent years, the world has become a global village and is considered a single market. Resultantly, the competitive level among businesses has increased. In the era of globalization and rapidly changing world economic order, entrepreneurship has emerged as one of the most dynamic force in the economy and the society. It is driving the technological boom, which in turn is driving much of the world's economic growth. This makes entrepreneurship process very important from micro as well as macro economic perspective. It has become a broader economic phenomenon that has a major impact on the economy.

As the globalisation of business becomes more widespread, this impact will be felt even more deeply in the days to come. Again the scope of what entrepreneurship involves, will continue to change and evolve because environment in which entrepreneurship operates is constantly changing and evolving too. On the other hand, globalized world markets and economies have encouraged entrepreneurial organizations of all sizes and national origins to foster entrepreneurship throughout their operations. However, due to all relevant economic, political and cultural factors, the total path of business opportunities in entrepreneurial process is not so smooth and straight. Entrepreneurs need to be very dynamic and opportunists to find the global as well as regional ways of profit derivation and optimization. This research paper would deliberate on the relevant opportunities and challenges of entrepreneurship. With secondary database and methodological appliances, this paper will examine the emerging global issues (opportunities and challenges) faced by a few well established entrepreneurs in general. A set of policy prescriptions is the ultimate outcome of this research study.

Entrepreneurship for Development

Entrepreneurship is a complex and vast concept. Conceptualizations, definitions and understandings of the phenomenon have attracted scholars and practitioners from a very long past. After forty years of intensive study of the phenomena, the research community still spends much energy on the definition of entrepreneurship. This shows the complexity of the area of entrepreneurship. Many scholars and academicians have tried to provide a specific definition for entrepreneurship. All these make entrepreneurship distinct from other forms of economic and management thoughts and behaviour. Table 18.1 showcases a few broad definitions on the nature and behaviour of entrepreneurship opined by various experts in the field.

Going further, according to Kizner (1973), entrepreneurship has two main aspects. First, entrepreneurship is the 'alertness' to new opportunities. Second, entrepreneurship means seizing opportunities by taking further innovative actions. According to this, entrepreneurship brings alertness which leads to the discovery of new opportunities. If the opportunity is identified as an actual one, the entrepreneur will take action. Consequently, we can assume, alertness necessarily leads to innovative actions and entrepreneurship behaviours.

Table 18.1: Nature and Behaviour of Entrepreneurship

S. No.	Source	Definition
1.	Miller (1983)	A firm's actions relating to product-market and technological innovation.
2.	Kanter (1985)	The creation of new combinations.
3.	Gartner (1985; 1989)	The process of new venture creation, the process by which new organizations come into existence.
4.	Schuler (1986)	The practice of creating or innovating new products or services within the existing businesses or within newly formed businesses.
5.	Stevenson and Jarillo (1990)	The process by which individuals, either on their own or inside organizations, pursue opportunities without regard to the resources they currently control.
6.	Jones and Butler (1992)	The process by which firms notice opportunities and act to creatively organize transactions between factors of production so as to create surplus value.
7.	Krueger and Brazeal (1994)	The pursuit of an opportunity irrespective of the existing resources.
8.	Shane and Venkataraman (2000)	The discovery, creation and exploration (including by whom and with what consequences) of opportunities to bring into existence future goods and services.

Employment has always been a central issue in economic growth and development. In a wider sense, any type of job represents the means by which individual/s gain a sense of personal purpose and satisfaction; support themselves and their families; and contribute (direct and indirect) to the productivity of their local and national economies. The importance of job or employment to a healthy, productive and peaceful society is always there. Jobs can mean economic freedom for men/women; access to education and health services for children; and an alternative to violence for idle youth. Employment is crucial for successful and sustainable growth and development. Jobs promote growth, social cohesion, reduce poverty, improve gender equality and finally create a situation of development. Providing jobs for a growing population has always been one of the most pressing challenges faced by the developing world.

Lack of job opportunities is a very big problem for each and every developing economy, including India. The present job scenario in the country is quite serious. Unemployed and underemployed people are sacrificing their lives and skills year after year. A good number of people are adding themselves as unemployed each and every year. Unemployment rate both in rural and urban India for males, females and as a whole for all is briefly given in Table 18.2.

Table 18.2: Unemployment Rate in Urban and Rural India, 2004-05

Country	Rural			Urban		
	Male	Female	Person	Male	Female	Person
India	1.6	1.8	1.7	3.8	6.9	4.5

Source: Indiastat.com.

Unemployment in urban India is becoming a serious concern. This is due to the rising trend of urban density of population.

Again, unemployment rate specifically for educated persons in urban and rural India is given in Table 18.3.

Educated unemployed are also more in urban than rural India.

According to International Labour Organization (ILO), at present, there are more than 200 million people unemployed worldwide. Population projections suggest that the world will need 500 million new jobs by 2020, the majority of them in developing countries as their relatively young population enters the workforce. As the youth population matures and enters the workforce, competition for new jobs will become more intense. Workforce is growing, the number of job opportunities is shrinking (due to continuous technological inventions) and therefore the issue of entrepreneur and entrepreneurship is in big force.

Table 18.3: Unemployment Rate for Educated Persons of Age 15 Years and Above, 2004-05

Country	Rural	Urban
India	6.5	7.1

Source: Indiastat.com.

We have randomly searched the scenario of entrepreneurial development in Assam and analyzed how it can be used to tackle the problem of unemployment in the state. The following secondary information has been collected. Table 18.4 shows the number of persons employed in the enterprises in Assam during the six year study period.

Unemployment and Youth Considerations

Youth unemployment is one of the principal social and economic challenges of this decade in India and around the world. This is a significant issue as youth unemployment can lead to long-term negative economic effects and social unrest. Long spells of unemployment can have serious effect for individuals, such as reduced earnings and social exclusion. Studies on unemployed youth have found evidence of an effect called 'scarring', which refers to the long-term effects of not being able to find a good job after leaving college, leading to an imbalance in self-confidence. This ill-effect is compounded by the fact that employers are less likely to hire a young person who has experienced a long period of unemployment. It is estimated that one year of unemployment during youth can reduce annual earnings at age 42 by up to 21 percent (Gregg and Tominey, 2005) and that an extra three months of unemployment prior to the age of 23 results in an extra two months of unemployment, on average, between the age of 28 and 33 years (Gregg, 2001).

Table 18.4: Number of Enterprises and Persons Employed in Assam

S. No.	Year	No. of Enterprises	No. of Persons Employed
1.	2001	2,512	98,862
2.	2002	2,695	96,031
3.	2003	2,760	94,473
4.	2004	2,923	96,677
5.	2005	3,070	1,05,452
6.	2006	3,182	1,12,794

Source: Statistical Handbook, Assam.

Prolonged unemployment magnifies these problems and increases the chances that they are passed on to their children. In addition to these pronounced individual costs, the unemployed represent a significant stock of unused economic resources that lowers output and the potential for economic growth. Studies have also found a link between unemployed youth and political unrest and violence. There are 74.5 million youth unemployed in the world and the International Labour Organization believes that another half million will fall into unemployment by 2014. The impact of recent demographic trends coupled with today's economic slowdown, means there are not enough jobs for youth that are transitioning out of colleges and into the working world.

Entrepreneurship for Increasing Employment

Today, with the rapid development of our society, entrepreneurship has become one of the most dynamic forces in the economy. It is driving the technological boom, which in its turn is driving much of the world's economic growth. This aspect makes entrepreneurship very important from a macro economic perspective. As the globalization of business becomes even more widespread, this impact will be felt even more deeply. The scope of what entrepreneurship involves, will continue to change and evolve because environment in which entrepreneurship operates is constantly changing and evolving too.

Fostering entrepreneurship means channelling entrepreneurial drive into a dynamic process, which takes advantage of all the opportunities that an economy can provide. Entrepreneurship requires an entrepreneur to be a person of superior ability who pursues his or her goals despite obstacles, opposition, setbacks, and failure. He or she must persist in the face of adversity, confront unknown challenges and risks and learn from failures, have confidence in his or her capacity to deal with the world, and take practical and rational steps in pursuit of the goals. A successful entrepreneur tends to be a visionary, competent, independent, action-oriented, passionate, confident and a virtuous person who uses reason to focus his or her enthusiasm on reality in the efforts to attain the goals.

Entrepreneurship has often been cited as a key factor to improving economic growth in developing as well as developed countries. Evidence is there to suggest that entrepreneurs create more employment than non-entrepreneurs. Entrepreneurial activities encourage the development of new enterprises. Entrepreneurship is seen as an important way to deal with issues relating to poverty. Entrepreneurship creates new jobs and fosters a climate of innovative thinking.

From the past and present, entrepreneurs have greatly affected our societies, economies and industries. According to the concept of entrepreneurship, the prime mission of an entrepreneur has been to create wealth and business growth. There are various examples of the successful entrepreneurs (Henry Ford, Bill Gates and others) who created both personal wealth and public prosperity and their innovative products greatly affected our society, resulting in progress and advancement of an improved civilization. Accomplishments of this mission results in additional benefits to members of the society, whether the entrepreneur intends it or not. For example, customers benefit because they are able to fulfil a need through the purchase of a product or service. In addition, venture capitalists, lenders, and shareholders benefit by attaining returns on investments or interest through the entrepreneur's business. Moreover, employees benefit by earning income through the business's growth and prosperity. As a result, employees then become customers that have the purchasing power to buy goods and services that entrepreneurs produce.

Due to the dynamic nature of entrepreneurship over time, many entrepreneurs began to focus on a new mission towards improving society (Svikolos, and Carraher, 2006). It is important to mention that entrepreneurship and society are closely interconnected. Because entrepreneurship, as a part of our society, operates in societal environment, entrepreneurship and society are complementary to each other. Consequently, as both concepts of society and entrepreneurship are dynamic by their nature, not surprisingly, that as the society evolves over the time the role played by the entrepreneurship also changes.

Although young and adult entrepreneurs tend to have similar motivations for entrepreneurial activities, they often have different approaches and run different types of businesses. Accordingly, many young entrepreneurs focus exclusively on local markets because of familiarity and because they lack the knowledge about opportunities in other markets and how to take advantage of them (Chigunta, 2002). However, at the same time, they are likely to be more open than adult entrepreneurs to international activity (Cassia et al., 2011).

Entrepreneurship encourages high levels of innovation. Innovation is important because it can lead to more high-value productivity chains and technological change, resulting in a wide range and better quality of goods and services. Entrepreneurs stimulate innovation as they are responsive to potential new markets and seek opportunities to create new ventures, products and services. Entrepreneurship thus forms part of the process in shifting developing countries from factor-driven economies based on natural resources and unskilled labour, to innovation-driven economies which compete by providing new and unique products and services.

Youth Entrepreneurial Activities and Attached Problems

The proportion of youth involved in self-employment entrepreneurial activities varies across countries which may indicate variations in barriers and opportunities. Youth appear to be facing barriers preventing some from turning ideas into projects. Barriers arise in the areas of social attitudes. Lack of skills, inadequate entrepreneurship education, lack of work experience, under capitalization, lack of network and market barriers etc. are the some of the barriers towards youth self-employment and entrepreneurship. Some of these are systematically discussed below.

1. Young people are affected by their families, teachers and society as a whole. Important role models such as parents and teachers are often not aware of the requirements and opportunities of entrepreneurship. This lack of awareness results in a lack of encouragement for entrepreneurial activities, or even negative social attitudes that act as obstacles to youth entrepreneurship.
2. Prior work and entrepreneurship experience is a major determinant of business start-up and entrepreneurship performance. Young people typically lack human, financial and social capital necessary both to set up and successfully run a new business venture. Relative to older individuals, younger people are less likely to have sectoral, managerial or prior business experience and are more likely to be unemployed. They may, therefore, lack the skills needed to set up or run their business.

3. Entrepreneurs with greater initial financial resources are more likely to succeed. Young people are in a disadvantaged position because they will have low personal savings and would find it more difficult than adults to obtain external finance, including debt finance. Banks apply a set of parameters in the assessment of loan proposals, which include credit history, past business performance and collateral, which are likely to be lower in youth-owned firms.
4. Young people normally have limited business networks and business-related social capital. This may have consequences for setting up and running their businesses and building 'legitimacy' amongst key stakeholders (e.g. financiers, customers, suppliers).
5. Market barriers also affect youth entrepreneurship. Financial markets may be biased towards supporting youth businesses. Youth-owned businesses may also face 'discrimination' in product markets, with customers who can be sceptics about the reliability of their products or services. Similarly, due to limited resources, youth-owned firms are more likely to enter industries with low entry barriers where competition is fierce.
6. The youth population is a heterogeneous one and there are some significant differences across groups in their potential for entrepreneurship and the barriers they face. Some groups that face particularly strong labour market challenges include ethnic minorities, those living in deprived areas, those from low income families, and those with low education levels.
7. Entrepreneurship can play a role in supporting employment creation and attachment to the labour market and has done so over recent decades with various types of programmes. However, we know from years of experience that there are no quick fixes to ensure that all youth are integrated into the labour market. While some countries do a better job than others, all countries face pressures and

challenges in helping their youth.

8. There is evidence that young people are enthusiastic about starting businesses. However, it is also clear that few young people actually start businesses relative to those who express an interest and that their failure rates exceed those in older population groups. This reflects a number of barriers affecting youth entrepreneurship in areas including skills, networks and financing; barriers that are often particular to youth or more severe for youth than for adults.

Prescribed Policies for Implementation

It is important to note that barriers are inter-related, which implies the need for a package of policy tools, rather than a single one-shot solution. Some of important prescribed policies are stated hereunder:

1. In order to be successful, entrepreneurs need skills such as creativity, problem-solving and communication skills. Many a times, these skills are learnt through experience—often from entrepreneurial failures—that help an entrepreneur finally arrive at a successful venture. These skills can also be developed through entrepreneurship education and training programmes specifically targeting enterprise founders and owners. Such programmes focus on providing individuals with practical education and experiential learning that builds both soft skills, such as communication, social intelligence, and critical thinking, as well as hard skills like accounting and financial management. Additionally, such programs foster networks of like-minded individuals that support each other and can lead to the creation of entrepreneurial ecosystems which can promote increased entrepreneurial activity.
2. Increased entrepreneurial activity is dependent on many factors including the quality of training, adequate infrastructure and the local business environment. Nonetheless, better access to quality entrepreneurship and education can have a beneficial impact on the success of

entrepreneurs and thus the development and growth of innovative new businesses.

3. Care needs to be taken in assessing the particular barriers affecting different groups of young people. While there are some barriers and policy measures that are broadly the same for all groups, there can also be a need to vary the scale and nature of support for different youth target groups. In particular, a distinction can be made between disadvantaged youth—those who may be unemployed or inactive, live in a difficult environment or have major gaps in financial, human and network capital—and other young people who face less substantial obstacles but at the same time also represent an opportunity to increase entrepreneurship participation with appropriate policy intervention.
4. Entrepreneurship can be a route to decent work and sustainable enterprise for young people. However, 'the structures and delivery of mass education in most countries often thwart or throttle the natural entrepreneurial impulses in youth'. Therefore, educational systems across the developing world (and beyond) need to be reformed. Providing young people with more entrepreneurial training and exposing them to entrepreneurial role models can give them the tools to create their own employment.
5. Technology can also provide ways to improve youth employability. Mobile phones and online educational programmes can reduce both the costs of training, provide youth with virtual experience and allow young workers to combine on-the-job training with academic instruction. The use of educational video games and online web portals can also help to train young people with the skills needed for certain jobs.
6. One way to increase the employability of a population and promote job creation is to improve the quality of education. Education contributes to overall economic

growth by improving the efficiency of the workforce and leading to higher rates of individual productivity, which in turn leads to a higher demand for qualified workers. Education can provide individuals with the necessary market skills to be relevant in the economy. However, this can only happen when the quality of education is ensured. In order to change this situation and maximize the benefits of education while increasing the employability of graduates, collaboration is needed between governments, the private sector and the educational institutions. Such collaboration could support the preparedness of workers by aligning the supply and demand of skilled graduates while ensuring that the system operates in a favourable policy environment.

7. In particular, financing should be sufficient to allow young people to start businesses outside the low entry barrier but high competition sectors towards which youth entrepreneurship is currently skewed, and this finance should be associated with more intensive business development support for these enterprises.
8. It is important to provide integrated packages of support rather than relying on a single narrowly defined support instrument. For example, entrepreneurship teaching supports the development of more entrepreneurial intentions and competences, but may need to be followed up with start-up support to turn these intentions and competences into business ventures, while the effectiveness of supplying finance will be enhanced when it is complemented by advice, coaching and networking. Finally, effort is needed to improve the evidence base on the impact of policy on youth labour market insertion, involving more robust evaluations based on clear targets and objectives for the programmes.

Conclusion

Youth entrepreneurship is not a panacea for solving the

youth unemployment problem but it does have a role to play in facilitating a route into the labour market for a limited group of young people with the ambition and wherewithal to become entrepreneurs. The evidence suggests that when designed appropriately, government programmes can have significant impacts on increasing the exit rate of young people from unemployment with reasonable results on value for public money. Evidence suggests that when designing and delivering youth entrepreneurship programmes, policymakers should pay particular attention to the consideration that the best approach to youth entrepreneurship policy must be the selective one. Although youth may not seem like a likely group for entrepreneurship because of their inexperience and lack of finances, they do have an interest in entrepreneurship and many of them believe that self-employment is feasible.

References

Cassia, Lucia et al. (2011), 'Youth Entrepreneurship: Proposal of an Assessment Scheme for Policy Initiatives', Conference proceedings from the 2011 Annual Conference of the International Council for Small Business.

Chigunta, Francis (2002), 'Youth Entrepreneurship: Meeting the Key Policy Challenges', Oxford University, Oxford.

Drucker, P.F. (1985), 'The Practice of Innovation' in Innovation and Entrepreneurship: Practice and Principles, Harper & Row, New York, pp. 19-33.

Gregg, P. (2001), 'The Impact of Youth Unemployment on Adult Unemployment in the NCDS', *Economic Journal*, 111(475), F623-F653.

Gregg, Paul and Tominey, Emma (2005), 'The Wage Scar from Male Youth Unemployment', *Labour Economics*, Volume 12, pp. 487-509.

International Labour Organization (ILO) (2013), 'Global Employment Trends (2013): Recovering from a Second Jobs Dip', Geneva: International Labour Organization.

International Labour Organization (ILO) (2013), 'Global Employment Trends for Youth (2013): A Generation at Risk', Geneva: International Labour Organization.

Kirzner, I. (1973), 'The Entrepreneurship', in Competition and

Entrepreneurship, Chicago: University of Chicago Press.

Maes, J. (2003), 'The Search for Corporate Entrepreneurship: A Classification of the Concept and its Measures', Policy Research Centre on Enterprises, Entrepreneurship and Innovation.

Report by the Global Business School Network (2013), 'Education, Employment and Entrepreneurship: A Snapshot of the Global Jobs Challenge'.

Shahidi, M. (2008), 'The Challenges of Entrepreneurship in Dynamic Society', Bang College of Business, *KIMEP*, Almaty, Volume 1(1), pp. 34-45.

Svilokos, A. and Carraher, S.M. (2006), 'A Comparison of Social with Traditional Entrepreneurship', Proceedings of Association for Small Business and Entrepreneurship Conference, Corpus Christi, Texas, USA.

World Bank (2013), 'World Development Report, 2013', Washington, D.C.

Index

Index